I0128384

Jane Ellen Frith Panton

**Bypaths and Crossroads**

Jane Ellen Frith Panton

**Bypaths and Crossroads**

ISBN/EAN: 9783744679336

Printed in Europe, USA, Canada, Australia, Japan

Cover: Foto ©Thomas Meinert / pixelio.de

More available books at **www.hansebooks.com**

# BYPATHS AND CROSS-ROADS

# BYPATHS AND CROSS-ROADS

BY

## J. E. PANTON

AUTHOR OF 'COUNTRY SKETCHES IN BLACK AND WHITE,' 'THE CURATE'S WIFE,'
'FROM KITCHEN TO GARRET,' ETC. ETC.

LONDON

WARD AND DOWNEY

1889

# CONTENTS

# BYPATHS AND CROSS-ROADS

To see England, to know in the least the heart of the country we are so proud to call our own, it is necessary to leave the beaten track entirely, and, careless of main roads and railways, plunge into any bypath that may look appealingly at us, and make our way into that dim mysterious land that is so near us, and yet might be non-existent for all that the generality of folks know of its existence.

Once away from the dust and turmoil of the highway, that which we discover is merely a question of eyesight: naturally some people would perceive little more than they do driving or walking; and simply using the road as a means to get from one place to another as fast as may be; but to those to whom every flower, every bird, has some especial message; the fields and hamlets, the brooks and winding lanes, have all so much to say, so much to show; that we almost long for the microscopic eye of a fly, to note each atom of life, each wonderful fluctuation of colour, and to make ourselves thoroughly conversant with every subject in at least one small corner of Nature's kingdom.

We may as well confess that we have not one atom of sympathy with the feverish haste and frivolous excitement that characterise this present day of ours. We dislike being hurried along with the stream of life, from one event to another; and, avoiding as much as possible, the current that sweeps big ships and little ones; straws and flowers; dead bodies and broken hearts; alike towards the great ocean of forgetfulness; we content ourselves with resting just a little way out of the tide; anxious only to be taken into the confidence of Nature, who never disappoints us, and who does her work quietly and patiently; or to learn from the animate creatures around us how marvellous is the scale of creation from the lowest to the highest note.

A perfect summer day does far more to restore the wounded warrior who has fallen out of the fight, disheartened and troubled by the desertion of friends, the falseness of his nearest and dearest; than any amount of human sympathy; and in such enjoyment the world seems powerless to harm us.

Who has not known such a day? Who cannot paint for himself the picture? As we write, such an one rises before us.

It is very early morning. The pale dawn is just rising; a quivering soft gray haze is filling up the beautiful hollows on the hillside in front of our windows, and hanging its festoons over the swiftly-running little river. Then the sparrows in the eaves begin to stir in their nests; a questioning chirp announces that the father is aroused and wants to know the plans for the day. Insensibly the light broadens; great rosy clouds suddenly appear over Creech Barrow; beyond the meadows a cuckoo is shouting out its monotonous song, as if it were challenging the world to wake; and then the meadows themselves come into view, and draw our eyes to look upon their perfect summer beauty.

We can see now that a gentle breeze has arrived, and is

whispering to the flowers about the coming day. Not a month ago the meadows were golden with kingcups, but they have vanished. Still, the wind discloses all sorts of secrets. The brown grasses shade to gray as it glides over them ; a pink flush speaks of the willow-herbs ; a yellow one of the buttercups, that are almost buried in the luxuriant growth above them ; and the white dancing blossoms, curtsying hither and thither as the breeze takes them ; and crowding along the edges of every "lake" in the meadows are the lovely marguerites or ox-eyed daisies, who little know how fashionable they are just now, and are in happy ignorance of their fainting, dying sisters crowded into London window-boxes, and withering for want of the water and fine air that are denied to them, and which they perish for without ever knowing what they really lack.

Then in the "lakes" themselves we are aware of the stir of waking life. These narrow ditches, dug to drain the meadows into the river, are full now of lily leaves and buds. The reed-sparrows are chattering vigorously, and drawing attention to the whereabouts of their curious little nests, perhaps careless of this fact because they know they are so cunningly concealed, so daintily hidden among the thin spear-like foliage, with water about them on every side, that they are almost unobtainable by the ordinary bird-robber ; and just at the corner of the bank a moor-hen has ventured out, and is calling to her little ones to tell them to come from the sheltering spear-bed and take their morning exercise.

By this time the garden flowers are aroused, for, like human beings, the garden ladies sleep longer in their luxurious couches than the field flowers, who have nothing between them and the rousing breeze. The starling who lives in the chimney-bend of our neighbour's house is already at work on the lawn; and the roses are languidly opening their eyes and gazing abstractedly down at the geraniums and calceolarias at their feet; much as a "carriage lady" or member of the county regards a less favoured personage, or one that is compelled to walk.

Here it were well to pause and point out how extremely human flowers are. They have undoubtedly their preferences, their likes and dislikes; and will bloom freely and kindly for any one who understands and loves them; resenting unfair treatment, or unequal treatment and neglect; and repaying a hundredfold all the thousand and one attentions they require; and thus rendering a garden or conservatory as exacting, yet as delightful, as a nursery full of human plants; while a close observer will learn that a rose has pride that it were well to humour, and that a geranium has its fancies that are worth respecting. For, place a rose in unworthy company, crowd her, or refuse to acknowledge that she requires rich and generous food, and such conduct has only one result; and to crowd geraniums and deny them light all round and through their foliage can but produce a spindled, pale, lanky growth, that reminds us of a town child, or a starved and puling infant. Nature, say you? Well, so be it. Still, what is Nature but a strangely human thing, and who shall say where sense begins and sensitiveness leaves off?

Were it not better to confine ourselves to one thing at a time, we could moralise on this subject at length; for it is one of which much is learned in a sojourn among the bypaths of life, and has much to suggest to those who really care to study it; but we would now confine ourselves to the summer day of which we were speaking, and which we left somewhat abruptly to moralise over the manner of behaviour of our roses, who, as the morning advances, faint and pale beneath the impassioned kiss of the sun, who is shining gallantly down on the whole lovely view before us.

But before he arose in his might and donned his glittering armour the soft swish of the swaying scythe broke on our ears; then the scythe was whetted; the gardener's whistle vied with the blackbird's, and the strong scent of the dying grass perfumed the lazy air. Every now and then a child's voice called through the stillness; the breeze died away entirely, and the mulberry leaves hung motionless in the quivering atmosphere.

Then came the exquisite, perfect noontide hour for rest, when in the silence we could lie on the grass, and gaze straight up through the grand dark foliage of the ilex into the immense vault of heaven above; then it was possible to feel how powerless was the world outside to harm us; then a feeling of perfect calm, of perfect happiness, entered our breasts and remained there as conqueror. An almost indescribable feeling, too, for then dream after dream passed through our brain; we felt separate from the body, and deemed ourselves floating in a perfect sea of rest and scented beauty, accentuated by the thousand and one scents and sounds around us.

For if the birds were silent, as indeed all save the cuckoo are silent at mid-day, the insects were busy enough; the air is full of their voices, from the sharp spiteful " nipping " of the gnat to the deep organ-sounding note of the bumble-bee; while the fluttering wing of the butterfly flits past, and, a long way off, a persistent burr speaks of a late threshing-machine at work, and a clatter, rendered musical by distance, tells us that haymaking has begun, and that soon a soft, pale, uniform emerald hue will replace the present varied carpet, spread for us yonder in the stretching meadows.

Perhaps the idea of that makes us look forward to the evening, when we shall glide out in our little boat for a lazy excursion on our friend the river; for before the edges of the fields are shorn we want to see our flowers once more, if only to bid them a fond and last farewell. So when wonderful and dreamy shadows begin to wander about the chain of hills whose beauties never pall; and towards whose perfect, restful hollows we would fain turn our eyes when all else earthly is fading from their sight; we go down through the garden, where once gallant gentlemen and fair ladies dallied in the precincts of an old, old castle, of which nothing remains save a name, and one clump of stone, at one time part of the foundations; and pushing out our craft on the lazy tide we are soon yards away from the garden, going under the long gray bridge, over which the folks from the town are leaning, watching to see if we can shoot the arches of the bridge without ignominiously coming to grief. Soon we have passed Redcliff, and are out in the mouth of the harbour; we have mounted a sail, and are going merrily enough before a small breeze; we watch the great gray herons, sitting meditatively, and watching for the turn of the tide; we see the crows watching as well, and then discover the salmon-boats coming down the river after us, to wait too, when they will proceed to draw the first pool.

But we are in no mood for murder this calm summer evening, and go back, right up to the top of the river, and, resting underneath the bank, look through the sedges at the wealth of flower and bird and insect life around us. A corncrake is creaking away; the night-jar is whirring in the ash at the bottom of the garden; the swifts are screaming violently round the church-tower about the fine weather we are still to have; and the reed-sparrows have more than ever to say, and pay small attention to the willow-warbler who is singing away with all its small might.

There is a bunting-lark repeating its two notes on a furze-bush, and a couple of wild-duck fly up and make for their shelter a little higher up the river; then we see the water-rats come out; we watch them washing their faces, very much as a cat does, and then swim across the river again, to have all their trouble once more on the other side, rustling through the forget-me-nots with their pink and blue blossoms, and shaking the flowering rush that hangs out its pale pink flowers right gallantly in our meadows.

As it begins to darken the cockchafers boom past us; the bats dart and squeak close by our very ears; a thousand gnats are executing military movements, wheeling gravely to and fro, as if at some unheard word of command; and a belated dragonfly glitters as he darts head first into the grasses that doubtless afford him a shelter for the night.

Then a broad yellow moon suddenly appears over Redcliff, and hangs suspended there in a clear atmosphere, like a golden ball; damp mists begin to gather about the rushes, looking singularly ghost-like, and reminding us of our childish belief that these mists hanging about our low-lying fields are merely the spirits of the departed; who are allowed thus to revisit the earth they have known and loved, and to glide voiceless and with veiled faces about those places that in life were their accustomed haunts; and very far away a late nightingale attempts a song that should have been hushed a good month ago.

So fades the summer, and the autumn comes—the time of paradise for dogs and sportsmen. The early morning then is drenched in tears, yet the noontide sun has his revenge, and beats down upon us with ten times its mid-summer heat. Who can forget the first walk through the roots, when their great leaves are full of water, and turn over and wet us thoroughly ere we are half across the field? or who forget the secrets we discovered in a lazy saunter, gun under arm, through our small preserve? For although we knew the haunt of every brood of partridges, and almost knew them each by sight, it remained for September to disclose to us where one nest had been—so close to the road that we could but wonder how it had escaped the notice of the ubiquitous poacher; we could see exactly how the foxes had crept from their earths to our cherished coverts, and had carried off our best-beloved and our one ewe-lamb,—the cock-pheasant of whom we were so unduly proud; and we watched each field corner, full of our enemies the rabbits, so playful and enthralling in their manœuvres, when thinking themselves unwatched, that the naturalist in us conquered the sportsman; and, regardless of Joe's wrath and the bailiff's dismay, we remained looking at them instead of playing havoc in their ranks with the gun. A serene contemplation of the scene before them seems to constitute the happiness of a mature rabbit. He or she lies close down to the ground, occasionally blinking or twitching its ears, but the young ones are never tired of scampering hither and thither and playing with each other so ludicrously: that an untoward laugh on our parts sends them scattering back to the bank, in which an acute ear can hear them padding up and down their intricate passages to their holes like a small army. We have always envied Alice in Wonderland her excursion into the home of a rabbit. Those neat, well-planned passages are always so extremely interesting, must positively lead to some mysterious and unknown quarter of the inside world, that we have often wished to be small enough to glide after the tip of the white tail of a rabbit as it disappears to the music of Joe's enraged bark, and see for ourselves what his domestic arrangements in the bank are really like.

Sometimes birds are struck with this same notion, and

some are very fond of using a disused rabbit-run as a shelter
for their nests; and a tiny feather hanging on the opening
will tell us of the robin who has established herself within,
or of the burrow-duck who has placed her home so far inside
the sheltering passage that no one can possess himself
of her eggs.     Into these holes, in the severe winter of
1881-82, thousands of red-winged thrushes and fieldfares
crept for shelter, only to die there in such numbers that we
ourselves have seen none since that most disastrous time for
creatures—when we found plovers dead close under the
hedge, where they had been blown in dozens by the force of
the gale, and small birds crept close to the windows, looking
in like little children, with their tiny heads against the pane
whence streamed out the light and warmth into the dark
night, as if asking—piteously, silently asking—to be taken
in and given shelter and heat.     But it does not do to
encourage sparrows too much, for they become in that case
very much like small children once more—there is no getting
rid of them; and though they are very cheery companions,
once let them get on speaking terms and there is no stopping the flood of their eloquence; for one of the things one
learns in the quaint bypaths in which we love to tread, is
the practicability of holding sympathetic communication with
the feathered denizens of the air.     An intelligent chirp will
invariably be replied to by a sparrow; a good-humoured
whistle will attract the respectful response of a blackbird,
and of course a starling or a jay is only too glad to answer
should we speak to them quietly when they are close beside us.

   This knowledge is possessed in a great measure by the
fishermen in our harbour, and it is charming to see how
the gulls will stop in their flight when called or "tolled" by
the man lying motionless in his small gray punt, and will

circle round and round, replying or questioning as the voice alters its note, and looking in vain for the friend with whom he expects to have further converse; indeed, so great is the power one or two of the men possess that they can "toll" birds near enough to be within shot; still this seems such a cruel manner of securing our prey that we should be loth to resort to it.

All animals are singularly attached to the human race, and would of course become more so were it not for boys, and our pernicious habit of shooting and slaying every small bird or creature that comes in our way; and the careful study of nature opens out such a wide field of speculation that it is necessary to guard against becoming enthusiastic, or else we may find ourselves recounting things that sound too like fairyland for this prosaic age of ours.

When autumn is dying slowly into winter is perhaps the worst time of the year for an abider in the country: all seems so hopeless; we see our beloved flowers close their eyes and return to the earth from whence they came; the swallows and swifts that made life so pleasant to us have finished their remarkable flights across the river and back again twenty times without stopping, as if to prepare themselves for the long journey before them; the sparrows leave the haunts of men, and, gathering themselves together in vast flocks, frequent barn-yards and open fields, and scarcely trouble themselves to return home for the night. The blackbirds and thrushes are miserable, and only the cheery little robin sings to us, full of faith in the possibilities of better times coming sooner or later.

Still to the sportsman there is then occupation indeed. The pheasants are at their best; the wild-fowl entice him to spend long silent nights out of doors, and the rough shooting in the islands at the mouth of the harbour is not to be despised; while for some there is the fascination of hunting, with which, however, we have not the very smallest sympathy, save on our feet, when we can learn another phase of Nature, and pray that the fox may escape its pursuers speedily.

That there are bypaths even within a perceptible distance of London we have endeavoured to show in one or two papers farther on in this little book: bypaths in London itself where, "out of the tide," or in attending first nights in unfashionable localities, we learn much of another phase of life.

To us every well-known corner in the south of England has such bypaths, from the Kentish cobnut plantations to the far limits of Dorset, where a wholesome dread of Bonaparte still lingers hand in hand with traditions of smugglers and wild legends of shipwrecks and haunting ghosts; while every inch of the ground is rich with associations of the olden times, and full of lore about birds, beasts, and flowers, that is patent to all who choose to see it.

Watch, for example, this long, straight, dusty road, going straight away like an arrow from the great noisy city to a fair Kentish town; at times on each side are mean squalid houses, or again it passes through a quaint old market-place that was once the first stage to Tunbridge Wells. Here John Evelyn was stopped by footpads, and here Henry Esmond changed horses for the last time on his hurried visit to save his dear cousin, Lady Maria, from the hands of the bailiffs: now its nearness to London is all that keeps it alive, and its old square houses are rapidly disappearing before the love for red-brick turreted houses that is one of the features of the present day.

Even on the highways there is much to see, but more still off them. Take for example of what we mean the

great thoroughfares of London, with their vast apparent
prosperity, their crowded shops, their clean pavements
and their civil policeman; yet wander away from Oxford
Street or Regent Street but for a quarter of a mile, and what
do we find? Dirt, squalor, vice; crowded birds beating
their breasts and wings against the narrow bars; rabbits
that almost bring tears to our eyes when we see their eyes,
that all but speak, looking agonisingly at us; and then think
of the free, happy, gray creatures we know so well; weakly
children, down-trodden mothers too ignorant to be miserable; ay! and at times noble institutions; hard working
men and women anxious to amuse as well as preach;
and indeed all sorts of wonderful and painful things that are
unknown by those who simply drive or walk between the
rows of houses whose faces are so fair, and whose backs
are placed sometimes in these very bypaths. And leaving
London and passing through the market-place, what do we
find in our bypaths? It is late spring; the foliage is at its
very best; the golden oak, much like a baby's fluffy head of
hair, is changing into a maturer shade; the chestnuts are
dark and dignified; the pale hue of the larch still is accentuated by the darker firs among which it grows; the silvered
poplars and aspens quiver and wave like tortured things;
the road is on this side and on that; we are between the
two, and miles, so it seems to us, from every trace of human
beings! Presently we come upon one of those delightful
cross-roads through waving grass or growing corn that are
always so wonderfully suggestive and mysterious, and that
may lead direct to fairyland for aught that we know to the
contrary: unless one has time to spare in mooning, it were
well to avoid such paths as these! The very stile is
seductive: it suggests leaning thereon, and a comfortable
contemplation of the summer's crops, or, as at present, a calm

looking in upon an expanse of yellow buttercups that glitter in the flood of their spring sunshine that is vouchsafed to us. The path is very narrow, and we cannot tell where it may lead. Perhaps if we wander down it we may come to the land where our dead await us; we may meet and walk with her shadow whom we so loved on earth; we may tell her—ah! if she knows it not without our telling—how never a day passes without our thoughts going out to meet hers; or we may come upon enchanted ground full of suggestions. Shall we climb the stile and brave the walk? On and on goes the path: here lazy cows scarcely trouble to brush off the flies that buzz around them; there tall hanks of poles show where the hop-gardens are; and presently we are in a miniature village that has once been in the heart of the country. An old, old cottage, the upper rooms overhanging the under rooms, stands still, as it has stood since 1645, braving the elements, content to see the wonderful procession of the seasons, the march of life and birth; all ending in the silence of death; passing through the walls that last on contentedly as shelter to the life, and not to those atoms who hold life for the moment; while an open pond, in which ducks stand-ing on their heads in the water paddling with their feet out behind; a garden full of wide-mouthed monthly roses, and a red-roofed barn, form together a picture that is perfect; across the road is an "oast-house" with its cowl-shaped chimneys; and the one public-house stands at four cross-roads, with a lean finger-post pointing out the different routes possible for us to take.

We choose one with two deep green hedges for shelter; we pass beneath the shade of gigantic oaks and elms, each the resting-place of many a bird's nest; here we see the curious nest of the magpie, with its whimsical roof to keep out the bad weather, and in a ditch we see a robin's nest with four small featherless creatures who open their mouths wide in response to our chirp; expecting doubtless to have fine juicy worms dropped into the yellow chasm below us. Listen then a while to the delicious chorus of birds around: in yonder trees the wood-pigeon never stays her note; the blackbird is singing as if he could never be grateful enough for the glorious burst of fine weather; the thrush is singing too; and every atom of creation joins in, in its way, from the rustling leaf on the trees to the tiny insect that gravely circles in the delicious air. Away, away, as the eye travels slowly from one beauty to the other, it rests at last on the far horizon that, banded and belted in with magnificent trees, is hidden under a dense blue veil, as if the sky were resting there; we see another village, an ivy-covered church, a deserted house with shuttered windows looking over a neglected field, and then to our astonishment we are once more on the main road, within a short walk of which all this charming country is to be seen.

Or, again, we can take you to a wide, heath-covered, furze-scented stretch of common land: here in spring the numerous finches abound, and the golden gorse glows warmly under the blue sky; a great disused windmill stands up gaunt and black against the horizon; we can look away, away, over deep azure distances, until we come to a dark cloud, which is London; or resolutely turning our backs thereon we can stand on Cæsar's Camp and bethink ourselves of the Roman invasion, and how, maybe, our conquerors stood here looking down on the low city by the Thames that represented to them the haven where they would be.

Is it not almost appalling to wander in some such places as these and know certainly that the men who made history have been here too? Yonder rough block of masonry looks nothing, but the rough tile cropping out here and there shows that Roman hands formed it for some unknown purpose, that will soon now be lost entirely to knowledge, because such spots as these are being improved off the face of our native land.

It is with a hope that we may in some measure present, if only on paper, some of these almost unknown corners of the south of England that these papers are now collected in one volume; and if the perusal of them may in any way draw attention to places like them that exist at every one's back door, we shall be amply repaid; for to our minds England is full of interest, and the faint lovely echo from the olden times with which she is replete is far too little studied and loved by those children who use her, it seems to us, as acrobats or swimmers use a plank on which they stand to obtain a good spring; thus enabling themselves to get as far away from it as is possible.

## ON THE SKIRTS OF THE CROWD

THOUGH just on the very skirts of the crowd, our suburb is unlike any other suburb, and we naturally pride ourselves a great deal upon this fact.

True that we are between two very ordinary ones, but standing as we do off the highway, and a little in a corner, we are quiet and select, and, from our vantage ground, somewhat look down upon the denizens of other less favoured spots than the one that we inhabit. London lies like a vast octopus, stretching its lean and hungry arms on all sides into the country; and as these arms grow it has claimed and clasped our small corner, until it has almost lost all its appearance of country, and bears no more resemblance to what a real dweller outside cities would understand by that word, than does an imprisoned lark to the free singer revelling in fresh air and blue skies, far from the haunts of man.

Indeed, though it is almost treason to confess it, we cannot help saying that the immediate vicinity of London is exactly like a lark after some months of captivity; for is there not the frayed appearance about its trees and hedges that the lark's tail gets with rubbing against the bars of its cage? to say nothing of the spurious free-and-easiness that a lark has when it attempts to sing in the old willowy

fashion ; for although we have several real country possessions still left us, we should advise the rash new-comer to
pause ere tasting one of the new-ripening blackberries that
adorn the hedgerows, else will he surely receive a lesson to
leave them alone for the future ; for immediately he does so
his mouth is full of dust, with a queer dash of taste suggestive of a chemist shop, thrown in by way of a flavour,
that once experienced he never forgets.

Yet it is something to have hedges and blackberries, and
to be able to see a wealth of foliage round us that is as
luxuriant and beautiful as the New Forest itself produces ;
still, as years go by, and the arms become longer, it is
grievous to watch year by year how delightful parks are
gradually chopped up ruthlessly into eligible sites for building.

Great old trees that have stood the blasts of many a
winter's wind, and the scorching of many a summer's sun,
fall low before the axe.   And where once stately ladies rode
quietly under avenues of beeches towards the hall or the
manor, the enterprising builder has begun to dig up the
ground in the very superficial manner that suffices him for
a foundation.

In one particular case, close to our suburb, we own to
feeling this state of things most acutely, for it seems to us
that this uprooting is personal, and that far more than the
mere park will disappear ; when the final work of destruction
is over, and it is all laid out into "eligible sites for building."
For we have known it at all times and seasons of the year,
from the deep winter silence, when we walked together with
him who was the owner, rustling our feet in the dead leaves ;
and looking for the mosses in yonder corner ; through lovely
spring, when the whole place was carpeted with bluebells
and anemones, and summer's wonderful luxuriant peace, to
calm decay in autumn time, when we bid good-bye to the

C

summer and laid her to sleep, well knowing that next year should give her back to us again.

Now the shutters are up in the round thatch-roofed lodge, and the gate that once swung open wide constantly to admit visitors to the great house is padlocked, and bears on its shabby front the disagreeable notice that trespassers will be prosecuted; while on the old oak we always regarded with deep veneration, is displayed that odious board, that announces to all whom it may concern, that the sale of timber is to take place on such a day; after which the park will be considered as a series of sites suitable for gentlemen's residences.

Yet what memories will not go with the oak? up into his gnarled and twisted arms we have often enough climbed to look for nests and to watch the growth of the polypodium fern that looks down knowingly at us even on such a sad day as this. And do we not remember well enough how it was our ambition for our childish arms to meet round his trunk as we stood in a ring, that somehow or other was never destined to be complete?

It is not three months since the last owner of the place went through his gates in that dismal carriage that comes once only for all of us. It is not yet two months since the sale, yet the rust is on the hinges of the gate; a spider has spun his web across the latch, and on the paths that were wont to be so neatly kept, moss creeps and leaves lie thick; while the whole atmosphere that appears brooding over the spot is full of decay and damp and misery.

It was in early winter that the fiat went forth for the destruction of the place, and defying the hints to trespassers we entered once more the old familiar avenue, and wandered unchecked beneath the bare brown branches that were so soon to fall under the auctioneer's hammer.

Here all seemed silence save for the occasional chirp of a robin, that did not break into his usual clear, bright, cheerful song, but seemed insensibly to share the sense of decadence and death that pervaded the spot.

When we reached the house, turning its sightless, blinded windows towards the west, and stood on the doorstep where we were wont to receive always ere now our heartiest welcome; we paused a while, for knowing surely we should see the place no more we were fain to gaze at the scene before us, thus imprinting the lovely picture on our memory's page; much as a mourner, standing beside a coffin, gazes on his beloved's countenance, and implores memory to be his friend, and keep for him, for ever, that of which death has so cruelly robbed him.

Away to the east lay London; but there was small trace of that that quiet winter day. Only just there where we knew it existed the gray atmosphere seemed a little grayer, a little heavier; and we think more regretfully than ever of its ever-growing presence, its ever-increasing requirements, that render necessary such terrible sacrifices as the one we were deploring. For not so long ago our park seemed quite in the heart of the country. Folks went to the tiny church, long since improved out of all knowledge; while the sweet bells at eventide made the whole atmosphere vocal. Small boys and girls in clean white pinafores walked demurely through the park on the look-out for the squire, who had ever a smile for them all; but this is all over; and where we saw a long line of graceful trees, their beautiful bare limbs plainly visible in their winter nakedness, raw red villas will arise, or sham Queen Anne abodes be built that are only bearable because they are less hideous than the ordinary stuccoed mansion, dear to the retired tradesman's heart. In front of the poor old porch the gravel and lawn were cut up with the heavy waggons, and wreaths of damp straw were curled round the passion-flower and wistaria that we planted as children, and believed that they would never, never grow. Now that they have reached the nursery window, and are twined around the bars, the fiat has gone forth, and they will be cast away, heedless of the hopes and fears that they were once the source of in our hearts.

The flower-beds, so gay but only in the summer, had the remains of their gaudy blossoms still remaining in them; but the heliotropes and geraniums were dank and dead and blackened by frost and rain, while in one sheltered spot vast clumps of Christmas roses were unfolding their delicate pink-veined white buds; unknowing that they shall have no longer a sheltering glass to keep their purity from the pitiless weather; and indeed should hardly have time to open out before the scaffold poles are erected, and they are trampled into the ground by the workmen's feet.

The fountain that used to throw up its glistening spray against a summer background of purple beech and white flowering syringa was broken, and the shattered Cupid, thrown roughly down from his pedestal among the just-flowering violets, looked singularly like a little lost baby who had wandered in there, and having become weary had laid himself down to die.

In the distance the purple air that ever clings about the undergrowth in a winter wood did not stir, for evening was coming on, and there was no wind to move the quiet mist; and as we gazed away, away before us as far as we could see, it almost appeared to us as if the ghosts of the people who once had their habitations here, were allowed to wander about the place to the last moment, striving vainly to protect it against the coming bouleversement of the old regime.

Yet were this so, there were surely no worse punishment for the greatest sinner among those unhappy spirits; and for certain will they see their very names and abode entirely banished from the world.

As long as places and things exist as they used to be, there remains something tangible to connect us with the past and with those who were the inhabiters of it; as long as the great elms stood like a serried rank of soldiers, always drawn up at "attention" on each side the drive, it was impossible that we could forget the charming face and lovely smile that were hers who died so young, so pure, so sweet, that we can but think of her as one of the angels lent us for a while to teach us what the denizens of the other world are surely like.

For down that avenue how often have we seen her walk with her father, her arm in his, skipping beside him, and anon turning to lay her soft round cheek against his shooting jacket as she seemed as if she could never get near enough to him, or let him see how much to her were those lovely evening walks. From the long shadows we can raise them both once more; but when the elms are gone, we shall have nothing on which to hang the picture we so love to contemplate.

And here too where we wandered in the sweet spring evenings counting the primroses, eager to discover what work had been done on the earth by the soft drifting April rain, and by April sunshine, since the night before, will be dug cellars; and here where we stood to watch the bridal train, that before another year ran its course was replaced by the funeral one, will see homes raised that knew us not —the shadow from whose walls will obliterate all traces of that dear dead time.

Ay, even the shrubbery behind the house will go; which

is a sacred spot to us, for there our first brief love-tale was told, and there we wandered agonised, alone, and inconsolable, unable to bear our own pain, or face her parents' anguish when they returned home, after leaving her alone in the churchyard.

The house and woods are crowded by such thoughts, such associations as these : remembrances of bright days of happiness, of people once brilliant and young and beautiful, of whom it is impossible for us to think of now save as old and miserable and broken by care ; almost as impossible as it will be to realise, once the bricklayers are let loose there, the quiet and beauty that even in its very last days are yet to be found in each distant corner of the old park.

And in the last spring that the park, as a park, is ever destined to see, these beauties appear fairer than ever to our eyes ; and the trees, gay in their luxuriant garments, have never looked as lovely as now when they fall one after the other beneath the axe : it is the last flicker of the light, "the light burning before death," and adds many a pang to what we are enduring.

The bluebell dell, once almost unknown to us, so well hidden was it, and returning to us each spring as a glad surprise, is rifled by each child who once would never have ventured in beyond the straight path ; the closely lapping-over oak fence, rich with many a lichen, and crept over in places by the tiny ivy that clings with its own little fingers, and plants its own tiny feet into each crevice, and needs no nailing, has kept out intruders for many a long year, yet can do so no longer. Just when the pale green ivy leaves are pushing vigorously on, eager to make the most of the time for growing, it will be destroyed, ruthlessly torn away, and thrown aside by those who have neither time nor inclination to spare its beauties.

The thick thorn hedge, its symmetry broken every now and then by the glistening holly, has never yet been disturbed by nest-hunting urchins; in yonder tree a wood-pigeon has reared her young every year since we can remember, roosting there with her two children huddled up close together on a lower branch than the one selected by their mother, who thus appears to watch over them quietly; and out of the stump of the big oak on the lawn, broken in a famous storm more years ago than we care to count, came every summer evening regiments of bats that swept past us uttering their shrill uncanny cry; while we teased them by throwing up small stones that made them believe they saw their prey, the booming cockchafer; and now all these pictures are vanishing; all these dead memories going; and the living creatures must seek another home; for their old abiding-place is given over to the present day, that is too utilitarian to see in our park aught save its advantages as a valuable and eligible site for more houses for the ever-increasing population around us.

And yet the very fact that we are deploring is partly the cause of our delight in our own especial suburb.

For we too were once a great estate stretching away up a valley, calm and secluded, and belted in and adorned by trees; gradually the place was broken up, doubtless dealing a deathblow to some one's fancies and memories, and one after the other roads were cut, and houses sprang up hither and thither, yet preserving as much as possible many of the characteristics of its ancient state.

And to that we are indebted for several of our most loved and cherished possessions; for do we not own a hedge that is as fresh and beautiful as any you can find in the very heart of the country, and have we not trees on which we can gaze enraptured, as one after the other the seasons pass by, doing their divers works diligently? In autumn our hedge is covered with convolvuluses, and decked with hips and haws and oak-galls; it glows with the dark red leaf of the bramble, and has delicious tints of brown from its beech and oak leaves. And in spring all sorts of surprises are constantly provided for us, from the early-opening, somewhat consequential-looking, wild arum, that we call "lords and ladies," to the white anemone that comes up somewhat sparsely, and as if somewhat put out to find herself so much in evidence. In sheltered nooks we have primroses and more bluebells than we can count, that all suggest the seclusion and aristocratic origin of our one especial corner; and in our trees we can watch the rooks wheeling grandly to and fro in the autumn, as if they were being regularly put through their paces in a series of autumn manœuvres before flying off; for the especial small colony that belongs to us always joins a larger one in the winter, only returning when spring comes back to beautify our newly-budding hedgerows.

Autumn is a very silent time of year in our suburb; every one flies away, rushing to the sea, that as every one knows who is a real ocean-lover is always at his worst then; but then it seems to us that we like it better than ever. London is accessible at any moment should we require amusement, and our surroundings are so beautiful that we realise that we have all the pleasures and none of the pains that accompany a life really lived in the great city.

In days of fog that we can see brooding grimly over the dark line in the distance that means the metropolis, we have nothing worse than a soft gray atmosphere that is soothing and restful, and that gives way about noontide before the sun, that shines down joyfully on us for an hour or two, and is as exhilarating as a cup of wine.

After a few hours in London, and twenty minutes of rail, we forget the draggle-tail of our lark ; and not contrasting our surroundings with the purple hills of Purbeck, or the warm, bright Bournemouth chines, but only with the oppressive air just left, we welcome them gladly, and revel in a sunset that begins to render radiant the groves of trees, where yellow patches and a certain appearance of thinness mark that autumn is here indeed.

The robin sings shrilly from early morning till late evening, triumphant, as it seems to us, in having the whole world of song to itself. The swifts have gone, and the swallows are reduced to one or two ; but the martens linger long, and dart about the newly-springing houses with as much gusto as if they were a hundred miles from town. And, indeed, in the end of the first October we ever spent in our suburb, we watched a very late and imprudent swallow, with her nest full of little ones, with all the cares of her family on her hands, when she ought to have been well on her way to Africa.

We cannot understand now why she went into house-keeping so extremely late. Although we knew of the nest, we did not realise her intentions until we caught sight of her singularly wistful eye, watching the manœuvres of the last of her companions ere they departed and left her behind ; one of them lingering just a little as if he were expostulating about her foolishness in remaining where she was ; but she stuck to her post until the last week in October, when we saw her feeding the small birds, and encouraging them to learn a flight that could never be strong enough to escape the coming long cold winter nights. Unfortunately we did not live near enough to her abode to learn what really became of her, but the next time we went past her place of banishment she was gone, and all her children had vanished too. They could not possibly have flown to Africa, and doubtless hid about in chimneys and near warmth, in the way swallows sometimes but rarely do ; and that may have given rise to White's notion of them hibernating at the bottom of a pond, for we have twice ourselves found swallows in midwinter, and once had a little one, in an empty room, that was frozen there, owing to a sudden and severe frost. He appeared one evening at a window that was half-way open, slipping down between the two panes in a way that was agonising to witness and difficult to extricate him from, and we made him free of the room, where we dared not have a fire for fear he might fly into it and be frizzled to death ; and there he died, much to our sorrow, for we longed to save him for the joys of another summer.

And perhaps our swallows may have sheltered in some of the empty houses. Yet we saw nothing of them until the following April, when the whole place was pervaded by them for a short time as if they were house-hunting ; and then they went elsewhere, only coming about occasionally as if to pay us a visit. However, it is really curious to note how many rare birds we can see, especially in the autumn, or after a strong wind has blown them a little out of their reckoning. There are two herons that are to be seen regularly in an autumn evening, heading towards the east steadily just before dark : in a neighbour's pool, somewhat secluded in greenery and silence, wild-duck have paused a while ere proceeding on their journey. And we saw a specimen of the glossy ibis, so rare that we cannot understand how they escaped being shot ; and put it down to the fact that the ordinary suburban resident, being usually immersed in money-making, is neither a sportsman nor a naturalist, and knows very little of the creatures who live close beside him.

Only in the early spring we were visited by the peewits, whose familiar note, and the sight of whose graceful walk, made a strange feeling of home-sickness arise in our breasts; and in the winter we spent hours in feeding the birds, who gave us endless enjoyment in watching their different manners and customs, from the humble little robin, who waited until the rest had gone, to the consequential bull-finch, who had quite a stand-up fight over a piece of crust to which a blackbird had unfortunately taken an equal fancy.

Were it not for the evil-minded bird-catcher, and the eager grubber-up of every root and fern that were once superabundant here, we should naturally have still more attractions to write of. In autumn the stretching commons are purple with heather and knee-deep with bracken. There are lawns as umbrageous and silent as those supposed to be sacred to Devonshire, and there are woods, too often protected from the public by "trespassers will be prosecuted," but very beautiful to see even from a distance—in winter because of their delicate tracery against the clear sky; in spring because of the faint flush of brown, that tells its own story of the rise of the sap; in summer because of the deep silence and beauty of the mature foliage; and in autumn because of the thousand hues that deck them then. Still we pause a while, and wonder if we have not said so much for our suburb that we shall be inundated with human beings, eager to share in the pleasures of such a retreat as this; and for fear this may be the case, we turn on the dark side of the picture; for the suburban builder as a rule makes life unendurable by reason of his curious notions of what should constitute a dwelling-place, and has a manner of finishing his work, solely and wholly with an eye to a future, spent by him mainly in doing it all over again, that is apt to cause bad language from those who are his victims.

Building houses is at present a lost art, and any one who can design a plan where the whole internal arrangements are not specially formed for anything, save rooms in which to dine or sit or sleep, has, we feel convinced, a long, honourable, and lucrative career before him.

More especially, less confiding simplicity about the doors and windows would be advisable; for though we are very rural and innocent, the alarms of the gentle burglar that arise the moment the days " begin to draw in " should suggest that French windows opening out to the ground, and with no locks or manner of fastening save a simple screw, and no bolts or bars anywhere, argue an Arcadian confidence that might not be abused in the wilds of Dorset, but that is singularly malapropos ten miles from town.

And have not we who write cause to consider carefully how to prepare for that season, that seems to set in every autumn, with unexampled severity; for do we not call to mind a Sunday evening that can never be effaced from our minds, when, combining the simplicity of the country with the cunning of the town, we sent the domestics to church, having kindly dined early ourselves, and resolving to stay at home to guard our household gods?

About the time when the psalms were in full swing, as near as we could calculate, a mysterious small knock came at the back door; we took no notice; then the bell rang softly and mysteriously; we looked out of the window, and saw a manly form at the door; we went down, and demanded in our deepest bass notes, Who is there? but no response came, and after waiting a moment or two we boldly flung open the door and perceived nobody. We were beginning to think we had been deceived by our own eyes, when a frightened neighbour rushed in to tell us how all her silver had just been swept off the table, laid for supper—as is the suburban custom, before the servants depart to worship. And our servants came back (churchless) to tell us of their being asked questions by a couple of men, who roused their suspicions by wearing indiarubber shoes, and being most particular to know where such nice young women lived.

"We were sure you'd be robbed and murdered, sir, so we came back at once, to see if we could help," said they, and then proceeded to be of the greatest possible assistance by fainting in a heap (of two) by the kitchen grate.

However, we rose to the occasion, and despatching our man for the rural policeman we restored our damsels, and promised them his especial care during the coming hours of darkness. The suburban policeman is an excellent soul, and on being fetched from his supper—ruthlessly torn from his board at duty's call—he kindly consented to share ours, while we recounted our adventures, and heard from him how much evil these gentry had done in the neighbour-hood ; after which he interviewed the white and shaking domestics, obtaining by means of the most obviously leading questions more or less accurate descriptions of the men, and taking care that these should tally entirely with his preconceived notions of them.

By the time we had obtained all the information we could, and our friend had closed his note-book and bound it up with the elastic with a loud snap, we were a little more composed, and we were about to pass to lighter matters, our equanimity was again disturbed by our man, who tore in breathless and sank on his knees. "Oh, sir, I've just seen 'em," he gasped, "they've agone by the window. I saw their shadows, and so did Martha" (his wife, who refused to remain alone in the stables until the burglars were caught). Out we all rushed naturally, to find the people calmly passing on their way home from church, and casting their shadows as they did so on the kitchen window!

Then our friend the policeman saw his opportunity, and proceeded to make the coming night hideous to us by long and appalling stories of all the burglaries he had ever been assistant at, most of which were accompanied by bloody murders of the most atrocious type, and were generally committed by individuals exactly like those we had just been disturbed by. He pooh-poohed our notion that we were safe once four o'clock had struck, and said he had known the "worstest cases" about six, when any little turmoil caused by the householder resenting his throat being cut could be put down to the servants being about pretty early; and he finally demolished our last hopes of safety by showing us how, with a fair amount of skill, a diamond ring, and a sheet of brown paper smeared with treacle, any plate-glass window can be rendered practically useless in almost five minutes. Then he declared he must be off, and left us lamenting, but feeling secure that he would look us up constantly during the night, thus rendering sleep utterly out of the question. However, burglars are few and far between, and in those days of fogs, when London is practically unlivable in for three or four months in the year by children or delicate folks, the suburbs are really well worthy of attention, and perhaps in time burglars and builders may alike reform, and so allow of there being no drawbacks, at least for those who inhabit our one particular suburb.

# III

## A SUBURBAN GARDEN

But perhaps, after all, our most delightful possession is the garden itself. It is small enough for every bush and tree to be a familiar thing, yet large enough for the privacy so dear to the British mind, and for the ubiquitous tennis court ; while our trees form a shelter for our dear friends the birds, and are a never - failing source of enjoyment for us—from the time when we watch the leaves creep out of their sheaths, to that when they gradually become tarnished ; before they strip themselves one by one of their garments, and allow us to see all the secrets that they hid so carefully from us in the summer, when the foliage was too dense for us to perceive the thrush's nest that we knew of, yet could not discover, and that hid successfully the form of the nightingale, to hear whom we invited our friends, as in town one is invited to hear a prima donna ; but in our case with the certainty that our songster would neither sulk, nor have a sore throat, nor be deterred by the weather from appearing.

Was it not from the birds that we received our first intimation of the coming spring? for before we were aroused to the fact that the drowsy light of early morning had begun to look in on us, much earlier than we had been accustomed to see it, the sparrows had begun their animated chatter over the circumstance.

First of all there was a prolonged note, that told us at once that we were right in informing the children that we had heard what species of day it was from our dwellers in the gables, long before they came in to announce the pleasing fact that at last the south wind was paying us a visit; for after that comes a regular chorus of joy, and it needed but small imagination to know that big and little birds were congratulating themselves on the delightful change in the atmosphere, and that they were laying plans how best to employ the time of warm moist weather that was certainly now before them.

Any one who is only conversant with the ways and manners of our feathered friends in the depths of the country would regard a suburban garden as an utterly hopeless place in which to study their customs; the un-trained eye sees only the circumscribed space, the meagre bushes, the stinted trees, and the apparently futile attempt at culture of flowers—"All this must," say they, "leave little shelter for your birds to be attracted by, and must only make you long more than ever for the wide heaths and commons; the deep, quiet, decoy ponds; and the thousand and one creatures that day by day flitted over the garden there, or passed you in your walks and rides."

Not at all, my dear good soul, we answer cheerfully; come sit by the window with us and watch. You will soon learn, as we did, that there is all the difference between those wild Dorsetshire creatures and our suburban acquaintances that there is between the town and country human beings themselves. Look, for example, at yonder starling, emerging at daylight from the chimney where he has his nest. He has none of the free impertinent assurance of his rustic prototype, who is pretty sure he is safe in the spot he has selected for his home, and who returns year after year to the same place certain to find it ready for him. But he is a cautious, educated soul, who is wary in all his movements, and while knowing full well the house below him is empty, is yet aware that a tenant down there will soon put an end to his domestic hopes and joys, and so appears prepared for either fortune.

He even seems to know quite as well as we do what means the stopping of a fly drawn by the suburban horse : who is himself a character, and is so used to the work of house-hunting that he can never be got to pass a board with the fateful inscription "This house to let" on it without a struggle : for he just flies to a tree in the garden, and appears to be grateful for the look of sympathy we give him, as we watch the descent of a couple of agitated females, accompanied by several children grasping "orders to view" in their warm and sticky paws, who proceed to spread themselves over the house and garden, while we watch in dismay, fearing lest we should soon have neighbours far less interesting than those that are already in possession.

Next door, again, a tiny bit of loose slate has caused one of the starlings who lived in the colony in the chimney all the winter to migrate. He could not resist the delightful seclusion proffered him rent free among the rafters ; and day by day we watch him as he waits for a few moments, before going in at the aperture, that is so small that it looks to us like a pin-prick in the hard slated roof.

He puts his head on one side and then on the other, as if considering the best way to set about it, then he crouches down on the shoot as if lengthening himself out, and finally disappears in an instant, as if he had suddenly learned a conjuring trick and was able to make himself small at will.

The starling is a clever and persevering bird, and has a very high opinion of his own capabilities.

His note is not melodious, for example, but he is quite persuaded in his own mind that if only he had time to practise he could sing quite as well as the best of them. Sometimes he becomes impatient of the effortless, glorious rush of song poured from the quivering throats of our thrushes and blackbirds, who sing all day in the wood across the road ; and he has more than once betaken himself to the extreme top of an elm in the corner, and perched there, giving vent to the most remarkable sounds that ever a bird was guilty of.

We are quite positive of his intentions : there he sat, swayed to and fro on the fragile branch, while the east wind blew through his feathers unheeded !

First he said, " Chuck, chick, chuck," then gave birth to several quick sounds as if he were gnashing his bill with rage ; then he tried a queer strangled-sounding note, then he contented himself with chirping again, and then he appeared to pause, waiting a while of course with his head on one side, deliberately listening to a blackbird in an opposite tree.

When the blackbird had finished, the starling began again, and this time really warbled quite respectably for half a second or so, until another starling came up, and so very evidently jeered at him, that he pretended he was busy, and made for home again as quickly as ever he could.

It was an endless source of amusement to watch the regular stages of family life through which these birds passed. We know exactly when the little ones are hatched, by the ardent manner in which the parent birds forage for them all day long.  When the hen is sitting, early morning and late evening seem to suffice for this occupation, but the instant those hungry little mouths are opened, up there in the roof, the starling seems to spend his days in collecting worms, calling attention to the fact with his sharp note.

Then later on, sudden rushes into the bushes cause us to notice the young ones, who have left the nest and are beginning to do for themselves—little plump, almost tail-less creatures they are, that can hardly fly, and that flutter about among our ferns in blind despair as they hear us approaching, and who learn to fly with the accompaniment of shrill squeaks of anguish that would be amusing were they not so incessant and so very ear-piercing.

But as it is utterly impossible to stop them making this noise, it is best to obtain what amusement we can from watching them cling to the boughs, shrinking, until they are almost pushed off by their indignant parents : when, finding they can use their wings, they flutter down to the ground, where they run about until disturbed, when they fly into the nearest bush, where they fondly imagine they are entirely concealed from sight.

Then, too, in winter and very early spring the sparrows were a never-failing entertainment, though it was hard even then to forgive them their mischief, and the calm manner in which they appropriated our eaves.

But though they did an amount of harm that was rather trying, and made enough noise to wake the dead, we looked upon them leniently, considering them essentially as children or rather schoolboys of the bird world, and so endeavoured to console ourselves by watching them, for the destruction they wrought among the buds and yellow flowers in the garden. And indeed it was curious to notice their undoubted preference for yellow, for while not one crocus of that colour escaped their sharp little beaks, the white and purple ones passed unscathed through their short and charming lives.

Naturally, the drying east wind had parched up every morsel of green food in the garden; the sparse grass on what we call our lawn was dry and crisp with frost; there was not an appearance of a bud on any one of the trees; and there was literally nothing save the crocuses on which they could feed; but their preference for yellow was again displayed when the primroses came out; for while the mauve and white double ones were untouched, the single yellow flowers that we had brought up from Dorsetshire were all nibbled round and spoiled, just as we were rejoicing in a glimpse of their familiar faces; and the yellow winter jasmine was stripped of its blossoms in an adjacent garden entirely by those wee marauders, the sparrows. Still it is very amusing to watch their little preferences for each other's society, their vigorous fights, their ardent, untidy housekeeping, their calm demanding of our hospitality, their unaffected delight in every tree that puts out green leaves, in every lovely promise given, and alas! very often broken, by the spring.

We know how to accept these pledges, but the sparrows believed every sunny hour meant summer, and made a regular tour round our circumscribed space every fine morning, just to see exactly what had been doing in the world since the night before.

How else account for all the noise they combined to make as they flitted about or hopped trustfully along the grass, knowing that most cats are excluded from our garden, save and except two fair creatures who are too well fed to do more than give an occasional glance at the small things that can be out of their reach before they have got over the stretching, mouth-watering process : which is very prolonged indeed, in the case of those cats who are allowed in our precincts.

Then, too, when the hedge was discovered to be in leaf in a sheltered part there was a regular chorus of joy, every sparrow coming in turn to investigate the wonderful sight; and one was so moved by the spectacle that he possessed himself on the spot of a long straw, and sat with it in his beak, meditating long and profoundly on a proper place where he could commence building his nest.

All this was very delightful, and we felt quite *en rapport* with our small neighbours. We wasted a dreadful amount of time in watching them; and we almost fancied we were beginning to understand their different notes, and that we should begin soon to be able to converse with them, when a change came o'er the spirit of our dreams, and we began to find out more than we expected.

The first symptoms of discontent came from the higher regions. The children woke at unearthly hours owing to the noise made by "they dratted sparrers" in the eaves, and began to chatter too; bits of nests and smashed eggs embellished the window-sills, great lumps of straw stuck out from every corner; and we were beginning to falter in our allegiance to our birds in a small degree, when suddenly the climax came and we gave in altogether, and ordered a speedy and summary eviction. One night we were aroused by a most curious and uncanny sound in the house, or outside it—we couldn't quite tell which. It might have been caused by the cats rushing up and down in the passage, and we arose and cautiously looked out. There wasn't a sign of a cat—all was peaceful there, at least—and, willing to believe that we were the victims of an hallucination, we retired to our couch, determined to make the most of the extremely few hours of darkness that were before us, knowing full well that, once we had daylight, anything like sleep would be perfectly impossible, owing to the birds by which we were surrounded.

But the noise continued : flutterings as of wings seemed on every side, and presently small frantic squeaks accompanied these uncanny sounds.   The solution of the mystery was easy : the walls were, we knew, hollow, and to our horror we came to the conclusion that some of the birds had crept in under the eaves, or at one or other of the loopholes left by the kindly builder—who was evidently determined we should never lack fresh air,—and were dying in agonies just behind our bed-head.   We shall never forget the terrible sensation that seized us at that instant : that within a few inches of us a little soft brown bird was beating itself to death in the darkness was appalling, and the cessation of the sounds, far from consoling us, made us long to get out of what felt like a chamber of the dead ; and we were thankful when the clocks announced an hour at which we could descend without causing every one to think we had gone mad.

When the men came with their long ladders, the birds, evidently believing that some house-cleaning process was going forward that need not trouble them ; though it was certainly somewhat disturbing for the time ; flew right away on a pleasure excursion, and only returned at night when the work of destruction was complete.

And this was indeed done in a most systematic way, and helped us to discover the source of many a draught that had sought and found us at our fireside during the winter, defying every curtain we placed or precaution we took to circumvent it.   Wherever a draught could come these "squatters" of ours had crept in and taken up their abodes. There were a few completed nests, with two or three eggs already placed therein ; but in every available inch were

preparations for housekeeping, that must have resulted in
our being obliged to vacate our apartments in favour of the
nurseries under the eaves; for no living person could have
stood the noise that would have been made.

It was rather a sad sight to see the heap of straw and
bits of wool, and tag-rag and bobtail of all descriptions, that
went to make up the nests—for all seems fish that comes
into a sparrow's nest, — but a sadder one awaited us.
Having ascertained that the birds that were the cause of the
eviction had escaped by the way they came in, and that
our sympathy and sleepless night had been wasted, we were
going into the house, when we suddenly became aware that
the sparrows were returning, joyous and full of life after
their holiday.    It was quite appalling to see the manner in
which they behaved.

Fancy, if you can, returning after your day's work in the
city, to the old accustomed street where your house has stood
for more years than perhaps you care to count; think of walking joyfully along, your step waxing insensibly lighter as you
pondered over your dinner; and perhaps thought of your wife
and bairns; and then imagine the sensation that would seize
you, could you perceive that, like Aladdin's palace, your
house had entirely disappeared, and a great gap or a blank
wall represented the familiar door-step and the place where
the steps should be;—fancy all this: and then you may be
able to understand the sparrows' feelings, when they came
back to find a hard cement wall, where once had been a gap
into which they crept, sure of a warm and sheltered corner;
or a pitiless piece of wood barring the entrance to what was
once a remarkably eligible residence.

It was exceedingly curious to note the divers stages of
feeling through which they passed, going from the deepest
surprise into the wildest tempests of rage.

At first they really imagined they had come to the wrong house, and after a few futile efforts to find their accustomed haunts, they departed next door, as if they were quite of opinion they had taken a wrong turn ; but a very little time convinced them that this was not so, and back they all came, scolding, squeaking, and raving over the untoward and unexpected state of affairs.

Surely never before were birds in such a quandary! They flew against the house and beat at it with their wings ; they perched themselves on the beams, and they chattered about the chimneys ; but try as they would there was no inlet left, and they came to the conclusion that they were hopelessly and emphatically given notice to quit.

One sparrow had seized a feather out of the mass of débris and sat with it in his beak, as if nothing should daunt him, but the rest flew, as night came on, sadly and solemnly, into the trees, and no doubt during the watches of the night laid their plans for vengeance.

Shall we ever forget the heavenly peace of the night that followed the eviction ?   Alas, never, for we have not yet had its fellow !   True, we felt rather uncomfortable " inside," as the children say, when we thought of the homeless wanderers in the trees ; but sleep after all is one of our best possessions, and we do not like to be defrauded of it, so we turned on our pillows like the sluggard and congratulated ourselves on a good day's work.

We might have spared our jubilate !   The very next day the sparrows returned *en masse* and took possession of our eaves, putting their nests into old martens' nests, or tucking up their untidy clumps of straw stolen from the stables under the overhanging rafters, or into shoots, or indeed anywhere where they could possibly find a resting-place ; and though, of course, we declined to allow them to remain in the shoots, we ceased the warfare and allowed them to bring up their families undisturbed; obtaining what consolation we might, from watching the agonised expression of one papa sparrow, who returned from his foraging expeditions more and more perplexed as to his safe entrance into his nest, that, being perched somewhat on a slant, very lightly, under one of the eaves, required an almost acrobatic education to reach surely and without accident.

He always perches first on the chimney and gazes at his nest; then he crouches and prepares for flight, but losing heart rests again; again he crouches, again he stays; but at last with a supreme effort he flies straight, gives himself a side-way twist and vanishes, and we can almost fancy how his loving family receive him, patting him on the back, and calling him a fine fellow, for performing a feat to which our cruelty has condemned him.

However, we have at times much more aristocratic visitors than the sparrows; these are our neighbours' doves and pigeons, who alight on our chimneys and make day hideous with their moans like "a soul in pain," as a sentimental visitor remarked, but that to our minds resemble far more a domestic in the first stage of hysterics; and does not a smart, brown-coated, red-breasted robin come always all the winter long, and, perching itself on one particular spot, sing to us at the one hour of the day when life seems at the lowest ebb, and for about the same length of time on each occasion?

In fog or snow or bitter wind he was there, and if we were dull before, the sight of his cheery little person and the sound of his warble gave us something to think of, and somehow or other seemed to brighten our whole day.

We cannot quite make him out; we are quite convinced he has a history, but what it is we do not quite know; he never has a friend; we have never seen him save alone, and on this same gate-post; none of the other birds know him either, and he has no wife as far as we know; but all winter we had an idea we kept quite privately to ourselves that the spring would disclose that small wife's existence; and that if we only watched long enough we should learn that his pretty song was all about what the spring was going to bring him, and that he knew quite well that it was good to be cheerful, because better days must sooner or later come to all!

Opposite our very windows in a park we pretend to ourselves is ours—as indeed it is ours, because we enjoy the sight of it just as much as the owners do—is a charming rookery. The secrets are all open to us from the moment the birds return in spring from spending the winter in the larger rookery some distance off, to the time when the parents in the busy spring come and forage for their young beneath our windows: when the cares of children are making them silent in the trees, there is always something of the profoundest interest going on. It may be weakness and a work of supererogation on our part, but we must own to digging up divers worms that are left about to attract the rooks to our garden (though of course the worms retreat, wriggling back again out of reach long before the rooks see them), but they only come at very early morning, preferring to make for the ploughed fields or the newly-springing wheat and barley, where they can forage undisturbed except by others of their own kind.

Often and often jackdaws fly scolding over our heads, and reminding us of that distant castle in the gap of the Purbeck hills that is so beautiful: and we could, an we would, have a series of dog visitors, who are too apt to turn gardeners to be quite as welcome as we could wish.

Still there is one poor little white creature that has
formed a hopeless and sad attachment to our white terrier
that is quite pathetic; he was bought a sweet little ball
of fluff, with brown ears and nose, on Bournemouth pier,
and was warranted never to grow. When put down to run
he raised the laughter of each rude boy he met. When
carried by his mistress, his wee head confidingly pressed
against her, and his comical eyes looking out of his fringe,
he was the envied of all beholders ; but alas ! he grew long
and hideous, and with such an affliction in his hind legs,
owing to a liberal allowance of gin in his early youth having
undermined his constitution, that all his friends prophesied a
speedy demise, and his enemies suggested poison as an easy
termination to his ludicrous and ugly little life.

But his mistress loved him and would have none of this,
and he still exists to haunt our garden and appeal to
Belinda—who is too old for these vagaries, and whose heart
was buried in Boffin's : our red spaniel's : grave some years
ago—to smile upon him ; but she is profoundly bored by her
small lover, and laughs at him with the other dogs in a way
that is not quite kind, but that has no effect whatever on
her admirer ; for he drags his head that belongs to a Maltese
spaniel, his body that is somewhat like a fluffy dachshund,
were this a possibility ; and his tail that was originally
designed for a retriever, after her from early morn until
dewy eve ; and creeps under gates or through hedges reck-
lessly : to have a moment's look at the object of his affections.

It would take too long to walk round the garden and
make the acquaintance of our ferns that grow here far more
brilliantly and luxuriously than in the lovely hedges and hillsides from which we took them in their infancy : and perhaps
they would not tell others all that they do us. But for us
they are a perfect picture-gallery, for the *Osmunda regalis*

brings back to us in a moment the very day and place where we first made its acquaintance, and our lovely Dorset Holme Lane is almost our own when we look into the heart of *Filix mas* and *Filix femina* that we brought up from that scented, calm, and beautiful place, hidden like a gem among the wide stretches of the arid heath. As each frond unfolds, and waves its banner in the wind, we see a different scene, and we can but advise other suburban residents to make their visits to the sea-side or country equally profitable, and bring home with them ferns that do wonderfully in soil where nothing seems to flourish, and that will bring back to them each spring complete vignettes of the places where they were born, and the summer surroundings that were theirs when the collector's trowel made them his own. Things that are really lovable should have associations; and these almost everything in a suburban garden can have, which gives it one of its greatest charms; for no one can complain of " nothing to do " who is fortunate enough to care for what folks term "inanimate" things, and birds and animals; for there is always enough to interest them ; while the small glass-house, called by courtesy and the advertisements a conservatory, gives wet weather occupation, and in our own case brought us an amount of knowledge that was no small addition to our small previous stock on the subject of a suburban garden.

## IN SEARCH OF FLOWERS

WE made the acquaintance spoken of on the last page one day in the very middle of winter, when there was not a flower in the garden save an occasional violet, so modest and unpresuming that it had buried its face in the miry bed and refused to raise its head on any pretext whatever. A stunted primrose, looking as if its edges had been nibbled by an inquisitive rabbit, was not much better, and as we must have flowers some time or other, we set out boldly in our attempt to procure something to replenish our vases, or perish in the attempt. And it is very nearly this latter, and, if mud were fatal, it would be quite, for as we turned out of our gates we were well-nigh engulfed in the best imitation of the Slough of Despond that we have ever seen. Close to London as we are, we have not become sufficiently advanced in civilisation to have a footpath, and we ploughed our way through clay that almost swallowed us up, and that rendered our boots the scorn of all beholders, and caused our man to give warning on the spot when asked to clean them. If it were not for the mud we should have enjoyed our walk mightily. The old year was sobbing itself away very gently. A soft south-west wind moaned sadly through the beautiful bare trees that swayed softly to and fro as if they were rocking themselves to sleep to the tune the breeze was singing.

When we reached the top of the hill we could look for miles, and see nothing save an occasional church spire, while the middle distance looked intensely purple under the gloom of the winter afternoon sky, and the few stunted broom bushes on the hillside appeared already as if they were beginning to think about the spring, and produce from their store their bright golden blossoms wherewith to gladden the hearts of the children who play among them, unchecked and unreproved.   To the left we caught just a glimpse of a dull silver pond, and of a big farmyard where the cows stood knee-deep in straw, and looked contemptuously at the rooting pigs that will investigate their carpet, sniffing here and there in a way that must disturb their meditations greatly ; while on the right our apology for a river crept like a thread of water, or, more like yet, the trail that a snail leaves on the ground, and made us think of another river many miles away, so sorely, that we remember the object of our walk, and with an impatient sigh proceed, trying to forget and succeeding not at all.   But we do forget when we get to our nursery, and at once, as is our wont, begin to ask questions. The window of the tiny shop was full of flowers—heaths, looking frail and wax-like, yet in reality the hardiest of crea-tures, only requiring plenty of water, a cool equal tempera-ture, and small attention when in blossom to last for weeks in any ordinary room ; the thin pale Roman hyacinth, strong of scent and frail of existence ; quantities of geraniums blossoming as if it were July and they were glowing in the summer sunshine ; one or two strange human-looking creatures, full of expression, that are orchids, and sundry great white arums looking proudly down at their humbler friends and appearing very much as if they would like to blow their own trumpet.

Our friend the gardener was very busy, but never too busy

to tell us about his flowers, which he loves, and treats as one would treat a child. He had just packed three great square wooden boxes for Covent Garden, and had a whole range of ferns and palms being denuded of any small brown particles, or dead fronds or leaves, and having their leaves tied up and folded round, to send to the same market; but there was no appreciable difference in his houses, that were full of everything beautiful and pleasant to sight and smell. The fern-houses looked cool and green, but did not feel the former when you enter. The pipes being full of hot water kept the place at an even temperature that was very pleasant; while out of the crevices in the brickwork tiny ferns and mosses sprang spontaneously and flourished vigorously, showing distinctly how well they like the damp warm air with which they were supplied. There was a cooler place than this, where maiden-hair fern was kept solely for cutting for "bo-kays," as our friend naturally called them; for if this lovely, graceful creature is grown in a cool house the fronds last much longer, and do not suddenly turn black in the face and frizzle up, as do their sisters forced fiercely into maturity by greater heat. Flowers, you see, are much like human beings, after all. Then in those cooler houses we found more arums, and that wonderfully long-suffering and useful plant the aspidistra, with its wide white-and-green striped leaves, that is by far the best plant for any one to have for room decoration—for it requires small attention and lives on, caring nothing for a gassy atmosphere, irregular waterings, and bad position as regards light—that might teach its own lesson to the thoughtful possessor of one of these kindly creatures. Naturally, if well treated, they respond immediately to kindness, and keep beautiful for ever, increasing greatly and multiplying year by year; for we, who had one plant, now twelve years ago, have five or

six, all sprung from the original one that has gone through
many vicissitudes; but certainly it does not do to think of
the great graceful palms, if we speak simply of decoration,
for nothing exceeds both their beauty and usefulness; still,
they are more expensive to buy, costing 10s., where the
aspidistra costs 2s. 6d., and they require an immense amount
of heat and attention, else surely will the leaves crack and
turn brown at the edges in a most distressing manner.
Beyond where the palms live were eucharis, with their great
starry flowers, and stephanotis, just beginning to bloom;
while a strong scent attracted us to sundry gardenias, which
at that time of the year fetch 1s. each wholesale in Covent
Garden, and are doubtless sold by the retail florists for much
higher prices than the gardener gets. In this house the
flowers were principally white, and kept—O curious contrast !—for weddings and funerals, when expense is for the
moment not considered, and the only thought is how best
to deck the pure white victim or heroine of the day. Sometimes the cross for the coffin and the bouquet for the bride
lie side by side in the little workshop, and doubtless have
their own thoughts on the subject of the pageants at which
they are about to assist. But of course these flowers were
too costly for us, as indeed were all scented varieties just
then. Jonquils and cut Roman hyacinths were about 1½d.
a spray; and when we gazed longingly at a soft mossy bed,
out of which peeped about a dozen lilies of the valley, we heard
that 6d. was quite a low price to obtain for each tiny cluster
of bells, and so turned our eyes in another direction. Here
were the last of the big white Japanese chrysanthemums,
flowering freely, and almost knocking their heads on the
glass roof above them, and these fetched 2s. a dozen; while
literally hundreds of geraniums were sold at 8d. a dozen
heads, ready fixed in their places with gum, a process that

keeps them fresh and usable for about a week, and allows them to travel their short journeys without dropping their petals in the manner they naturally would otherwise do. The best geraniums for cutting from at that time of year are, we believe, those called " Vesuvius." There is the white geranium of that name, and one of a clear vivid scarlet, that looks wonderfully cheerful and bright ; but the gem, to our minds, is a new very dark red, called " Henry Jacoby," which, being new, fetches a comparatively high price, and was at that time not cut, but sold only as a plant. There were houses full of geraniums and primulas—some double, some single, all lovely—all ready to fall victims to the scissors, or rather the gardener's knife. And standing on the floor were ranks of the scented-foliage geraniums that always somehow remind us of summer garden-parties, or bouquets sent with quivering hearts to the object of one's latest affection in the far-away days of one's youth.

But the orchid-house was the place where are the gems of the collection, and where each orchid stands on an inverted pot, it standing again in a saucer of water on a charcoal floor, for they require damp and to be well drained at the same time, and where we see curious spotted plants, wonderful mauve creatures, and spiritual, graceful sprays of white blossoms resembling strangely our ideas of angels. As we listened to the gardener discoursing on his occupations of the year, that never cease, are always changing, and are invariably among beautiful and pleasant surroundings ; when we hear what he learns from the bees, and from noting how one flower will not live with another ; and that some are such enemies that they refuse to be together, and die immediately should they be put in water with a stronger foe ; we begin to think what an excellent opening there is here for some of our younger sons who have nothing to do, and refuse the occupations we offer

E

them as being ungentlemanly. Every year the demand for flowers increases ; a capital of £1000 is quite a fortune to the gardener who means to go in exclusively for flowers ; and though, of course, great care is required, the occupation is easy and charming in every way ; and as we wandered home through our enemy the mud, and thought of our friend whistling cheerfully among his cherished blossoms, we began to have doubts, as to whether we should not do well to abandon literature, in favour of raising cut flowers for the London market ; while on reflection we came to the conclusion that many of our girls, who form subjects for newspaper articles, as victims of boredom and poverty, could pass a great many happy hours in cultivating plants and flowers, that, even were they rich enough to be able to do without them themselves, would be received with rapture in many of such nooks and corners as the one we visited not long after making the acquaintance of our friend the gardener.

## OUT OF THE TIDE

THE steady roar of the tide goes on unchecked. Hurry and rush of man and horse go westward; but just out of the tide is a quiet square that might be miles away from the great thoroughfare, out of which we turned on our quest for the place whither we were bound. The square was very wintry. The damp trees, about which the fog clung like a winding-sheet, scarcely moved; every now and then a sad yellow leaf fluttered down, and seemed to fall with a sigh among its sere and faded brethren on the sodden lawn. And indeed life, once a very real thing in these great houses that have had their day as fashionable residences, seemed as wintry as the outside world, and appeared stationary for a while, ere being engulfed altogether, and turned into warehouses and big shops should the tide ever run in their direction again, which, however, is not likely at present. There were positively no signs of life, and all was very quiet, and we rang at one of the square, solid house-doors with rather a sinking heart, for surely a ghost will open it, and we shall find ourselves ushered into the company of many others, resident there since the time of good Queen Anne, the date of whose reign is yet extant somewhere above our heads. And within we shall surely expect to find many treasures dear to the heart of an art decorator of the present day—costly

china, maybe, or queer antiquities; beautiful chairs and
sofas in rich brocade.    Indeed, we almost expect to see
Harry Esmond come swinging along, or note a heavy coach
and four draw up, and graceful ladies alight therefrom and
glide in before us up the staircase.    But a cheerful little
maiden answers our timid knock, and ushers us into a quiet
parlour, where a sweet-faced lady, clad in a long black
garment, welcomes us and leads the way upstairs.

Here, in a big square room with window seats—whereon
doubtless long-dead lovers have rested from the dance, and
looked out perhaps on the square, white with snow,—were
rows upon rows of beds.    There was nothing of the hospital
look about the place, however; no long whitewashed wards,
each more cheerless than the last; but it was looking as it
must have done in Queen Anne's time; though, instead of red
satin couches with spindle legs—a spinnet perhaps in one
corner, and stiff embroidered screens dotted about—we
found long iron couches, on each of which lies a child.
The room was a room essentially, and a room in a home.
Insensibly pity wells up in our hearts, for the children were
all flat on their backs, and not one out of the number could
put its foot to the ground.    We think of some other children,
restless creatures, who are never quiet, even in their beds:
who when awake rush hither and thither, and whose weekly
attendance at church is a very penance, because of the
enforced quietude: and we looked here naturally for impatience, tears, and querulous questionings of their fate;
but we found nothing of this, nothing but busy hands and
cheerful faces, and a very natural amount of curiosity about
us and the world from which we had just come: a world
that generally produces, marvellously enough for them,
spongecakes or beads or dolls spontaneously growing in
that outer atmosphere that exists for many of the children

only in fancy. Some of them come from courts and alleys
where their ailments are regarded impatiently; where the
aching little backs and the pain-tortured limbs have no
couch softer than the cellar stones, or the hard floor of the
attic; where other healthier children swarm, and their moan
of pain is often silenced by an oath, or, more sadly, even by
a blow. For how can the poor be aught but impatient with
illness, particularly with such an illness as hip disease? Life
is hard enough even when health abounds, and to have to
provide for sickness is unendurable, because of its impossibility. What wonder, therefore, that our sick children have
cheerful faces? though to us the divine patience of sick
childhood can never be really cheerful, because of its deep
appealing pathos. This hospital, so clean, so nice in every
way: would that we could say so home-like: is their idea
of heaven. There is nothing but kindness here, and even
does the doctor hurt, as hurt he must, he has such kind
words and such a skilful hand that the child almost forgets
his pain, because he knows it is all done to do him good.
Some of the children are lovely; and when we look at
" Punch," with his beautiful curly head and bright eyes and
noble brow, we think what some rich childless people would
give for a boy such as he is; but, poor little soul! he has
double hip-joint and spine disease as well, and will most
likely never again leave this quiet home except for the still
quieter churchyard. He is a play-loving child too, and has
quite his own opinions on the merits of cake and cocoa for
tea, and boldly proclaims us " a goose " because we declare
cocoa is not our pet beverage; and a very small amount of
encouragement would result in a dangerous and irregular
game of romps, but this cannot be allowed, for the smallest
exertion flushes the round cheek and damps the wide fore-
head, and a word from one of the nurses is quite sufficient

to restore the brown head of curls to its place on the pillow, from whence he winks at us knowingly as we nod good-bye. A slight disarrangement of the bed-clothes displays sundry complicated straps, and we are shown how the little creatures are kindly kept in the best position to enable them to have a chance of recovery, and, though seldom really cured, there are often remarkable results in the treatment the children receive in this charming house. "Granny," for instance, who announces her age as seven, but is gravely assured by the matron that she means 700, was brought to the hospital condemned to lose both her legs; yet the doctors thought she could never stand the shock, for she was but a baby of four, and weak and puny besides; but now after three years of bed Granny has been drafted to the branch home at Bournemouth, with every hope that in a short time she will be able to get about on crutches, which indeed she may cast away in time, and progress on the very legs once utterly condemned as most useless and dangerous possessions. Granny has without exception the most hideous and battered specimen of a doll in bed with her that ever one's eyes fell upon; but to Granny it is the embodiment of female grace and beauty, and is loved with a love that is most pathetic, for we can but think it is to her a species of reflex of her own battered little self, and that she gives to dolly some of the care and affection that are so lavishly bestowed on herself; and not even hearing of the attractions of a wonderful doll's house, given recently to the Bournemouth Branch, will induce Granny to leave her antiquated plaything behind her, for she is sure that it would cry "drifful" after her if she did. Indeed Granny, though longing to see the sea and the beautiful pine-woods, about which other children returned therefrom for further treatment have told her, is full of compunction. She cannot understand what her dear, dear lady will do without her, and she holds the lady superintendent's black dress with one thin little claw of a hand and gazes at her as if she would rather see that kind and loving countenance than the broad blue Solent and the white and red cliffs of which she has heard so much. Even her bed receives a share of her sorrow, and having slept thereon for the most sentient part of her small life, she almost believes that neither bed nor ward can possibly exist at all, once she has gone away from them.

It was very pleasant to sit and talk to any one of these children. They were all so well-mannered and sweet-voiced, and boys and girls alike are all occupied with some sort of needlework. Here a roguish mite hides her work as the lady-superintendent passes, then beckons mysteriously to us, and under the bed-clothes displays a corner of a beautifully-worked case, that is being prepared secretly for presentation at Christmas to the lady-superintendent, who, of course, knows nothing whatever either about the work or the necessary materials, and will be most profoundly surprised when the presentation is duly made. The big rooms were visited one after the other, and in all were sweet and childish faces, all merry and happy, even in the case of one dear little maiden whose eyes were heavy with tears and sleepless nights, but who, being promised she should sleep when it became dark, gave a ghost of a smile and whispered Couldn't it be made night at once? yet was quite contented to wait for tea-time, sure that after then she should have rest in sleep. When another Christmas dawns in some house where death's hand has lain heavily during the past year, and taken away a child from the home, it were well if some child in the Hip Hospital in Queen Square could represent to the bereaved parents that child who left them early in the day. It were well on long dark evenings for girls, tired out and bored to death by imaginary dulness, to gather in each other's houses, and organise working-parties to make the smart little red jackets that cover so much pain and real fatigue and misery; and well indeed for those who will step aside from the great hurry and rush of life, and who will go and see for themselves the beautiful patience, the pathetic calm suffering, of these poor little creatures, whose one happy time of life is spent in the hospital, where so much is done for them, and where money is always needed badly. These little children make us ashamed of our selfishness, and we longed to cause the stream of wealth to turn into Queen's Square and help the hospital on a prosperous voyage; even though it must rest quietly and peaceably doing its noble task, just out of the tide; and for those who shrink from seeing pain and sickness, even only hinted at, we can say, as we said before, Turn your minds to flower culture, and send the results to these hospitals, where the sight of a lily and the scent of a rose does more good sometimes than either pill or potion; and where the simplest flowers lend an air of home and beauty that is a great help to nurses and children alike !

VI

## A FIRST NIGHT IN AN UNFASHIONABLE
## LOCALITY

In a very unfashionable part of town is a closely-populated district, so densely inhabited that the houses appear to have no room for their elbows, and most of the denizens seem to spend a great portion of their time promenading the streets or hanging over the low shop-doors and in at the open shop-fronts, while they eagerly discuss among themselves the price and quality of the articles before them, generally without the smallest regard for the owner's feelings. A subtle scent of fried fish permeates the air: fish seems to be indigenous in the black mud that decorates the side walks; and fish of all sorts and sizes, in its dry or smoked condition, is laid out on barrows or slabs, to tempt those who may have resisted it in its fried state; while at one side vigorous shouts draw attention to prime cuts at fabulously cheap prices; and a general air of gaiety is spread over all by the presence of sundry merry-go-rounds; in a tiny square to the right, where an organ grinds perpetually, petroleum flares wildly in the slimy air, and wooden horses go round and round in a manner that can only result in severe sea-sickness to the riders, who, however, seem not only unmoved, but positively radiant as they gyrate. The streets are literally

overflowing with human beings, but they are principally of
the female and juvenile orders of mankind. The two or
three public-houses that we pass seem ominously quiet, and
have no loungers round their doors, but appear to remain
closed in a manner that speaks volumes for the impaired
traffic through them; and as we emerge from one of the
side streets into a species of square (pronounced "squeer"
by the habitués thereof) we are enabled to account in some
measure for the dearth of the nobler sex by seeing hundreds
congregated round a small door, wholly inadequate to admit
the host that wishes to enter.

It is curious on entering the hall to closely examine the
sea of faces behind us. There is not a woman in the place;
there are none but bona fide specimens of the working man,
who evidently mean to enjoy themselves thoroughly, and
without putting on any of the usual first-night critical spirit
that distinguishes more exalted audiences, they study the
programme with fixed attention, and eagerly look out for old
favourites and friends in the songs and performers. The
whole affair is managed by invitation; for did they pay for
their seats they would consider they had a right to object
to any song or recitation that did not fall in with their views
and that might be suspected to teach them a moral lesson,
like a powder in jam; but as guests of the committee a
respectful attention to all is, in a measure, enforced; though
certainly this first night everything received the warmest
possible applause and appreciation. Watching the men's
faces and listening to their comments would do much for
the embryo legislator; for, ridiculous as it may sound, the
working man is very like a highly-strung harp, and responds
warmly to light and sympathetic touches, while a harsh or
masterful hand produces nothing but discord. There is not
much sympathy for the ordinary mawkish ballad of the

drawing-room, but a song that speaks of the sea, an old-fashioned melody, or an heroic deed, rouses the audience to enthusiasm, while part-songs are invariably encored, and recitations from Tennyson and Bret Harte were freely handled by the critics in the front row, and pronounced in the one case "pretty broad," and in the other as "bosh." What brought down the house was emphatically a song with a chorus, joined in melodiously and heartily by the roomful. This had been repeatedly demanded from one gentleman, who was evidently an especial favourite, under the name of "Powder-Monkey," and as these cries followed every song he sang, we began to imagine that this was his name of endearment, for opprobrium could not be possibly hurled at the head of any one who was so enthusiastically applauded as he was. However, the mystery was solved by his singing the song, which might have gone on until the present time had he sung it as often as it was asked for. That their applause was sincere was emphatically proved by the fact that after a song sung by a gentleman and his wife, to which an encore was demanded, the lady was requested not to sing too ; very politely but unmistakably requested ; because the audience wished her husband to sing alone some song that had been remembered, and looked forward to since the last series of entertainments in the winter previous.

It may seem hard on the women at first sight that they are rigorously excluded from these delightful concerts, where the music is so thoroughly appreciated by many of the wealthier classes that the strictest care is required to prevent the tickets getting into the wrong hands, but in reality it is the kindest thing possible. Saturday night is the busiest time for any good working woman. There are the children to see to, the house to clean, and the absorbing walk in

search of provisions for the Sunday's dinner—purchasable
with a clear conscience and ready money, because of these
very entertainments that keep the husbands out of the
public-houses, where their wages would inevitably be squan-
dered on drink. No man can be expected to return home
to sit dully in an atmosphere of soap-suds and crying
children, to stumble over a pail, or to be scolded by an
over-tired woman, who is anxious he should not go out, but
is too overstrained and busy to do aught but grumble at his
presence when he is least wanted; and the advocates and
captains of the Blue Ribbon Army would do well to visit
one of these entertainments, and take a leaf out of the books
of the People's Entertainment Society.

During the whole two and a half hours the concert lasted
the attention never flagged for a moment. The "Leather
Bottell" was sung enthusiastically, and as enthusiastically
encored; but temperance and enjoyment seemed to walk
hand-in-hand, and silently and impressively taught the necessary lesson of temperance in all things. In all the long
slippery walk to the station we did not meet one single
drunkard, not one man even slightly "elevated"; and the
streets were filled by shoppers and gossipers, all seemingly
happy and contented; and we could not help wishing that
some day the People's Entertainment Society would see
their way to provide a rational good concert of sacred music
for Sunday afternoons, where the wives could go with their
husbands, and the children imbibe an early love for music
that shall afterwards fit them for the fostering care of the
Royal College of Music. It is ridiculous to say that the
English are not a music-loving nation. They are, if they
are given the right music; and though at present this may
not be a very high class of composition, and they may prefer
the easily-caught lilt of Moody and Sankey's hymns, the

well-known tunes of "Home, Sweet Home," and the good
old sea songs, and more modern "Nancy Lees," and
"Powder Monkeys," who shall say that from this succeeding generations shall not rise to Beethoven and Mozart;
or that great English composers may not spring from these
once eager listeners to the concerts of the People's Entertainment Society?  If any one should doubt these state-
ments let him go to this old, old suburb, where the clergy
house has delicious tiny panelled rooms, that must once
have been the boudoirs of fashionable belles; where Boling-
broke once lived, and where now mechanics and working
folk only reside; and let him watch the men's faces as they
sing the chorus of the "Powder Monkey," and he will soon
be converted to the belief in the music of the future; and
even if he is not, he will have spent a remarkably pleasant
evening.

Should he not be so fortunate as to be present on a first
night, the next best occasion is when the audience take part
themselves in the entertainment and endeavour to repay
some of the kindness they have received by presenting the
society with what they call a pay-concert.

On that occasion ladies are admitted—for Saturday night
is not chosen for these concerts—and the seats are paid for,
all the receipts being handed over to the funds of the society
that has done so much for them; but the principal feature
then is undoubtedly the band, that is played exclusively by
men who before these concerts were given had never
handled a musical instrument.  It is worth the journey to
our unfashionable locality, if only to see the faces of the
men as they play: the loving manner in which they clasp
their violins, and the amount of energy they throw into their
drumming, all pointing their own moral, and speaking
volumes for the kindness of the conductor, who, himself a

young man, gives up several evenings during the week to teaching others to amuse themselves ; and suggesting again to us that among these byways of life can be found ample food for reflection, ample work for any one who finds time hang heavy on his or her hands !

## BY COACH

THE St. John's Wood gardens were at their best the hot morning we passed by them on the top of the coach. Many-coloured rhododendrons, deep yellow azaleas in clumps, and brilliant golden laburnums, all flourishing mightily; and as we got nearer Finchley the lovely may-trees and bushes began to gleam like silver in the flood of June sunshine. There at Finchley the first change of horses was made, and we parted with our gallant team, made lovely by yellow rose-buds at their ears, for four others embellished with red rosebuds; and after a short pause the coach rolled forward once more, and then we began to leave the houses behind us and to get out into the wide beautiful country. Far away to the left rose the tall graceful spire of the Harrow Chapel, and all along the horizon on both sides lay trees, with here and there a mansion rising among them, suggesting human beings. But who can describe the trees! There was no air to stir the branches, and they looked like green clouds, the blue haze that was over everything lying among the clumps and softening colour and shape in a wonderful manner. There was a deep brown copper beech; there, the black buds of the ash, still unfurled, while the dusk-red early foliage of the oak and the more golden leaf when it is quite out, contrasted perfectly with the gray of the willow

or the bright glossy green of the beech; there were dark,
cloudy-looking places that tell us that the firs are present
with their gloomy foliage, now tipped with the pale tufts
that speak of summer, yet looking densely black among the
newly - clad trees, and the woods swept round until the
universal greenness merged into the purple misty distance.
Finchley seemed to be the paradise of nurserymen, for
there were acres of glass glittering in the sun; but soon
new houses began to get fewer and fewer, and at last we
saw nothing save trees and fields, these latter brilliant with
buttercups and evidently laid up for hay, for soon we smelt
clover, and saw patches of pale green where the grass had
already been cut.     In a field to the right a white horse
stood like a marble statue, except that he ceaselessly switched
his tail to sweep away the flies.     He was quite motionless,
and when we returned in the evening he was still there,
standing in exactly the same place as he was in the morning.
In every pool of water the cows were meditating knee-deep,
and the small sheep, whose thick fleeces hung . raggedly
about them, were all pressed closely against gates or hedges,
or grouped together under any scrap of shade they could find,
so intense was the heat.     Soon we came to a noble line of
chestnuts, the blossoms of which looked like fairies' Christmas-
trees beginning to die away; but here and there were deep
pink flowers that were just in their prime.     Then we came
to Whetstone, where the guard pointed us out a big-headed
dwarf, who saluted us languidly and with condescension,
and who we heard is a lazy little beggar, and generally
watches for the coach from his bedroom window; but on
that occasion he was up, and looked as if he wished that
he were not!     Past Whetstone to Barnet, where we stayed a
while at the Red Lion—an hotel that has memories of the
real old coaching days and takes small notice of the spurious

article, and where there is a quaint old garden, at the bottom
of which is a regular old-fashioned bowling-green—and then
off again we went, our heads well set for South Mims. But
at Barnet we were shown the fair-ground, where a large horse
fair is held, and this set our horsey friends off at once, and
we were largely instructed by them in many mysteries. We
listened entranced, until we changed horses once more,
having arrived at South Mims, which is represented by a
public-house and a large barn ; but this is only the beginning
of the parish, and South Mims itself is a long straggling
village, one side white, and the other lying in a hollow, and
very much like a Birket Foster ; being red, and looking
lovely with its foreground of water full of animated geese,
goslings, ducks, and ducklings, and its background of cloudy
green trees. The church has an old square gray tower with
a very modern body, and the churchyard itself looks placid
and quiet. Here we saw two men engaged in digging a
small grave, which when we returned was filled up and
crowned with roses. Who may say what hopes, what bitter
tears, were buried there ! But now we were off again, just
pausing to wake the echo that slept at the entrance of the
village, and gave back a clear answer to our horn ; and then
driving rapidly between hedges, where the columbine was
beginning to twine, and that were yet unladen with the dust
that was our only drawback to enjoyment ; and where we
saw numerous finches and sparrows disappear, their beaks
laden with worms and flies for their newly-hatched families ;
and where the orange-tip butterfly flitted up and down ; and
presently at the top of a long hill we were shown St. Alban's
Abbey standing high and square five miles away. The
whole scenery now was perfect : trees, more trees, where the
bright tasselled larch stretched out her green arms to hide
last year's dead foliage, hanging below her newly-covered

F

branches, and to the left we saw large mansions peeping at intervals through deep green clumps of trees, and now we were ascending the hill on the summit of which stands the quiet market town we have come to visit. We had an excellent luncheon at the George, where the slim gray-coated young fellow who drove us nearly all the way took the head; and the professional driver the bottom of the table; and then we wander out to the cathedral, which was resounding with the hammer and chisel of the restorer, and at the porch of which was a yew, very, very old and shady, and near which we rested a while listening to the ceaseless caw of the rooks and the shriller clatter of the young ones in the nests; and then we heard the sharp cry of the swifts, aptly termed screech-owls, as they dart and skim about; and saw, as we gazed at the cathedral, that two sparrows had nests that were built in the deep mouldings of the windows. One flew away as we looked, while the other sat still gazing at us motionlessly from her untidy home in the corner of the stone arch she had selected. After leaving the cathedral we wandered about the quiet dead-alive old town with its steep streets and narrow passages, and marvelled at the utter quiet of the place, where once sixteen coaches used to pass through in the day, and that is now quite deserted save by the solitary specimen we had patronised; and we could scarcely believe the account told us of the palmy days of St. Alban's by a venerable individual, who declared he had been ruined by railways, and had had to take to selling old china as a substitute for the occupation of driving that had once been his.

And very good and quaint was his old china too—here a cup and saucer dainty enough for the toast of the teacup times to be pledged in; there a beautiful bowl, that might have been the christening font at some ceremony where

the fairy godmother had failed to be asked; while sundry
odd plates and dishes, marked with crests or initials, spoke
volumes of a ruined family, or perchance a purloining
butler.

Always when coming upon such a collection of odds and
ends as the one possessed by the old collector, we cannot
help wishing profoundly that things had tongues, as well as
people; for a great many things would be much more interesting to talk to, than are the majority of human creatures,
who have nothing to tell us, and chatter aimlessly about
trifles when they do speak.   Fancy the stories a patchwork
quilt could relate, for example; each morsel of print or silk
or satin having its own particular history; or the delightful
old-world scandal yonder teapot could pour out if only its
lips were sentient; while the stones that compose any venerable building could communicate events that would make
the fortune of any lover of scribbling: but, fortunately,
the sound of the horn called us back to the present day,
or we might be conversing now with the old china-
merchant.

It was with great delight that we took our seats for the
homeward drive, which was, if possible, even more lovely than
the morning one had been, and the exquisite view of London
from High Barnet, where we saw it like a vague cloud far
away in the distance, was alone worth the drive; but if the
old coaching days were in the least like this experience of
ours, we can but be sincerely sorry that they are done away
with.   We had the cheery guard, with his different saluta-
tions for every one on the road; hand-wavings to the maids
evidently on the look-out for him; cheerful and playful
tootlings of the horn to several childish admirers; and
friendly greetings to grooms and stable-helps; and then
above all we had the steady up-and-down trot of the horses,

and the beautiful insight into the country, seen from the top of the coach.    Indeed, there is no pleasanter way of spending a hot day than by doing as we did, and, taking the coach in the middle of fashionable London, enjoy the delights of an entire day in the country.

# VIII

## TEN MILES FROM TOWN

It is like a dream to stand upon this eminence and gaze far away into the distance, for there, rising like a solemn prayer, or a wondrous mirage, is the dome of St. Paul's ; looking as if resting simply on a mass of cloud, that is poetical only, and has no suggestion whatever of the smoke and crime, the dirt and misery, that it represents.   Behind us stand, graceful, calm, and peaceful, the silver stems of a clump of beeches ; while behind once more we can look for miles over the wonderful Kentish landscape, that is finally lost in the deep blue vaporous veil, that tells its own story of the richness of the land and the wideness of the horizon that is before us.

Just at our side, field after field is deep with the rich brown grasses waiting for the scythe, that has been occupied until lately in the clover fields lower down the hill ; while every now and then, as the soft wind sighs through them, we see thousands of the great starry-eyed marguerites, which we instantly long to gather, regardless that in so doing we should doubtless do far more damage than the flowers are worth.

Every hedge is a study for a painter : white wild roses, densely white in places, and close - shut and sweetly-scented ; wide-mouthed roses, with pink lips and yellow centres, blossom freely, while the pale yellow honeysuckle creeps all over, and contends for our favour with the deeper pink kind, that is much sweeter and prettier, and grows quite as freely if it reaches the top of the hedge. As the breeze plays about the flowers and bends them towards us, we are fain to believe the blossoms are beseeching us to gather them kindly, and show them a little of the world that is so close to them and yet so far off. Red poppies and yellow tiny stars of the potentilla claim our notice, and wild geraniums and campions perk up their heads and almost cry out as we pass, "Pick me too, oh, please pick me!" while the big daisies are starred about everywhere, and pensively hang their heads, thinking doubtless of how much they are now the fashion, and that they only require a helping hand, not only to have a place in fashionable circles, but to be warmly welcomed and admired by the greatest of the great.

It is quite entertaining to the cynic, or to any one who knows much of the country flowers, to note how these common creatures (if one dare call them so!) have lately risen into favour, and into such company that even the rose fades before them, and to know how this sudden caprice is regarded in some circles. It were well to listen for a while to any farmer's wife, or regular country denizen,—for surely never was a better illustration of the proverb; "A prophet is not without honour, save in his own country"; and should any of these worthy folk penetrate into great houses, or pass balconies lovely with white and yellow daisies, the flowers would feel considerably abashed could they know how they are talked about in their native land.

For there they are considered such a nuisance that they are spoken of as "botherums" and "nasty weeds," and a dear old lady who paid us a visit from Dorset, not so long ago, flushed quite prettily when she saw our vases full of them, and on her return home sent us up a great basket of roses, so pained was she to see how low we had fallen since the days when she and we were neighbours. But here, ten miles from town, they are in so much request that on one or two days of a week a man is stationed up here by the beech-trees to keep off intruders, and make them, if possible, adhere to the footpath : which is one of those delightful, essentially English paths between or rather through fields, that lead us on and on, almost mysteriously, over stiles and through hedges, secure that at last we shall see something worth seeing.

While we were meditating for a while at the beeches, and talking to the man who is supposed to keep people off the daisy-lands, and making the acquaintance of one of those soft, rough, gray-coated dogs, with white noses and paws, and stumpy tails, that always suggest sheep, and are generally called Tip, and who have eyes that tell their own tale of a meditative soul, and a loving heart, fond of the country, their life, and their master, the quiet was suddenly broken by a tumultuous noise that was most distracting ; and we had to summon to our aid a large amount of affection for our fellow-men, and toleration for their peculiar manner of enjoying themselves, ere we could reconcile ourselves to the horde of barbarians, which now proceeded to make the beeches hideous by cat-calling, song-singing, and a perpetual shriek for Pol-lee that was most enraging to the ear.

However, we are thankful to say we smiled pleasantly as they trooped by, laughing and romping and screaming in the most agonising way. Here a girl in a pink frock and a draggled feather sang, "'Ark, I 'ear an aingel sing," while another chanted vigorously, "Buttercups and diysies," with a cockney twang on the last word that showed conclusively where she came from, and we discovered that these were a

party of costermongers and flower girls who clubbed together through the winter, paying so much a week, in order
to have one day in the summer in the country, to see the
home of the vegetables and fruit by which so many of them
gained their livelihood. How could we be angry with them
for coming between "the wind and our nobility" when we
realised what this day meant to them? and we could only
look forward to a good time coming when education should
teach them to modulate their voices and to take their
pleasure with a little less liquor to wash it down. As they
passed along, we went on our way down a shady lane,
listening as we went to the blackbirds and thrushes, and
watching our friends the sparrows a while, who just then
were engaged in educating their children with such an
amount of fuss and worry that one wonders how the poor
little creatures are ever brought up at all. In the first place
the sparrow's nest is built with an admirable eye to shelter
and safety, but with no notion of adaptability to the time
when the little birds will have to take exercise, returning for
the night to the place where they are born.

Here in the lawn, under the eaves of a gorgeous lodge
built in mock Elizabethan style, is one of the nests in
question. It is tucked up so tightly there, that the tiny
fledgling cannot re-enter it; though he receives elaborate
and energetic, if somewhat confused, directions from his
mother; who perches on the beam above her trembling
son, who clings shrinking to the wall; and never stops talking
until he sinks down on the grass again, and looks appealingly
at his director, whom he assures in perfectly understandable
bird-language that he cannot and will not go there again.

But his mother comes down, makes a raid into the
garden, and appears once more with something in her beak.
She feeds the small creature vigorously, scolding all the

while. We are positive she tells him there is a cat about, ready to pounce on birds who will not try to return home, and finally he makes a series of efforts, the last of which proves successful; and with quite a chorus of joy they fly into the nest, greeted by twitters and squeaks from her other children, who are presumably not yet old enough to go out for a walk, or fly among the strawberries.

It is really impossible to believe we are only ten miles from town, when, in quest of tea, we enter a tiny shop and ask where we should be likely to find that necessary article. The one inn is filled and overrun by the coster-mongers and their ladies, who are solemnly dancing to-gether in pairs, though the sun's heat is tremendous; and there are no trees; there is no shade of any kind before the place, so we cannot go there; the little shop seems our only hope, yet it is so very small and so primitive that we are almost afraid to ask lest we should excite derision.

It is one of those shops where everything is to be bought, and where candles and paraffin oil assert themselves over all the rest of the stock in trade in the most astound-ing manner; two baskets of strawberries are gradually dis-solving in the heat on a chest of tea; sugar and flies are amalgamated; and the weary mistress of the establishment leans over the counter with a heavy baby in her arms, and endeavours to extract from a very small child with a very large bottle what she requires to put into it.

She brightens considerably when she sees us, and we at once fall into the breach. The bottle suggests vinegar—is it that? Nah, says the child, smiling vaguely. We seize the bottle; the mystery is explained. Of course it is paraffin, and supplied with that and a pennyworth of sweets, the small maiden goes on her way rejoicing, and we are free to ask about our tea.

Again we say we must be many miles from London. We cannot be going back there when the hours get cooler, and the long beautiful shadows slant towards the east, for we are at once taken into her confidence in a manner that speaks volumes of her birthplace.

For it is only in the country, where time is a drug in the market, and folks have not utter disbelief in every one who is strange to them, that we can get to talk to any one outside our immediate circle. And now we know at once all about the keeper of the small shop. We know she meant to have had tea-parties "regular," but her husband had twenty-seven weeks of rheumatic fever, and that has thrown her back "terrible"; and she is now looking to her strawberries to pay the doctor's bills and keep her forward a bit until he returns to do his work as carpenter on a great estate close by. Anyhow, she will give us tea and straw-berries, and so we settle with her and have our tea, while she tells us her troubles quite gaily, and only to point or illustrate her surroundings, which are good, but would have been so much more to *our* liking had it not been for this illness.

Behind the house we find ourselves regularly in straw-berry land. The plants are doing their very best, and are producing fruit right gallantly. Regular rows succeed rows, and the pickers, arrayed in immense straw hats, are busy at work filling baskets with the fruit that will be in Covent Garden before the morning, packed securely in round baskets, and covered down under great cool rhubarb and cabbage leaves. The home demand is great too, for people live close round this place, a fact that is hard to believe, so well are the houses hidden, and so far off is the railway. And even while we are looking at the picturesque scene round us, several baskets are taken away by the ser-vants of the houses about.

Close to the hedge, outside the garden, a bent, bright-faced woman is gathering her apron full of grasses and weeds, a fine spot of colour being added to the green landscape by the saffron-hued shawl that hangs on her shoulders. She too gives us a bright smile, and invites us to come and see her curious family of rabbits, which have a remarkable parentage, and are the offspring of a hare and a rabbit ; and are her great amusement, for, poor soul, she lives all by herself, and has fits, which she mentions to us rather as if she considered them a mark of distinction. But like all the other people in this village she is perfectly cheerful, and has not a complaint to make or a fault to find ; and was quite enraptured to find any one as interested as herself in the small curious hybrids ; whose mother had been given to the keeper, and returned by him to her original possessor, because she would not live out in the coverts with the other rabbits, but would continually haunt his house, bringing the hare with her, and doing irreparable damage to his small attempt at a garden.

It is really no wonder that the village people are pleasant and contented. Perhaps their living so high up above the valleys gives them a feeling of exaltation, or causes them to rise superior to the ordinary frailties and foolishnesses of humankind. Even the noisy folks, who on Saturdays and Sundays render the quiet village simply odious, are looked upon indulgently—"'tis their one day," "they don't know what mischief they do," "bless 'em, they don't harm us," are phrases heard anywhere ; and not because the van-loads spend money, because they do not, for the very good reason that food and drink are brought with them, but because the villagers are simple and sympathetic, and most likely have themselves sons and daughters in that distant city, whose Mother Church never fades from before their eyes, save when a thicker fog than usual buries all that is usually seen from the beeches.

Even those who do not care (if any such exist) for birds, or fruit, or flowers, and human nature, must feel some slight access of enthusiasm as they look at the trees with which the country side is crowned and enriched.

In winter they are beautiful, standing out against the clear sky, each tiny atom of a twig distinct and lovely, strangely resembling the fine seaweed we used to float in water in our childhood, and then delicately spread out on a sheet of white paper. In spring each tree has its own peculiar dress; in midsummer no words can describe them as they stand solid, silent, magnificent, almost unapproachable in their loveliness, dark and dense as funeral plumes, yet with indigo shadows under the green that give an air of life to what would otherwise be rather gloomy; while in autumn each colour that a painter has for use is lavished on them. The scarlet glows on the chestnut; the oak is marvellously green; the yew is dark; saffron decks the beeches and elms, while a paler yellow falls upon the birch, that sighs out her life in a faint ladylike manner that is rather entertaining than otherwise; and, in fact, each season of the year has here as elsewhere its own particular beauties with which to tempt our sight.

We wander far afield; we dash across seas and climb mountains; we listen eagerly to strange tales of travel in far lands, of wondrous verdure and tropical loveliness: and it is well that we should do so. But all cannot do this; and it is therefore well even to know that homely beauties and charming people and scenery exist, even so close to the crowd, as our beeches, which are not more, after all, than ten miles from town.

## OUT OF THE WORLD

FAR away on the distant horizon lies a dim cloud that might possibly be the veil that hangs between us and fairyland. On the left hand a deep wide valley, with an almost imperceptible thread of water, to tell us of the time when a vast river three miles wide rolled along where are now trim fields and hedges. On the right hand another valley stretching away to a long range of hills, dotted here and there with churches or houses that seem to stretch their heads from the trees that surround them, as if to strive and see a little way away into the world. Overhead there is the curious sharp rustle of the beech and the rounder sound of the oak ; below our feet close-growing ling, just going off from the pale mauve hue of late summer to the rusty brown tint that tells us that autumn has already announced his first appearance as positively to occur immediately. The trees here are like no other trees, and are all lopped and stunted by successive generations who have exercised their forest right of "lop and top," and although they are never to be so maltreated again, it will take some years before they can be tall and stately monarchs of the forest, through which the wind can riot at will, bending and swaying them rhythmically in the way he loves to prove his right to rule over the woods. And yet, as we regard the plumy appearance of

the trees, noting the banks of undergrowth and the close
way in which the branches entwine, and then watch the
effect of this from a distance, we begin to feel contemptuously towards the ordinary tree, and are almost convinced
that the £5000 spent on satisfying the claims of the com-
moners is wasted.    There are small traces of common where
we are standing : we might be miles and miles away from
the haunts of men.    Presently we hear the sharp cry of
the jay, and catch the blue glint of his wing; while close by,
on the curious hornbeam, now tasselled with its autumnal
wealth of fruit, a red-waistcoated robin is singing away gallantly, rather proud to be the only songster who is undaunted
by the sense that autumn is here, and winter is hurrying up
as fast as he possibly can.    There are as yet small traces of
decay here, for the chestnut, who always loses courage first,
and allows his garments to fall into rags sooner than does
any other tree, is not represented here ; the close-growing
pollard oaks and beeches, and, above all, the hornbeam, are
all as dark and beautiful as if July, in full summer garb,
were present in the woods.    Yet as we turn away from our
vantage ground, eager to escape any trace of human beings,
we note the ineffable sense of autumn in the air ; and as
strong scents arise from mignonette and late annuals in the
gardens by which we are obliged to pass, before entirely
reaching the heart of the forest, and we notice a magnificent
magnolia, with its great pale-yellow velvet cups, we are
forced to confess that autumn has come, and that flowers
and leaves will soon be things of the past.    Yet as the houses
once more disappear, and the road leads us on and on and
up and up, we are at last landed in another glade that suits
our mood well, for here, indeed, Nature, though beautiful
and marvellously lovely, seems rather melancholy too ; and
as we penetrate beyond the bog, thick with rushes and

starred in places with sundew, we suddenly find ourselves in a place where surely the wand of the enchanter has been at work, and has surprised a band of the weird sisters as they watched, wailing and tossing their arms around the bier of their best-beloved, and with one touch transformed them into the mystic, wondrous beings we see all around us.   Beings they must surely have been at one time, for see how their silver shaded trunks glitter and seem instinct with life as we stand and watch them ; note their long thin arms stretching up to the blue sky !   Every now and then the wind comes rushing along, shifting the shadows from the leaves and letting a golden rain of sunshine glint down through them, which, as it falls on the dense, green mossy turf, lights up the whole place as if it would mock at the speechless agony of the surrounding trees.   Then a deer, startled by our appearance, dashes by, and we almost hear the horn wound, and the tramp, tramp of some unseen huntsmen as they hurry by us eager in the chase ; but the trees only seem to stand with their arms upraised, wailing ever over the futility of all that mortals pursue, and uttering prophecies as to the end that comes to all things alike in this weary world.

It is almost impossible to remain here long, so like an enchanted forest is it, and we fancy the monks, who once owned this particular corner of the forest, must come here at nightfall and once more lop the trees for firewood to warm the hearth that used to be theirs only, in the neighbouring Abbey of Waltham.   But this they cannot do ; long years must have passed by since they exercised this right, or the long thin arms of the pollard beeches would be less ghostly, less fearfully suggestive than they now are.   The forest is peopled with dead days, and on the side that overlooks the Roding Valley few folk come to destroy our illusions.

Here are the Ambresbury Banks, climbed over by wild
roses, and deep with brambles and ferns, and like nothing
so much as the hedge that surrounded the Sleeping Beauty;
yet when we have penetrated at last within the old earthwork,
we cannot find her, for she is buried deep in the dust and
earth of ages.   Yet, should we be sacrilegious enough to
arouse her from her slumbers, she would have much to tell
us surely, for these banks once surrounded a camp : perchance of ancient Britons or wilder, older folk than these,
whose strange flint implements were found at the lowest
part of the bank when it was cut through by some ardent
archæologists ; or she might have superintended a fight to
defend the fortress, when smooth sling' stones, many of
which were discovered in the ditch below the bank, took
precedence of bows and arrows, and, perchance, wielded by
our beauty herself, did deadly execution among the intruders.
Yet if this side of the forest be all dream-like, weird, and
silent, full of memories of Queen Elizabeth, whose open-air
drawing-room still exists ; if here the deer yet browse,
venturing out in winter when food is scarce, along the high-
road ; because they know the hay-carts travelling up from the
depths of the country to Whitechapel market, drop clumps
of hay on which they can feed ; and if the pollard oak and
beech are unvisited save by those who really love nature ;
still the forest has another side on which we are fain not to
touch, a side that begins at High Beech, whence we look
over the valley of the Lea and hear the popping of the rifles
as they are being tested at Enfield.   And when we turn
away from the exquisite view, feeling traitors in our heart to
the New Forest, that, though lovely indeed, is commonplace
when compared with Monkswood and Ambresbury Banks,
we are amply punished for our moment's lapse from loyalty
by the sight of merry-go-rounds, 'Arry and 'Arriet mounted

sans habit, sans straps, sans everything necessary for decent bestridement or riding of a quadruped, on the leanest of cab horses free for the day from harness; by the visions of a monster hotel and—crowning horror of all these mundane spectacles—of a sham lake, the pride of the Corporation, who are, we believe, going to extend this yet farther and to vulgarise this end of the forest quite beyond redemption. For not even the possession of a vast tree-stump called Queen Elizabeth's mounting-block, or the sight of her hunting-box, once possessing an oak staircase, up which her Majesty was believed to have been in the habit of riding her horse when she went to bed, can ensure it from being nothing save a gigantic tea-garden, very charming and delightful for those who like that sort of thing, but ineffably jarring to the nerves of those who have just wandered free and enchanted through a forest fit for dreamland, and in which one is certainly, for a time at least, quite out of the world.

# X

## A CORNER OF KENT

IT was on a calm peaceful October morning that we set out to explore this particular corner of Kent.

A soft blue haze hung over the landscape, and appeared like a veil decorously drawn across Nature's features to hide the work that death was doing there ; yet although a sense of decay was in the atmosphere, it was only suggested, and was so calm and peaceful that we insensibly felt soothed thereby, and almost thought ourselves in a dream as we drove along through a series of pictures that no pen can adequately describe, and that would require the brush of Cuswick or Linnell to bring before you the exquisite hues, the perfect mingling of colours, that seemed to drift by us. It is curious to note how when driving through Mid-Kent corn seems entirely to disappear and give place to the tall languid hop, and to plantation after plantation, field after field, of low-growing shrubs and trees. Standing on any eminence that commands a wide prospect, and where it is possible to see for miles around, the soft dreamy blue haze that hangs over the landscape broods over nothing, save low-lying silent stretches of country, with the curious hump-backed, hooded oast-houses dotted about ; and at the time we saw it, embellished here and there by a few white government-tents that yet remained as shelter for the hop-pickers, whose scanty task was but just over : for the hops that especial year were both few and late, and were only just done with, as far as the picker was concerned ; while whole gardens were left unpoled, that is to say, with the bine twisted sparsely round the tall poles, because there was no fruit to gather, and in that case it is always better for the hops to leave them alone, trusting that another year may be better and allow the hop-grower to recoup himself for his unhappy losses.

It was pleasant to turn away from contemplating this unsatisfactory state of things, to plunge into one of the plantations below us, where the well-known Kentish cobnuts flourished, doing as well as the hops had done badly.   There was a great sense of calm in the plantations.   The sunshine glinted down through the boughs of the apple-trees that were planted as much for the sake of the shelter they gave the nuts as for their fruit, which was almost as little that year as the hop-harvest.   Every now and then a thin yellow leaf fluttered through the crisp air, or a clump of nuts fell ; or among the leaves on the ground a slight rustle drew our attention to a small red-robber, who, anxious to fill his larder for the winter, was braving all sorts of perils in his quest for provender.   "Squirrels never take a nut that has a maggot either," said our guide, as he took a shot with a stone in the squirrel's direction, "and we have to shoot them constantly, as otherwise they would clear off a plantation in less than no time ; but he's welcome to a few nuts this year, for we have more than I remember for some time.   Just look here !" and he turned back the broad changing leaves of a tree just by, and showed us the russet-brown clusters hanging closely together underneath them.   The colour was really wonderful all round us, and there was not an inch of ground wasted.   The apple-trees looked grim and gray with their twisted, gnarled, yellow, lichen-covered arms, and

below them stood black-currant bushes in ranks, the leaves
of which were turning deep purple and scarlet; while the
nut trees, in serried lines, grew taller again, and in a more
symmetrical form than the other bushes; and were yet densely
green in places, and had only their ripened fruit to show
that autumn was well-nigh over. And beyond them again,
in every spare corner, young trees in pale yellow, or red, or
faded green dresses, were bending and swaying in the gentle
air, ready to be cut off in their youth for use as hop-poles
in the neighbouring garden.

Presently we heard a sound of voices, and boldly following our guide over muddy banks and in among the trees,
brushing as we did so many a gossamer-web from across our
paths, we came upon the nut-gatherers busy at their task,
and eager to make the most of the fine weather; for in the
damp the nuts do not harvest well, and, turning black, give
the buyers the trouble of drying them over brimstone to give
them a fine colour; which, being decidedly a trick of the
trade, is repudiated by the grower, who resorts to none of
these "dodges" for putting a better face on the matter
than it deserves. The gatherers were women and children,
who do not touch the trees, but simply pick the nuts up
from the ground as they fall from the boughs under the
shaking they get from the foreman, who takes a pick, and,
pushing it round the stool, *i.e.* the stem of the tree, shakes
it vigorously, nor ceases until the nuts cease to fall, when he
goes on to the next tree, followed by his group of women,
who scarcely stopped from their task to look at us as we
passed. One shilling and fourpence a day does not seem
princely pay for such back-aching work, but the women look
well and happy, secure of occupation in these parts, for the
weeds will next claim their attention, as the plantations are
kept quite as free from these plagues as are most gardens, and

they will be required for some time yet to root up the
American cress and long grasses that seem to grow the
moment the master's eye is off them.   No one would believe
that cobnuts require the amount of attention that they do.
To the uninitiated they seem such nice easy things to grow,
almost wanting nothing save sun and air ; but to begin with,
the trees will only flourish and bear fruit on the Kentish
rag, with a covering of loam or red sand, the "fleeter" the
better, and entirely refuse to fruit at all if white sand or clay
be given them for sustenance.   Then, too, the Kentish rag
is not the only rag they require, and after the fruiting
season is over the trees have to be plentifully "mended" or
manured with rags, sprats, and farm manure, the rags
coming down from London in wicker-baskets, that are afterwards used to keep the hares and rabbits off the young apple-
trees, as they are slipped over them, like a species of open-
worked crinoline petticoat.   But before the "mending"
begins, the ground all round the trees is opened, and the
long suckers that spring from the roots are cut off, after
which the trees are sawn and cut to retain their shape,
which is something like that of a cup, hollow in the centre,
and overflowing, for the boughs close to the ground
are the boughs that bear best and suffer least from the
maggot or from the late frosts, that, coming with any real
severity in May, can at times quite destroy any chance of
nuts for that year.   The cutting and sawing are done as
soon as ever the leaves are really off and allow the operator
to see the buds that will be first next year ; and when once
set to work, a skilful hand progresses rapidly, and it is pleasant
to watch the swift manner in which he passes from tree to
tree, until when he has finished his plantation it looks
curiously like a flat table, so even and regular has been his
handiwork.   The small pieces sawn out are made into

faggots for the use of the hoppers in the following autumn, for the hop-grower keeps his workmen in fuel and shelter, as well as in hard cash. Then the trees are "wanded," the long wands, or shoots from the roots, being pulled up, so that all the strength of the tree goes essentially towards making fruit.

It seems ridiculous that fashion should extend to fruit, but it does; for the sweeter but smaller filbert is being gradually eliminated to make room for his finer relation. It is impossible for an outsider to discern between each kind of these trees, until he is told that the trees resemble the nuts, and that the cob is a ranker-growing, bolder-looking creature, and requires a good deal of attention, or it would soon deteriorate, and, if let alone, would soon go back to its wild state. Some of the trees are very old—more than a hundred years old—but the principal plantation is about thirty years of age, as until the trees have been some time sedulously looked after they do not bear at all, and it is most interesting, first of all, to see them in the tiny square of ground, where about three or four stools, cut down and allowed to throw up as many wands as they like, provide stock enough to keep up the plantations, and allow of trees being replaced, directly one dies; to the schoolroom, as it were, where the small trees begin their independent exist-ence, finally settling down among their elders in the open plantations, becoming in their turn grown-up trees and use-ful members of society themselves. When the nuts are gathered, they have yet to be harvested, and after coming in sacks from the plantations are shot on the oast-hair, or the hair-carpet, in the hop-kiln, used as well for drying the hops, and which is capable of standing any amount of heat. Yet no heat is used in drying the nuts, and they are simply spread over the carpet and left alone till they are sufficiently dry to be packed into the bushel-baskets in which they travel

up either by rail or road to London ; where they are sold on
commission just at that time for about 6d. per lb., and are
bought by us at whatever our fruiterer chooses to charge us
for them.   The inside of the oast-house is most picturesque.
At one end is a raised platform full of nuts ; at one side a
step-ladder allows us to look down on the carpet, where,
clad in their shaded brown coats, the nuts lie, waiting to be
harvested, while the beams are used as store-houses for all
sorts of things, from the cut rushes, brought from Sussex,
and used for tying the hop-bines, to the long hop-poles
themselves ; and are also made useful to hold the ponderous
scales, that before iron was as cheap as it is now were made
of wood ; and are of a most primitive construction ; while
from the window on the left you may look down to a curious
oak-framed cottage built before the time of Henry VII, and
notable for the fact that it is guiltless of any sort or species
of foundation, as it is enclosed in a heavy black oak frame,
with ponderous beams and cross-pieces ; the weight of which
keeps the cottage stationary, and the interstices being filled
up in a most primitive way with rubble and mud and the
ubiquitous Kentish rag.

It has most likely been originally a farm-stead, for the
structure is larger than an ordinary labourer's cottage of to-
day, and would have been quite a princely residence in
those far-away times when it was put together, and that
may have been even earlier than that ; for the only way the
date was at all localised was by the finding of some coins of
Henry VII's reign under the floor when it was moved, as if
they had dropped there from the pocket of some lounger by
the hearth.

This consisted of a wide opening about the centre of the
house, and that was of the most primitive construction, the
smoke going up at its own sweet will, and winding in and

out of the roof and about the bedrooms, the walls and beams of which yet bear the traces of long-extinguished fires, over which folks, as dead as the embers, and not leaving half as many traces as they did, have doubtless warmed themselves, and thought of little save the heat they were bent on acquiring. The garden round the cottage was bright with autumnal flowers, and bordered with a brown-red shamrock that gave a peculiarly pleasing effect, contrasting as it did with the gray stones and lichen-covered paths by which it had planted itself.

The house where our friend resided was also of great interest and antiquity, and had a wide square hall, in each corner of which his venerable predecessor, the rector of the parish, long since dead, used to keep a butt of port wine. He began at one corner, and went regularly through the four, refilling them as he went, and thus ensuring that the one he began with should be replenished with wine old enough to drink by the time he came to it again. Of how many times he lived to do this history has no record, but the corners of the hall have a singularly empty appearance, as if they resented the port-wineless condition that was now theirs.

The old oaken staircase in itself could provide meditation for a poet for days : it is so venerable, so easy. We can fancy childish feet walking up them slowly, and as if they found the wide black steps a serious obstacle to that perilous journey between the drawing-room and the nursery. We see in the twilight long-dead brides flutter down in their wedding attire, returning new-made wives, to descend once more a little sad, a little anxious, to go away from that familiar house out into a new and untried existence. Again we fancy the mother or husband walking up slowly one day, not feeling very well, and as if somehow the staircase was

rather longer than it used to be, save in the long, distant,
childish days ; then anxious folks haunt the staircase,
the doctor goes up and down, silence falls, and then something comes down the stairs that shall never return again
to the old familiar haunts.

In an old house the staircase must always be the rendezvous of many a ghost ; as darkness falls and the wind rises
a little and moans in the chimneys, tapping with the rose-
branches impatiently against the windows, we can almost
fancy we hear their tread. The mysterious creaks that
break suddenly on our ear in the middle of the night can
thus be accounted for ; and we believe, as we lie and listen,
that we can distinguish once more the feet of those we
loved and lost as they pass up and down ; and know who it
is that lingers there, unable to lift up the latch and come
in among us. Ah, foolish waste of time in these days of
ours ! and ghosts are scoffed at by us, who know all too
sadly their impossibility in broad daylight, with the
screech of the train in our ears, and perhaps the telegraph
boy coming up to the door, whistling lazily, though for all
he knows life and death may hang upon the message that
he brings : but indulged in gladly and suitably, it seems to
us, in that old-world place !

But pleasanter still, maybe, is it to wander out into the
village in early morning, when the October mist lies heavy
on tree and flower, when the chrysanthemums look at each
other over the geraniums and talk of how they will shine
in golden, and red, and brown dresses, when the first frost
shall turn the scarlet creatures below them black in the
face : pointing an unconscious moral of how each thing,
each creature, has its day but once, and has to retire gracefully if it can into obscurity, while another than he takes the
stage. A moral repeated again when we reach the old

church, put quite a mile away from the village, on the
extreme top of a hill, as are so many of the Kentish churches,
for the builder thought more of the Canterbury pilgrims
on the look-out for certain shelter and succour, and a priest
whose presence should never fail them, than of the few
unlettered creatures who lived the lives of animals, in the
scattered huts, around my lord's or the farmer's house.

For in the church we find the names of many a goodly
knight and dame, who once lived and loved in a beautiful red-brick hall of Queen Elizabeth's time, where garish
ribbon borderings glittered and mocked their old-world
background with their modern formal colourings ; but now
when we turned away from looking thereat, we heard that
the family vault and a right to lie therein, are all that
remain of the possessions and privileges owned by those
whose names look down coldly on the stones beneath them ;
for the property has bit by bit gone into other hands,
and the original owners of the hall are wanderers on the
face of the earth.

It is pleasanter perhaps to look at the perfect scene
before us, and to gaze over the fair Kentish weald, than to
contemplate the *tempora mutantur* written on all in the
church ; yet it was interesting to hear how the long ride to
church caused an ingenious gentleman to start a trade at
the lychgate on Sundays, that consisted in selling a particular
cake of gingerbread for threepence ; and at the same time
presenting his customers with a glass of gin for fear they
might otherwise remonstrate at the high price of the
remarkably small cake tendered for their refreshment after
their ride.    This clever infringement of the revenue was
ultimately put a stop to ; but the receipt for gingerbread was
handed down to posterity, and the same species of manu-
facture can be still bought in the village.    In those days

pillions were the natural means of progression; and a story
is told of a doughty squire who never discovered that he
had parted with his better half, owing to some especial jolt
over deeper ruts than usual in the lane, until he had dis-
mounted, and was proceeding to tie up his horse to the rail
that yet bears traces of the use to which it was put, when
he found out his loss, and departed to seek her : thus
losing one sermon, doubtless to obtain another and a much
more emphatic one from his spouse, whose rage must have
been extreme, not only at her position, but at the spoiling
of her Sunday raiment that must have ensued.   At early
spring-time, when the orchards are full of blossom and
vocal with the nightingale's ceaseless voice ; or in summer,
when the bushes are laden with gooseberries and currants,
bought as they hang on the trees for jam-making purposes
by London manufacturers ; in autumn, when the hop-
pickers are at their picturesque work, aided and helped by
the hop-grower, who with his wife and children solemnly
open the campaign by picking a certain portion of a garden
themselves ; or when the nuts are gathered ; or even in
winter, when hunting is to be had, and the horses in a neighbouring training-stable are of the most absorbing interest to
all alike ; — there is always something to see, something to
amuse the onlooker ; and there are no words that can
describe the love and affection with which he or she who
lives there regards this quiet place, while any one who likes
open-handed hospitality and a peaceful lingering among,
and reunion with, the things of past days, cannot do better
than attempt a short sojourn in our especial corner of the
garden of England.

## A CANTERBURY PILGRIMAGE

NOT even the presence of the ubiquitous railway seems to make any impression upon the ancient gray cathedral city of Canterbury ; it is as quiet as if the steam monster never passed it by ; as sombre and " old-world " as it was in the days when the Canterbury pilgrims promenaded the narrow streets and swarmed in at the Chequers Inn and at the Falstaff, that exist now much as they did in those far back days. It is essentially a town that suits the ancient cathedral, that, gazed at from Harbledown, looks much like a great lion couchant, or a vast rock set fast in its midst, under the shadow of which safety and peace are to be found, and which suggests little of the strife and warfare that in earlier times surged round it, and filled the whole Kentish county with blood and fire and sword. For in those ancient ways stand queer closely-pressing houses, out of the windows of which it were possible for loving neighbours to hold sweet converse, and shake hands at meeting and parting, quite easily and without effort at all. Though it certainly jars on the mind that is seriously intent on olden times, and meditates a Canterbury pilgrimage on the ancient line, it is well worth the journey and the disturbance it is to one's mental " make-believe," to take the train and make our way all through the lovely Kentish land, regardless of the anachronism. It is still more curious when we start from town in a mysterious gray fog that entirely obscures our vision until we are past St. Mary Cray; when it suddenly lifts a little and allows us to see, looming out as if they were giants, sundry great creatures that, before we have recognised them for the ploughmen and horses that they are, have vanished once more into the fog; but now we leave that behind. A pale long line of yellow light appears behind the low range of hills on the left; we see primroses starring the hedges, looking strangely cold and out of place among the sparsely lying snow; we notice catkins and the soft velvet palm shivering in the chill air, that becomes keener every moment as we get nearer the sea; and by the time we reach Rochester the sun is out and flooding the scene before us with the thin bright sunshine of a somewhat frosty spring morning. How lovely, too, is Rochester from the railway, and how mysteriously do we seem to go round and round, never losing sight of the square grim castle, with its eyeless sockets gazing at the river; and which appears to stand guard in front of the small cathedral, that modestly lies back from the river, much like a small child shrinking behind his mother's sheltering garments; and how divinely beautiful and suggestive are presently the long stretches of mud-flats reaching away, away, until we see the red-sailed boats, drifting softly and quietly out to where a faint line of gray suggests the broad, wide, open sea; whence we note two visitors in the shape of sea-gulls flapping about the fields, investigating them for some worm or insect that shall be to them a change of diet after their sojourn by the shore. We see long gardens being made ready for the coming hop harvest, and we note, too, enclosure after enclosure given up entirely to the culture of low-growing fruit-trees, among which every now and then a weird-looking apple-tree stands high, with a coat of lime-wash or some such concoction on its bark, that makes it look like a ghost as it stretches up its arms seeking after the sunshine. But the sunshine has quite gone again when we reach our destination, and the grim gray atmosphere has returned and seems singularly suitable to the grim gray place, whence the train we have just quitted leaps eagerly forward towards Dover, as if it feared being caught and shown how utterly unfitted it was to disturb the venerable city by which it passes.

Small amount of imagination is required to bring back the days of old : albeit the fact that the square block of buildings that represents all that is left of the Castle, has been pressed into the service of the gasworks, is rather a shock ; but having proceeded through Mercery Lane to the High Street, we catch sight of the grand gate or bar leading into the close, and feel that not even the fate of the Castle will prevent our plunging straightway into the earliest ages of Christendom. What though the High Street : queer, twisted, gable-ended as it is, and having many a house in it embellished with a curious fishscale-looking tile : seems principally given up to public-houses and goody-shops. Surely these only remind us of the days when the annual stream of pilgrims passing up the street made plenty of accommodation necessary ; and of those more jovial times when in 1673, "the city did give a banquet to the Duke and Duchess of York and to the Prince and Duchess of Modena, consisting of the following articles, viz.—Canded cringo, dried suckets of all sorts, green citron, dried past (query paste), dried pears and pippins, quince past, canded lettuce, dried apricots, raspberry past, dried plums, rock candies, savoury ambers, smooth almonds, macaroons, iced march-panes, prince biscuits, drop-cakes, a large march-pane, with canary, claret, and white wines." Fancy the effect of such a

banquet in these days ! Yet surely we can forgive the pre-
ponderance of sweet-shops when we have such a link with
the past as they make. The city records are full of such
quaint things, and tell us also how in 1475, while the King
was on a visit here, the city gave an entertainment at the
Chequers, the site of which is still to be seen, when the
whole expenses of which, including a porpoise and 8s. paid
to the cook for dressing the dinner, came to 15s. 8½d.;
adding at the same time that the King came to the city by
night ; on which occasion the porch of St. Andrew was
illuminated with four pounds of wax lights, at the expense
of 1s. : a modest way of going to work that should commend
itself to the reception committees and other wiseacres of
this present day. But it is painful to feel that not more than
a hundred years ago, the city walls, gates, and towers all
stood as in centuries since ; and to know that only the one
leading into the close and the one at the bottom of the
High Street are left ; all the others having fallen victims to
the rage for improvement—save the mark !—that characterises (even in these enlightened days) such miracles of
learning and wisdom, as are crystallised and concentrated in
corporate bodies, and folk who are anxious to enlarge their
field of railway operations.

But if we would really feel like those pilgrims of the
olden time, it were well to wander into the city over Harbledown, pausing for an instant to gaze at the lovely view, where
there were no evidences of modern life to vex us by their
anachronisms ; and, indeed, the face of the country can be
but little changed since the days when procession after procession paused here and offered up prayer and thanksgiving,
ere proceeding on the last stage of the journey to the shrine
of the martyred saint. The city lies below us, with the
grand cathedral seated like a queen upon her throne, her

subjects at her feet, towering up above the low gray houses
lying closely beneath it, and all round the fertile country
sweeps away, away, reaching on the left a low hazy line that
we are fain to believe is the sea washing in over the Whit-
stable flats; while on the right, sundry hop-poles and fruit-
trees, just beginning to bud, tell their own story of the
garden of England. We can see, too, the venerable
yew-trees dotted here and there, planted by the pilgrims,
says one authority, to mark each passing of a pilgrimage,
or, as says another, to keep up, by order of the kings of
Kent, the supply of wood for making bows for the use of
their warriors; and we can see the great gate of the city
and the walk round the walls: which is the pride of the
inhabitants, and the most beautifully-kept corner possible.
As we wander along the road we are surrounded by the
ghosts of the past: we can fancy Chaucer's motley crowd
are with us, singing a little perchance, or praising God maybe at the sight of the beautiful church that contains the
goal of their hopes. Yet, as we pass into the High Street
we leave them, watching them vanish at the spot where
once stood the Chequers Inn, and where now are few if
any traces of the ancient hostelry: yet vestiges of those
times remain, for here are the most venerable houses in the
city, pressing so closely together and with such projecting
gables that we wonder how light and air penetrate into
the old rooms above. As we part with the pilgrims, more
modern ghosts attach themselves to us. Surely out of
yonder lattice-window peeps Agnes, watching for David
Copperfield, who may have gone to meet his aunt on the
Dover road, where each milestone makes us think of Mr.
F.'s unfortunate relative. We are quite sure we saw Mr.
Micawber just now; and Agnes's father vanishes into a
square sober-faced house over the way, that is everything

a lawyer's habitation ought to be.    Were it not for all these
phantoms the city would seem strangely empty to our eyes,
accustomed as they are essentially to every-day sights; but
once out of Mercery Lane and the High Street and our
ghosts change again: we pass under the ancient arch, and
are in the Close, with the rooks busy in their nests, and the
gray-headed jackdaws croaking mournfully over the same-
ness of life, and the monotony of nest-building that has to
be done year after year, year after year, for not much purpose
after all.    Vanity of vanities, croak the jackdaws, all is
vanity, while they flap heavily round the centre tower,
making excursions every now and then in search of straws
or twigs, which they proceed to push into every available
inch in the tower, from which they never seem to be absent,
and doubtless never have been absent since the days of old,
when Norman barons and knights clanged armour - clad
over the gray stones that lead us direct into the great
cathedral.

As we stand for a moment and see the long flights of
stone steps—worn and indented by the tens of thousands of
pilgrims, long since gone into dust and ashes—we can almost
believe their ghosts perpetually pass noiselessly up and down
the staircase vainly looking for the shrine that once stood
just a little farther on, and that at the time of the Reformation was broken, and the contents scattered, while the
chestfuls of jewels departed to enrich the treasuries of the
king.    Ay, even the stone that tradition represents as leaping
from the ring of Louis VII and fastening itself irremovably
into the shrine, when its owner felt reluctant to give it up,
went too, and was not endued with sufficient devotion to
enable it to refuse to adorn the thumb of the spoiler of
the place it had decorated so grandly.    We can fancy the
whole scene, can watch with our mind's eye the gradual

H

burning of the bones that had wrought thousands of miracles, depicted to this day on stained windows near by, that yet were powerless to save themselves, and the final triumphant carrying off of the offerings, on men's shoulders, through the great west door, maybe, that clanged after them, quite oblivious of the fact that they had now few treasures left to guard.  On this scene looked down the armour of the Black Prince, that with the heartless fashion of the world lasts on very comfortably, although the wearer to whom it was a shield is now nothing at all.  Still there is his casque, there his gloves, and the velvet surtout, with the lilies of France yet visible on the faded and torn garment.  Close beside him, in a rough brick grave, built on the pavement of the chapel, rests Odo Coligny, Cardinal Chatillon, who fled to England for safety in the time of Queen Elizabeth, and who, all danger past, was returning home to France, when his servant gave him a poisoned apple — why and wherefore there is no record—and he died there, and was entombed thus roughly until a chance occurred for his friends to take his body back to the land that gave him birth.  It seems somewhat bizarre that he should still be waiting, albeit the tidal train dashes past his resting-place so often, and it would take little time to restore him to his native earth. Doubtless his ghost, too, adds to the number that never leave the cathedral, and waits for the day to come when he shall see his home once more.

Living people have nothing much in common with Canterbury, and the present day is out of place in a spot where history is crystallised and old times are modern once more. The march of ages cannot teach anything or do anything for such a place as this; the present has little to do here, and we can only hope that it may pass peaceably and take nothing more away.  The archbishop's palace that has seen

many changes since the days when it was presented by King
Ethelbert to St. Augustine ; after which it was destroyed by
the Danes in 1011, and rebuilt by Lanfranc, only to fall
once more in the time of Charles II, when the great hall
was pulled down and the materials sold : is no more, it is
true ; but as we stand in the damp, bitterly-cold chapter-
house, where dreary gloom and green moss reign supreme,
and that looks on the untidy ruined-looking cloisters that
are such a strong contrast to the exquisitely - kept set at
Salisbury, where one can fancy sleeping very calmly and
gladly in their pious peace ; we can see that there is enough
left for us to recognise where it stood, and to show how,
when the knights sought Becket there, he evaded them, and
rushed panting through these very cloisters, his robes wrapped
round him, and caught up, to assist his flight over these very
stones until he reached the sanctuary—which, however, had
no power to save him ; for, refusing to bar the door, and
relying only on the holiness of the place he had chosen, he
stood waiting, and received his deathblow on the altar he
had looked to for safety.   Even his body had to be taken
to the crypt, or undercroft, and was watched there by the
monks through a grated window from the higher part of the
church.   And here came the king, sorry, when too late, as
are, alas ! many of us in these days, when we all have the
same feelings and ideas as the men of old ; and here he did
penance, weeping sore, and giving over his back to the
smiters, who after all, whatever they did, could not bring
back the murdered man to life.   Once more the undercroft
becomes a refuge : here are the French and Flemish refugees
received and welcomed by Elizabeth, and here they had
their homes, and wove silk raiment for the gallants of the
court ; yet, though they were constrained, it is said, to adopt
so many English lads to learn the trade, so that it might

continue in Canterbury for ever, the trade has disappeared ;
and all that is left are sundry rings in the vaulted roof,
whence depended the lights by which they worked, a few
inscriptions, and a walled-off space in which the descendants
of those very people yet worship and hold their services
twice a Sunday in French, just as they did in the days of
their exile.    Older days than these lie dormant in the small
church of St. Martin just outside the walls, where the earth
has gradually grown into an eminence, owing to the continuous burials in the yew-shaded graveyard : that have been
going on there so many hundreds of years that the character
of the ground is entirely altered, and has risen above and
around the foundations so much, that it would be hard, if not
quite impossible, to enter the church at the ancient doorway
recently discovered at the right hand of the altar.

Here Bertha and Ethelbert may have entered, casting a
glance maybe at the wedge-shaped gap in the wall at the left
of the door, called by the sexton a "leper squint," and that
as all know was used by the lepers to gaze at the elevation
of the Host without mixing with the congregation ; and which
seems to point out that another altar must have one day
existed there, as the "squint" looks entirely away from the
present communion-table.

In the churchyard itself the earliest known gold coins
have been turned up by the sexton's spade, that has further-
more discovered Anglo-Saxon beads, and yet other tokens
of far-off days before Ethelbert was king, and Bertha his
queen was a Christian and came from France.

Here Augustine stood and took his first sight of the
"rude wooden city embosomed in thickets" that Canterbury
then was, and here he was met by Ethelbert, who was by
him baptized in the church, in the very font at which the
parish babies are christened nowadays.

It is only people that depart the world; the very things we make ourselves outlast us, and mock us with their superior powers every day.

It were easy to spend many days in and around Canterbury and yet not have exhausted all it has to show and teach us.

There is St. Augustine's Monastery, looking very much as it must have done at its foundation, so ably has it been restored, with its great gateway and immense dining-hall, proudly pronounced by its custodianess as the very "holdest in the kingdom." There is the uncomfortable seat, sacred to the archbishops, where tradition says St. Augustine once sat and that all the kings of Kent were crowned therein; and that no amount of historical interest can prevent from being very cold and hard; being, as it is, made out of Purbeck marble, in four pieces, to allow of its being moved if necessary; and there are strange old-world streets and byways, peopled thickly by those troops of ghosts who must walk the city day and night for evermore.

It is strangest of all to wander along the raised walk called the Dane John, by some curious mental muddle between the donjon keep, the Danes, and John, and see the strong walls and towers, now growing trees and shrubs in their interior, instead of containing the weapons of warfare, for which they were made; and then to catch another glimpse of the ancient castle; turning at last to note the railway, that seems the only false note in all the echoes of the past, to which we have been listening; yet that reminds us that time is still going on, and that we must leave the past, and plunge back again into the present, without having seen half of what we intended to see.

# XII

## DECAYED GENTILITY

### A SKETCH OF AN OLD COUNTRY TOWN

ONE of the most pathetic traits of the present day is the manner in which life has ebbed away from places that were once of the greatest local importance, and has left them stranded, cast aside, and done with ; nay, even desecrated ; much as one throws aside a worn-out glove, or a once respected and respectable pair of boots ; little heeding what tramp may annex them, or through what muddy paths they may tread, or what grimy paws they may cover.

In such a manner as this has life ebbed away from one particular country town. Houses that were once proud to cover and shelter members of " old families " still stand, but appear protesting against the ignoble uses to which they are put in the present day, while one after the other they fall into the hands of tradesfolks, and are either converted into shops or inhabited by those who were once delighted to call at the kitchen door for orders.

Before all traces of its olden glories are departed we would walk in those wide well-known streets once more, and are fain to take others with us too, so keeping green the memories of those quickly-vanishing days. Yet ghosts seem to haunt those empty streets, and we can proceed but little way, ere our arm is taken by one, who has long since been at rest in the churchyard; yet who is very near to us when we walk in the place he knew and loved so well.

Straightway before our eyes rises the pageant of life as it used to be. We are very small once more; the street becomes wider and higher; there is a great noise, a lovely noise, all around, and we realise that it is fair-time and we are on our way to buy a fairing. It is a bright enough sight too! The town is built in the shape of a cross, and where all the arms meet is a great square, filled just now by booths crammed full of toys and gingerbread and all sorts of leather gaiters, gloves, and aprons. The venerable town-hall, that always had a mysterious interest for us, is crowded with farmers, who lounge around the walls and doors, and wander up into the justice's room; where it seemed to us some one was always being tried and condemned to unheard-of penalties for poaching: and sit in the reading-room downstairs arguing loudly over the wickedness of whatever government—Liberal or Conservative—happened to be in at the moment.

The pavement is heaped with cabbages tied tightly into bundles—why, we never could make out—and all sorts of fruit, for it is September; and then we thread our way through the crowd, angry at the manner in which our escort is detained to speak to a fresh friend every moment.

We could wander now for hours in the town and see scarcely one face we know; yet then the place seemed full of cheery countenances, all intimate friends, all kindly curious, intensely interested in the sparse events that happened in the families around!

For years the life between the four green walls by which we were surrounded appeared to pass tranquilly enough, with not even an under-current that might at any moment appear above the river to mar the even flow of the stream of daily existence.

Of course things happened: babies were born; a marriage or two bound the people together and added fresh fuel to the flame—made other subjects of conversation; but there was no sensible difference in the amount of folks who took their Sunday walk round the walls; or no falling off in the attendance in the church or chapels.

Then, too, the place was full, as indeed it is now, of interest to the antiquarian, for we possessed a past that was really old; and the associations therewith go back and back into the days when the Danes sailed slowly up the little river, and fought long and boldly in the low green meadows that surround the tiny town, over which for ever brood silence and sleep, heavy with dreams of a long-dead day, when it was a royal residence and the key to a wondrous hunting-ground, then only a vast sort of prairie land, with here and there a tangled forest to serve as a shelter for the many deer, which have disappeared with the kings that chased them.

As in those days so in ours, the whole town is surrounded by walls of unequal elevation, ascended at the end of one of the streets by a gradual green slope, and reaching, when we arrive at Bloody Bank, a sheer descent of some thirty feet. The walls are all green, dotted about with divers clumps of low-growing furze, and rough, prickly bramble bushes; gorgeous in late autumn and early winter with their deep purple and russet foliage; and in spring literally glistening in the thin yellow sunshine, with gold and silver buttercups and daisies; and while more prudent children seek the cup-like shelter of the Cockpit, now sacred to bonfires or an occasional circus, bolder creatures swarm about the walls and gather flowers enough to gladden the eyes of half the children in a bigger city. For the walls are almost sacred

to the town's children, and to sundry horses that graze
quietly, by order of the charter, from May until November,
when the grass is left to grow at its own sweet will, clothing
with verdure even the bank with the ominous name, earned
at the time when Judge Jeffreys held his ill-omened assize at
the county town near by, when he condemned seven gallant
gentlemen to die on our walls for the part they had taken in
Monmouth's rebellion against the king.

From Bloody Bank the view is lovely indeed; we can look
miles across the heath, decorated here and there by a curious
hump, that marks where the war-wave swept over the whole of
the south of England. Leaving these barrows to show where
once slept the illustrious dead, and from whence sundry urns
have from time to time been extracted, we can watch the
course of the tiny river as it creeps along out to the great
wide harbour; where tide by tide the long-legged graceful
herons dispute the rights of fishing with cormorants, and the
débris-eating crows; and where once, in the good old days
when guns were few in number and owned only by real sportsmen, wild fowl were always to be had, and where now they
are almost exterminated; and we can look right over the
town to the perfect range of our lovely hills, that at all times
of the year are full of colour, and, unchanging as they are,
are ever changing, by reason of the cloud or sunshine or
mist, that drifts ever across them, revealing every day fresh
beauties to him who knows and loves them thoroughly.

The town itself is commonplace indeed at first sight, and
seems to hold few attractions for a passer-by, but this is due to
the fact of a great fire that raged in the latter part of 1762;
and that until a very few years ago was remembered with awe
by more than one of the old folk who then were very youthful
inhabitants of the place. But it could not burn the legends
with which the place is stored; nor did it burn all the houses,

one or two of which exist as they were inside, in the time of
Charles II, albeit a new front has been added, or some difference has been made externally, that would deceive the eye of
him who merely passed quickly through the quiet town.    But
once step inside into the narrow panelled passages, and climb
the queer low twisted staircase, and wander in the unevenly
floored rooms, where we walk on solid oak that ofttimes is
as slippery as glass, and we find ourselves in another world,
where it was necessary to have a square hole in one of the
walls, through which the head could be thrust to receive its
last coat of powder ere sallying forth to sundry dinner or
quadrille parties ; and where queer bones, saved from the
cows' feet used in the broth that flowed freely for the poor,
were thought most excellent and charming material to use
for bordering the paths ; filled even now with quaint old-
fashioned flowers, whose names are almost lost among the
shadows that envelop the past.    From a window higher up
the street—now transposed into a grand plate-glass casement, but which was not so long ago one of those queer
chambers built on posts out into the street itself—was
watched one of the old evening funerals ; and it was delightful to hear from the spectator herself what a curious
awe was produced by the sight of the long dark procession,
lighted by torches that flared and flickered in the damp cold
air of that long-ago Christmas eve ; and of the relief she experienced when the last torch disappeared round the corner
of St. John's Hill towards the old church, where now at the
present day there remains a stone coffin where some say
Edward the Martyr lay for a while after his murder in Corfe
Castle, before he was taken to his longer rest in Winchester
Cathedral.    The church has been altered and restored until
there is little of the original structure left, and, though much
improved just lately, was unfortunate enough to have first

excited the desire of the restorer in those days of darkness in
the early Victorian period when whitewash, and galleries and
pews of the most hideous construction, represented culture
and artistic merit to the youth and beauty of those obscure
ages.    And so our church presented, as did the town, very
little of interest to the casual gazer.    Yet there are one or
two tiny priests' rooms, and an old side-chapel, a heavy lead
font, and other objects of interest, which would repay any
who, wandering so far from the beaten track, might pause a
while in the ancient borough.    Then they might learn of
the sixteen churches that were once to be found within the
walls; they could walk on the lovely common, where a low
sunken road, called the Roman road, leads (or led) straight
away to the county town; they might investigate the ghosts
that haunt the Priory, and find out the subterranean passages
that lead from that venerable stone building to the church,
and farther away to Bestwall (a corruption, by the way, of
"by the east wall"), where another priory is supposed to
have existed; or they might investigate the curious rights of
the charter, and contemplate, with whatever feelings that
strike them as being most appropriate, the procession of
mayor, recorder, and aldermen proceeding to church in nice
furry gowns from the town-hall, preceded by the town-crier,
who is arrayed in such gorgeous raiment that on the very
few occasions that we have been visited by celebrities he
has been taken for the mayor, and been singled out for
attentions that have seriously incommoded him and much
angered whoever happened to hold the office at the time.

In those early days, before we gave place to the ghosts,
we found some of our principal amusements in electioneering, and although most of the old families were of course
Conservative, after a long and desperate fight one election
we succeeded in returning a Liberal for our borough.

True, he had a duke for his grandfather, and was altogether a mild specimen of his race; but as a Liberal he was elected, and as a Liberal he was bound to vote; and so we walked erect, having at last shaken off the trammels of the Conservative yoke, under which for many years we had groaned, but which up to the present time we had been forced to wear.   The Conservatives, indeed, having been so long undisturbed in their possession of the seat, hardly worked at all, and treated our opposition as the usual form of protest; and, indeed, we were all astonished when our man headed the poll with the magnificent majority of twenty-five, but we triumphed meekly, and as those who possess a great treasure with trembling, scarcely believing that at last it is theirs.   At first the Conservatives were paralysed, speechless, and disorganised, so heavy and un-expected was the blow, and for many days after the election the county went about declaring that the Queen tottered on her throne, and the Constitution was undermined, and they gazed upon us as if expecting to see us decked in the bonnet rouge of the Republic, which we were supposed to be on the point of proclaiming at the Cross; but when events went on much as usual, and not even one county magistrate was fired at as he drove home across the desolate heath after the usual fortnightly meeting of the bench, the Con-servatives breathed again, and, laying their heads together, proceeded to map out a plan for cultivating the constitu-ency, and causing it once more to blossom with the sweet flowers of Conservatism and stupidity, and to raise again those hedges of "no-progress" and "down with education," that had so successfully separated them from the vulgar herd for so many years past.   The candidate was forthcom-ing in one languid youth, whose energies up to the present time had been devoted to Berlin woolwork, to singing mild tenor songs in a kindly patronising way at penny readings, and to tending carefully a long, dark, drooping moustache, which was the one thing every one remembered about him, as the only distinguishing feature in a very inanimate face.

However, he was well known in the neighbourhood; was county to the backbone; and the fact that he was ignorant and averse to progress simply made him a very fair representative of the class that proposed to array itself under his banner. Was there not the great Mac-Manchester, who had turned Conservative and Churchman when he set up his carriage; and who, after an industrious struggle of twenty years' duration, had at last penetrated into the outer courts of county society, and sat obediently on the doorstep ready for anything, from contributions to the latest laurel-wreath for Lord Beaconsfield to baby-linen for the destitute (Conservative) poor? Was there not also Colonel Carter and the Duke of Dunderhead, to say nothing of the incumbent of the parish church, and the small but energetic parish doctor? Yes; these and many other aspirants for county favours rose as one man, and began assiduously to work their best for the great Conservative cause.

Our member in the meantime was not idle. He went duly to the House, and voted on every division; he telegraphed to us every important event, and we as duly placarded the town with the telegrams neatly printed on beautiful pale-green paper; he sent money for blankets, for coals, for Sunday Schools (of all denominations); and he came down all the way from town to walk in procession with the Mayor and several others at the Sunday School Centenary; which sight moved to tears the oldest inhabitant, who, with an extremely dirty handkerchief clasped ready to wave in an even dirtier fist, declared between his sobs that a more beautiful sight had never been seen since the day when the foundation-stone of the town-hall had been laid by his grandmother amid the applause of hundreds. Did John Smith lose his donkey, the member was immediately applied to to replace the venerated animal. Did Mary Brown feel herself in want of a mangle, she at once, through the rector, demanded pence for that object from our unfortunate representative ; and in fact not one, either Tory or Whig, who applied for help was ever turned away empty ; so in less than no-time he became generally popular, and we began to feel that we had indeed secured a Liberal to represent us, and one whom it would be very difficult to dispossess of his seat. Naturally, this liberality struck terror into the Opposition ranks ; and on the publication in the local journal of the fact of the member's having presented Mrs. Smith with a complete set of harness and a new cart to match the donkey, they rose as one man and called a committee meeting, determined to put a stop to such goings on, or to die in the attempt. What occurred at that meeting we never could find out, but suddenly and mysteriously streams of benevolence began to percolate gently through the substratum of our society ; and very soon there wasn't a coalless cellar or a blanketless bed to be found in the borough ; and about a month before Christmas condescending and general invitations were issued for a ball at the Manor ; where the Conservative candidate danced with every one, and won golden opinions from the wives and daughters of the free and independent electors of the borough. On hearing of this festivity, our member, not to be outdone, gave two parties—one for the children, with Christmas-tree, magic-lantern, and other accessories, the other for the grown-ups, with champagne and flirtation galore ; and as a great many handsome Guardsmen were brought down from town for the occasion, the Conservative

bout was forgotten, or soon pronounced a very second-rate
affair.    Then the Conservative candidate organised a concert in aid of the aged poor, and sang lustily, with his fine
dark eyes well turned up to heaven, or rather towards the
roof of the town-hall; but the only result of that was that
for many days after, the male portion of the aged poor was
drunk, and the female part so bemused with the fumes of—
tea, that they became disrespectful when addressed, and
impertinent when reasoned with.    Then down came our
member again with his corps of Guardsmen, and in a trice
bills of the popular green were again hung out in every
direction, to announce the performance of an amateur band
of Christy Minstrels, when "Bones" was enacted by an
earl, and "Mr. Johnson" by the member himself, faces
blacked and all complete; seats free, and refreshments at
intervals.

   But this sort of thing could not go on for ever, and after
pronouncing the Christy Minstrel entertainment the most
vulgar thing they had ever heard of, the Conservative party
became serious, and organised a gigantic meeting where
London speakers should enlighten the bucolic mind on the
advantages of living under the Conservative regime; and so
they got down an individual who once stood for, and was
rejected by, a small constituency not a hundred miles from
York; well placarded the walls with bills of a deep-blue hue,
pressed into their service the Duke of Dunderhead as chair-
man; and proceeded to gather in an audience of whom they
could be sure, and who they knew would not dare to
dissent from anything they said.    We would give worlds if
we could report in full the speeches, long, sad, and weary as
they were.    They deserve to be recorded for ever in the
archives of the Conservative body.    How Mr. Gladstone's
ears must have burned that evening!    How the Irish

gentlemen would have raved and shrieked could they only have known what was said of them! but they were mercifully spared this. And then the rejected one rose and gave us his idea of how things ought to have been managed last election, and was kind enough to sketch us out a programme of proceedings for the next. The Conservatives were to form themselves into a body of moral police, and were each to take upon himself the task of converting five Liberals to the good cause (query, do five Liberals go to one Conservative, we wonder?). They were to keep an eye on the five, were never to leave the five, and, in fact, were to make themselves so indispensable to the five that they would never be found apart. If, after this was done, the five were not converted, then, indeed, had a black day dawned over the benighted borough in which he had stood; and then, winding up his peroration with a strong recommendation to fear God, honour the king, and beware of change, he left us, doubtless to return to act as moral policeman to the five Liberals under his supervision in the borough that had rejected him. Since that meeting we did nothing, as our member had to sit day and night in the House, and was not able to visit us; but we saw the moral policemen at work, and soon emulated them not a little. Five Liberals undermined one Conservative, and he was to be seen quite tame and penitent in a public-house, where he once was a bright and true-blue star, and where a voluble barber talks at him night and day to keep him in a proper frame of mind. Soon the moral policemen found out several very important facts; and one good young man, who spent his Sunday afternoons in reading chapters to bedridden old people, was so busy discovering who had paid the fines due from three determined Liberal ruffians aged six, seven, and ten, who had feloniously abstracted

buns from the baker's shop when he was out on duty with
the moral police, that he sat extracting the necessary information out of the eldest ruffian's grandmother; and was
so elated to discover that the secretary of the Liberal Committee was the payee, that he rushed off at once with his
intelligence to headquarters, and quite forgot the chapter.
Every one soon began to watch every one else, and caused
us all to become so good and so moral that we were rendered
rapidly uninteresting, except to the two parties who fought
over our bodies.    There was not a pauper in the place, and
even the drawing-rooms of the ladies were gorgeous with the
offerings of the member and his rival, the latter coming off
a good first by the fact of his sending specimens of his own
handiwork, in the shape of wool mats and fender stools;
while the former could only despatch curious and stripy
specimens of the latest thing in æsthetic table-cloths, that
are still to be found, we believe, in some of the drawing-
rooms where he was once an honoured guest.    But, alas!
time has brought round its own revenges, and there is now
no need for all the elaborate mechanism once employed to
ensure an election; and, being disfranchised, the county
has withdrawn its smiles from our town, and it is left alone in
its glory.    Still, it were as well to chronicle another form of
electioneering tactics before it vanishes into darkness with
other shadows of the past; and to relate how we used to be
asked out shooting, as an encouragement to us to give our
votes and interest in the right direction.

For we were very fond of shooting round our neighbourhood, and though our candidate had been severer than any
other man in the county on poachers, and folks even said
he used to look out for them himself round the hills in the
middle of the night, for fear his keepers should not be sharp
enough, he looked forward to representing a sporting neigh-

bourhood, and so sat no more on the bench, and the
poacher just then was a happy man. But when the big
battues were over, and February was advancing towards us,
we began to hear of large parties being organised, and Tom,
Dick, and Harry, chaperoned by the parish doctor and a
legal friend or two, met together round the Manor, and
had a real good time of it. It was a curious motley group.
Here was an athletic young farmer, who had a decided
hankering after county favours, and not finding farming
quite as profitable as it might be, had some idea of climbing
to gentility by aid of the Church. He had already been
heard at Bible meetings—getting his hand in ; and, as he
was very good, as well as a staunch Conservative and a first-
rate sportsman, he made an excellent whipper-in, and was
always ready to do anything from reading the lessons in
church to organising a shooting-party and giving advice as
to who is to be asked to meet who. Some folks won't meet
others, and the doctor, who could not be spotted as belonging to either one side or the other, so politic was he, was
apt to be huffy if all those he met were asked from the
lower ranks ; and the lower ranks were quite capable of
taking themselves home in high dudgeon if their bosom
friends, and no one else beside, were at the Manor on
their arrival ; and it required an immense amount of
knowledge to arrange one of these affairs properly, I can
tell you.

So while we began with the farmer, we looked round and
discovered the doctor, and then passed on—through two good
fellows to whom every one, Conservative and Liberal alike,
was devoted—to Smith, who had a knowing dog with a thin
body and long legs ; and nothing definite enough about his
make to enable us to say whether he was a greyhound or a
terrier or a Newfoundland ; but who did not wait for the

rabbits to be shot, but caught them the moment they bolted in the most scientific manner, and brought them to his master, who turned rather red, bit his lip, and gave a sideway look at the keeper, who was too well drilled by his master not to look the other way.    We had almost forgotten another mysterious person, who came with a boy of fourteen or so, with a squint, and elaborately attired as a gamekeeper would be in a play, to carry his cartridges and see to his little comforts generally; and who let off his gun constantly before he saw anything to shoot at; but he had a way of appropriating everything that was shot until the young farmer was almost inclined to slay him, and was only restrained from doing so by the knowledge that at least twelve votes depended upon our sardonic friend being kept in good humour.    The candidate was miserable, inclination pointed to the long barren side of the hill over there, where he said feebly they would get heaps of rabbits, and have a lovely view of the sea, but on hearing "Cuss rabbits!" from Smith, and "Blow the sea!" from the mysterious one, duty conquered; and he led the way down a delicious moss avenue, through thin brown trees, where the adventurous honeysuckle had already begun to open its blue-green leaves and twine about the bushes, and where we found a stray primrose, looking pinched and miserable in the keen air.

Smith suffered a good bit from his dog, which seemed to go by the name of "Hi, you," for it was never spoken to in any other way; and once when a halt was made, where the moss avenue divided into four ways, while the keeper and the candidate had a consultation, it was really beautiful to see him suddenly spring forward and catch a pheasant, which he brought with a knowing smile, its head and tail wobbling dreadfully, to his master.    Then on we all walked again through the wood, which might have been an enchanted one for all the game we saw, and back once more into the avenue. Here we caught sight of a pheasant; but as the mysterious one fired rather before he trod on it, so close to us was it, we found nothing much of it except a small heap of feathers. The rest was scattered about generally in such tiny pieces they did not seem worth collecting. The language over this feat was not quite parliamentary, for tempers were beginning to rise, and Smith and a friend who "came along" and joined him, were heard to say that the member's plan of putting a good-sized piece of ground in the beginning of the shooting season into his agent's hands was a much better game than this; and hanged if they did not go down there, where a man was always welcome, and could be pretty nearly sure of a snipe, instead of being purposely misled and taken where that chap must know there wasn't even a feather. The young farmer could not stand this, and went and had a few words with the candidate, who began to say he was awfully sorry, but the birds were so wild; he had shot so many for his good friends at Christmas time (and, to do him justice, he sent pheasants to every one just then, even to those who had Liberal coals to cook them by), he was afraid he must really ask them to come out of the coverts and try the hill. Out of the coverts they streamed; through a field where the young farmer potted a pheasant and Smith shot a hen pheasant, regardless of a solemn promise given before starting that hens should be sacred owing to the nearness of the breeding season; but as he remarked he had seen so few he did not know "t'other from which," the candidate had to smile and forgive him. It really was worth while climbing that hill to see Smith's dog with the rabbits; he pricked his long ears that looked as if they were the property of a spaniel, raised his long front paws that certainly had once belonged to a greyhound, wagged his tail eagerly, and with a wonderful expression on his fox-terrier countenance, waited. There was a rustle among the gorse bushes, a dart, a flicker of a white tail, and back would come the dog gleefully, his mouth full, and laying the poor little struggling beast at his master's feet, would be off after another.

Having been asked to shoot pheasants did not mean rabbiting, and already one or two of the party had gone home, while the candidate and the young farmer produced an excellent luncheon and some good wine; and by dint of this and affable conversation tried their best to make up for the absence of game; while we looked at the view and moralised muchly on the sufferings of those unfortunate men who want to get a seat among the lawgivers of this wondrous island. As far as we could see lay the heath, with here and there a brown excrescence that meant a cottage.

Our poor little town was away in the distance, and for miles and miles the hills swept away to the moor; and the moor to the distance; and there was small evidence of life, and positively none of cultivation. Most of the land belonged to the candidate, whose time had been spent in shooting and occasionally law-giving in the neighbouring town, and who knew about as much what was good for England as his own pheasants. But luncheon was now over, and we descended the hill, where we turned out a hare, and startled a couple of partridges that looked suspiciously like a pair, though it was not the 14th of February, before which date birds are supposed to go about in flocks; and just under the hedge we found three hen-pheasants, doubtless laying plans about future domestic arrangements, when the youth with the squint, who had never left his master's side, shrieked out, "We came out for pheasants, master; by gum we'll have 'em." The mysterious one fired at them as they

rose at the boy's noise.  There was a rush from master and
man.  The farmer stood speechless; the keeper swore
roundly; and the candidate, after standing aghast for about
five minutes, turned his back and walked home.  And one
by one the party broke up, resolving itself into fine air, or
disappearing altogether among the furze bushes, for the
members thereof never, somehow or other, met again at the
Manor.

Not long after this celebrated party we received the awful
intelligence that we were to be disfranchised, or rather in-
corporated into another larger place; and that gave the
death-blow to the town as it used to be.

Yet signs of decay had been visible for some time had
we only been able to perceive them, and it only needed this
last blow to develop what very shortly would have happened
whether we had retained our member or not.  We, I cannot help saying, but we have no more in common with the
dear old place: it is only in memory's wonderful picture-
book that we still retain our place among the bygone inhabitants of the little borough; but moving over those pages
we can see once more the hale old lady living across the
heath, in a sheltered nook below the hills, who invited us
to a garden party to celebrate her golden wedding, and whom
we met *en route* mounted on her horse by her husband's
side, having just completed her usual ride with him round
the little place he owned and farmed himself.

At the time we write she still exists at one hundred and five,
a wonderful specimen of the healthy action of her open-air life
among the hills; and as she tells us of the battle of Waterloo,
when she had been married five years, and then of "the dear
old man" to whom she was married "sixty years and four
months," we begin to wonder at the shortness of time and
the very nearness of the past, that had seemed so distant

it had been impossible for us to have aught in common
with it.

Yet the small wrinkled hand we touch reverently, because
of the tears it has wiped from the old eyes and the years it
has seen : has touched in its time the hand of a man who
saw the head of the Princesse de Lamballe carried on a pike,
and who said, as he told the mournful story, "she looked
so pretty I could have kissed her," and who was at the
theatre when the ill-fated king was brought back from Ver-
sailles and made to go with all his family to the play to show
his subjects he was still among them. At her words all the
scene rises before us : the agony he must have endured
seems very real ; and we can almost feel how the play must
have appeared to mock him as the imprisoned king sat
watching it, knowing full well the tragedy that was to follow.

It is even more curious to realise the tremendous bounds
and strides that have been taken in the world in her lifetime.
Naturally all those things that are to us every-day occurrences have first of all presented themselves to her mind as
chaotic dreams of some scientific enthusiast ; then she has
watched them gradually embodied ; and finally has seen the
realisation of steam and penny postage, and the curious
wonders of electricity develop themselves. She, who lived
in a time when the poor, and even the middle-classes, ate off
wood or beautifully-polished pewter plates, has seen china
in the possession of workhouse babies, and indeed may live
still longer to see the marvellous light of the future flooding
our streets and rendering the vice that "walketh in darkness" almost an impossibility. There were other wonderful
people in the town, who are all dead and gone away : the
dear old lady, who always sat to work at her little table
where she could at the same time keep an eye on the comers
and goers in the street, is laid to rest in the churchyard in

the particular corner that was set apart for her family, from time immemorial; and where she could not bear people even to stand in her lifetime, so great was the feeling of proprietorship she had in it.    Still, how well we can picture her as she looked up from her netting or the making of endless warm petticoats for poor children, made out of list begged from all her friends, and greeted us; invariably taking us at first for some relation who was years and years older than ourselves, and then finally recognising us, when she would say with her plaintive smile, "I was one of one-and-twenty, my dear," proceeding to entertain us for hours with old-fashioned politeness that never failed her, even when memory had quite gone.    Perhaps the best part of our visit to her was the display of relics with which we were entertained: when we were shown love-letters, the writers of which were dead years and years before; tiny invitations to dinner at three o'clock, apologising for the lateness of the hour on the ground that the haunch of venison sent by the squire could not be properly dressed before; and that showed that, even in those distant days, electioneering was carried on very much as it was in the present time before our town was disfranchised; and wonderful little bags, worn on the arm before pockets in dress skirts were invented, and that never matched the dress, as the taste of the wearer was displayed by her discerning a "sweet contrast" in colour to her garment in some material out of which the bags were manufactured; and which were used to carry their love-letters or wondrous handkerchiefs, with initials embroidered thereon with hair, taken first from the abundant tresses of some schoolgirl adorer, and then from the sparser locks of him who afterwards developed into a commonplace enough husband. How delightful it was to go there on a calm, summer Sunday evening after church was over!

The garden was in itself a picture, on which the tiny drawing-room opened with wide windows framed in by a verandah covered in the season by a giant wistaria. Here we would sit talking over the sermon, saying perchance how the rector had aged and how troublesome were all his numerous sons.

On the table inside was the large-printed hymn-book, with the spectacles in to keep the place; the piano would be open, with *Hymns, Ancient and Modern*, erected on the stand; the cats would sit solemnly winking at the bats; and the stores of beautiful old china would gleam out in the half-light that began to creep over the hills. Then we would get up and wander slowly down the narrow pathway, where mary-lilies would be throwing out strong scent into the heavy air; pausing to look into the chapel burial-ground, and talking softly of those whom we knew and who were among us so short a time ago, and who now were out of this troublesome world, having got through life and entered the silence of death, glad to know it was all over.

Then we would wonder at the height and beauty of the monkey-puzzle tree, the araucaria, that was the pride of the town; and we would endorse her opinion that the old tree-stump on the lawn should still be allowed to stand there, because a great white rose-bush had climbed all about it, and hung there making it sightly and beautiful with its branching foliage and blossoms; albeit the gardener condemned it because the lawn was rendered untidy thereby, looking sometimes as if a June storm had swept over it, by reason of the showers of petals that would fall from the roses in the night.

Suddenly the clock would boom nine: Emma would come rushing with goloshes and shawls to say supper was ready, and the dew was falling; the green gate closed behind us ; we said good-night, and watched her led in by her good old servant, who almost seemed like a mother, now that her mistress's second childhood had very nearly come.

Then we pay an occasional visit to a queer old man, who lives all by himself in a grand house, from which wife and son have vanished in body, and only linger round those stately doors in spirit, if at all.

He leads us with trembling steps into her room, and shows us her dresses; it is the occasion for the quarterly airing of them, and he displays them to us with a vast amount of pride. Here is a ruby velvet dress he gave her after her son's birth, fifty years ago ; here a black velvet, given when his son obtained a commission in the army ; here the son's uniform, spick and span, for dissipation took him off long before he could wear it ; and here endless stores of raiment, rotting and useless, of value to none save to the poor old creature, who, revelling in the past, cannot and will not see that the present has any claim upon him.

When death claimed him too and led him away from his relics, the things were worthless and moth-eaten and had to be thrown away, for none remained who could conjure up his Elizabeth's features in the fine raiment that she had never loved, and when he died they were discovered to be the useless old-fashioned things they really were.

After all, our town was full of these imaginary, unreal possessions. The red cloak adorning the comely shoulders of our one cheerful jolly old maid, at which we youngsters jeered as old-fashioned and inappropriate, represented to the wearer the acme of splendour, and the proper thing in which to attire herself for the party or concert at which it was worn. Ah ! we did not know then that she drew it round her soul, so to speak, which was as young and pretty and capable of enjoyment and admiration as ever it was, and not over the somewhat overblown charms that we called Miss Medina Batterson, but that was really only the case that hid her from our unappreciating sight. We laughed then; now we are fain to weep as we think of our ill-timed hilarity.

There is nothing so piteous as decayed gentility, and now that is all that is left in the poor deserted place; our accustomed haunts are neglected; our houses inhabited by strange people, who are not as we were; and all the rooms are full to us, not of the folks who really are there, but of ghosts of people, ghosts of fashions, ghosts of old follies, old loves, old hopes, and old beliefs!

One after the other English country towns are declining; centralisation goes on; gentility exists no more; there is not time now to be genteel—all is hurry and rush, all hanker after money, money, money; so perchance it is as well to linger lovingly about our streets, even if the inhabitants are no more; even if all our days of excitement and shooting and electioneering are past, and nothing is left but the sense of decayed gentility that characterises our old country town.

## THE DAWN OF THE SPRING

A SOFT gray haze lies over the winter landscape, that looks wintry only because of the stripped appearance of the trees and the insight given by the leaflessness of the hedges into the domestic arrangements of last year's birds. For in sundry niches still hang curious black clumps that were once comfortable homes for thrushes and hedge-sparrows : looking at present much as a house looks after it has been for months uninhabited. In the tall trees opposite remain the deserted habitations of the rooks, which, being but a small colony, have joined another larger one some distance off, only returning here occasionally, as if to ascertain that their residences are yet in existence : for it is a curious fact that small colonies of rooks never face the winter alone, but invariably disappear from their summer haunts to join some larger company, separating from them once more as surely as the first break in the weather suggests the return of spring.

The winter is dissolving in tears, that hang in drops all along the branches of the trees ; and the trees are already turning from the blackness that has been their hue so long to the clear brown that suggests the rising of the sap. One of the rooks has been standing on a great elm, gazing motionlessly at sundry very black sticks massed together, where doubtless he and his wife raised last year a fine family; but the old bird cannot make up his mind what to do. Something tells him that it is full early to begin to restore that dilapidated home of his : yet this soft, sweet-scented weather is surely spring, and it is as well to go with the times, even if one cannot quite understand them. So, with many misgivings, no doubt, he begins to think of restoring the structure. First he spends hours gazing at it ; then he hops a little farther off, as if he were turning his back on temptation. Again he returns and looks at it once more, with his head on one side ; keeping up a species of monologue all the time that is not responded to in the least by any of his companions, who are busy feasting on worms and other dainties. At present he is perched by the nest that is all hung about with dewdrops ; and, although he has not touched it yet, he holds a small twig in his beak, as an indication of what he means to be at as soon as his friends will see the folly of their ways and the wisdom of his, and will come, as is their yearly custom, to talk over how best to rebuild the old home, or to determine if after all it is better to make an entirely new one : rooks, be it remarked, requiring much help and advice, before even one twig is finally laid, or one stick placed in a permanent position.

The dawn of the spring, being so gentle, has roused all the bird-world ; and our mornings are no longer silent, or made musical alone by the cheery song of the robin. The sparrow has already begun to fight vigorously and hustle his friends off any branches to which he thinks he has taken a fancy, though he knows perfectly well he cannot build upon them all ; and the flocks of these pert little creatures that infest every hedge and rick-yard in the neighbourhood, already give signs of breaking up their winter companies, and forming into couples for the love-making period of the year. The soft weather is a delight to the sparrow, who is miserable only in bitter cold, that causes him to hunch up his feathers, and speechlessly beg for crumbs and warmth in a manner that is piteous to behold, spite of the many grudges we owe the little mendicant at every other time of the year. For does he not render our lives a burden to us by reason of the untidy nests he makes under our eaves? Does he not punctually nip our budding hopes as regards gooseberries and currants? Worst of all, does he not persist in waking us before even the laggard dawn of February mornings with his ceaseless chatter, that is purely domestic and that never rises beyond the bread-and-butter region of things? Rooks remind one of business-men— steady, prosperous, regular, not easily cast down. Sparrows are like those housewives whose one object in life is to rule the house, and who love to tell their friends exactly how much trouble they take to live. The sparrow's eager cease- less note has never a touch of music in it; and though the little creatures are cheerful and busy, they are so only about trifles. The robin too is domestic, but he has the poetry of home life centred in him; while the thrushes and blackbirds are sweet singers and fair-weather creatures, who represent to us the art and song and culture of bird life. And what, then, do the starlings represent? Ah! there is not much doubt of that. Over yonder there is an empty house—very melancholy to look at. There are bars to the upper window, whence once the children used to gaze across and beckon and smile to us; and the lower windows, whence a hospitable stream of light used to shine out like a friendly greeting, are shuttered and closed. Yet the house has tenants at last. The starlings have been in possession there all the winter; and they are very pleasant creatures to watch. They do not rise very early just at present, and there is always one that gets up first. He emerges from his particular chimney, and takes a look round at the weather, sitting at first on the water-shoots, where he occasionally has a bath and where the sparrows alway do : then he has a short flight, returns, looks down the chimney, as if to call up his friends, and then waits a while on the side of the chimney, gazing meditatively at the scene before him. Presently, one after the other, the rest emerge ; and they then sit about the roof until breakfast suggests itself to their minds, when they all fly down into the garden and strut about until they are satisfied. Then off they scatter, and we see them no more until the next morning, when they rise to the day's work in exactly the same routine.

As spring dawns, Nature seems like some enchanted princess waiting for the kiss from the fairy prince to awake her out of her sleep. Here and there the earth is pierced by a tiny spear : a yellow crocus stretches up its hands, begging the sun to call it out from its dark chamber into glorious light and air. Wee buds are already on the lilac ; and the shrubs have none of the pinched-up, black, starved appearance that makes winter a season of dread to the garden-lover. The present promise may be broken, snow and frost may return ; but now the whole atmosphere is full of hope. The birds rejoice, and Nature allows us to see signs and hear sounds that speak of spring and whisper of the summer beyond. The days are growing longer. Darkness has not quite so much of his own way as he had ; and we are allowed to feel that the worst of the year is over.

## THE NORTH FARM NOW

Now ; for it does not do to think of it as then.

Then it was quite a different place ; albeit not one inch of ground has altered, and but few trees have fallen since those days, fifteen long years ago, when we saw it first. Yet perhaps it is as well, ere painting the picture as it is to-day, to pause for a moment, and raise the soft gray veil that hides the semblance of those dead hours, when all seemed joyous enough, and we were all too oblivious of the presence of the tiny rift within the lute, that, like that in the poem, has widened until the music is indeed mute, and mute for ever.

How could we perceive it, when from every window streamed the hospitable gleam of light that, brightened by the warm crimson blind through which it came, seemed to say to us : Hurry, hurry out of the wild January storm into the quiet haven of rest and peace on which I am now shining !

And what a night it was ! The tiny station where we got out, stiffened and wearied from our five hours' journey from town, seemed to shake and shiver as the great north wind tore up the valley and threw itself in all its fury on the building that is but an atom of a wooden structure. Great swishes of rain swept past us, and we were in despair, until

a cheery voice called to us through the darkness and disclosed the whereabouts of our host, who was buried out of
the storm in surely the queerest vehicle ever invented by
man, and that seemed like a cart with a head on, in which
we sat sideways, and which was driven through the window
at the extreme end.

Into this we got, and then plunged down head first, as it
seemed, into the black night. The wind howled and raved,
and the rain pelted down on our carriage roof, sounding
like a perpetual shower of peas falling from the loose grasp
of a child. We bumped over stones and rattled round
corners, and seemed to undergo various and many imminent
escapes from sudden death; and all this time our host talked
gaily, expounding to us his plans for our amusement, and
confiding to us, with a jolly chuckle, his wife's mental
agonies and perplexities as to what she should possibly do
with company from London, and the Squire coming the very
next day, dear, dear ! to shoot the home coverts.

We drew ourselves up (and then we were not very high)
and thought ourselves equal to any amount of squires, pensively wondering, too, what the Squire would say to our gun,
the first we had been trusted with, by the way, and which
we had carefully carried with the tenderest care from Waterloo station until the present moment, and which was pronounced by all who had seen it the very best specimen of a
weapon that surely was ever possessed by youth ; and that
drew forth from our uncle a long account, given to us as he
held the gun and gazed at it, spectacles on nose, and head
on one side, of how he used to go shooting, making his
preparations himself, punching out wads out of old hats,
and getting gunpowder and shot-belt ready, and starting as
soon as the sun was up, with his dogs and one man ; walking miles through dank turnips, and then through blazing

hot stubble fields, returning to eat his brace of birds at a
six o'clock dinner, and then sleeping like a top in his arm-
chair, only roused to read prayers and tumble into bed,
rising again at early dawn, to carry on the same process
as long as the shooting season lasted.

" That was sport," said he ; " now 'tis very different, but
the world goes too fast nowadays, and there is no time for
anything.   And even when you go shooting you are all too
lazy to find your birds, but require them brought to you.
I've no patience with such ways ; not I."

As we heard what the Squire generally did from our
hostess, we felt constrained to believe that for once old
folks knew more than we young ones, and that our uncle
was right.   Yet we looked forward to the morrow, and, ere we
went to rest, flattened our faces against the many-paned
window, and wondered what we should see outside it when
the dawn came and the darkness fled away.

Surely never was there such a room, or such a heavenly
place for perfect slumber : not dead, heavy sleep, mind you ;
that is not in the least perfect ; but a warm, genial, tired
feeling, when we were just conscious that outside the wind
raved through creaking trees, and that rain flung itself wildly
against the window ; that later on we dreamed of lavender
and rose-leaves and a slow walk in an August garden ; and
then once more we heard life had begun again ; a cart
creaked away down the lane ; carters called to their horses,
and presently we heard the curious sound of the handle of
the pump and the ring of the pail on the stone-paved yard ;
then came the voices of children ; a gleam of sunshine told
us it was late, and the robins singing down in the garden
seemed to call us to arise and make the most of our time in
the heart of the sweet, pure, distant country.

Naturally the great event of that day was the visit of the

Squire, who was much more like a squire in a book than any real living man. Strange enough stories were told of him, to be sure: farmers who had pretty daughters never allowed them to be at home when the Squire was coming, for his character was as bad as his language; and that was of the good old-fashioned kind; and instead of the adjectives that are lawful, was seasoned by wild, strange words, that were heard all over the farm should things be not quite as he liked them at the moment. He was a thoroughly typical specimen of a thoroughly bad landlord, and in those days used his shooting solely as a means of ascertaining what improvements were done on the land in each place he went to; if the land did not satisfy him the tenant had notice to quit, and if all were in order, gates up, and the land yielding its utmost, owing to the expenditure of the farmer's time and money, up would go the rent, and the farmer must either be prepared to pay or go.

No wonder our pretty, smiling, agitated hostess quivered when she heard what was expected; no wonder we shared her indignation at having to prepare her cosy rooms for an incursion that would result in either raised rent, or a fiercely-expressed reprimand to get ready a meal, that would be eaten to the accompaniment of great oaths that would send the servant-maid shaking from the room; and to a coarse volley of chaff directed at his host, who could afford such luxuries as were put before him, and yet objected to a slight rise in the rent.

It was a curious experience for a Londoner! Neither our host nor ourselves were expected to shoot; nay, indeed, we were not allowed. We could walk with the shooters if we wished, and our host was obliged to do so, or would be ordered to, in terms more offensive than can be imagined in a free country, while the birds, fed on the farmer's corn, and the rabbits, the curse of the country, fell before the guns, and were carefully counted and taken away, with perhaps a brace of pheasants and a couple of rabbits thrown on the yard pavement at the farmer's feet, just as the dog-cart drove off. Then the returning to luncheon was surely another martyrdom. The coming in at five o'clock, when ordinary people had theirs at one; the muddy boots on the tidy green carpet, that had been down something like twenty years, and that must last as long as a carpet was necessary; the agitated creature, the Squire's toady, who was divided between his dread of the Squire's anger and a still more abject dread of catching cold, and who would make hurried excursions in search of the hostess to procure dry stockings, and to see that his hat remained warming in front of a fire from the moment it left his head until he required it on leaving; the tobacco smoke all over the house, and at last the tipsy keepers and beaters to get rid of, and satisfy, before any peace was allowed to enter into the desecrated home. All these things made us thankful indeed that the Squire only shot his coverts once during the entire season, and that all the rest of the year the birds might go free, only coming to grief occasionally when a poacher passed their way, or the keeper was ordered to shoot a few brace for the Squire's table.

It is pleasanter to turn from this recollection to the drive to the meet across the meadows, when the frost gave suddenly, and the river crept up the lane and entered the low " four-wheel " as we went; the cheery greetings, the magnificent view as we waited for the master on the site of the old Roman camp, surrounded by its three rings or walls and a couple of deep ditches, and crowned by the clump of fir-trees, in which the wind never ceased moaning softly; the great white fleecy clouds rushing along over a pale blue sky;

the sight of the men ploughing a little way off, taking no notice of anything save the straightness of the furrows and the movements of their horses; and then, as the hounds went away, the rapid drive across down-land, and through fields, cutting off corners, and coming into a lane, where we waited in lonely silence, listening to the gurgle of a wee brook, the busy wind among the hedges, the wakening of the bird-world, and the distant sounds of the hunt.

These had grown distant indeed, when suddenly, out of the copse to the left, the hunted creature crept.   Our host started up to give the view-halloo, but something stopped us ; the eye looked so appealing, the movement was so abject, that we silently regarded each other and said not a word ; while, as if interpreting our very thoughts, the fox crept under our "four-wheel," and lay low there, panting hard.

Was it a lie when a red-coated stranger, bursting through the brushwood, and asking had we seen the fox, we merely shook our heads and turned the subject ?   Well, lie or not, we did it, and remained where we were until sounds told us of the finding of another victim, at whose death we assisted nobly a little later on in the day.

How our conduct was regarded by our hostess we knew not, for she was too gentle to do aught save point speech-lessly to her poultry-yard, where the next morning lay the headless corpses of sundry turkeys and noble motherly hens, who had fallen in the night-time into the mischievous clutches of perhaps the very fox we had so foolishly saved, and who had only mangled the poor creatures, as it was too early in the year for him to carry off more than he wanted at the moment ; that being reserved for the time when a large and hungry family requires support, and for the which he forages ruthlessly, taking turkeys from the nest, and ducks and hens or chickens, in fact just whatever falls into his way first.

Then the year creeps on, each season embellished with a most appropriate picture. A mile away from any other habitation, the farm was a village in microcosm, a tiny kingdom with our host as a king——a king uncrowned then, but now talked of with bated breath as the good man, whose first thoughts were for his men, and his second for the land, and his last for himself, and who could not rest were the cottages ; the landlord's property, mark you ; unfit to house the men who worked for him. And then his passionate attachment to the land was in itself remarkable.

It was joy to him to plan for the welfare of each field, as if it were some separate and well-loved child ; and each season of the year brought to him subjects for thought and lovely suggestions, given out to us at times, and telling their own story of the silent poet, with whom we were for a time permitted to dwell.

He it was who taught us to watch the gentle travelling of the cloud-shadows over the swelling downs ; to see the soft flush in the trees that told of spring ; to joy in the tender different tints of the distant copses ; to note the divers ways and habits of the creatures and birds ; to tell from the shades of green in the distant fields which held barley or wheat or swedes or turnips, laughing at us until we overcame our ignorance and got as wise as ever he was in time.

Winter scenes rose up before us, when all is white and silvery and we follow up the tiny half-frozen stream with him in search of duck and teal ; evenings when we crouched in a furze bush, clad in curious gray night raiment, holding the dog back until the last line of yellow light got entangled in the rushes, and the whirr of the snipe told us to look out, because " flight " had in truth begun.

Spring scenes, when it was joy enough to know we were
alive, and that summer was really coming; when we found
every flower again, even to the white violets in the lane, and
the wonderful golden lent lilies in the copse, among the wan
anemones and yellow primroses; when the lane was full of
mysterious soft amber-coloured stuff we called sago pudding,
and that in time gave place to myriads of tadpoles, that we
never could resist disturbing, even when we were in our
Sunday clothes, and marching religiously to church; and
when the hedges were white with blackthorn, or flushing
with velvet palms, that somehow or other always look pink
in the distance, although they are yellow enough close to.
The meadows were full then of cowslips and cuckoo blooms,
and great marsh marigolds glittered in the sunshine in the
"lakes," as we called the ditches dug for draining purposes;
and the village children looked on angrily while the big iron
roller went to and fro over the fields; marking them out in
broad ribands of pale and dark green that crushed the
flowers down, and made it apparent that these favourite
play-places were "laid up" for hay, and were therefore no
longer open to all who liked to walk them.   Summer and
autumn have all such golden memories, memories of drowsy
Sundays, when the hot walk to church behind the servants
was enlivened by our hostess's strictures on the gorgeousness
of the broad embroidery-trimmed petticoats of the damsels,
or "maidens" as we always termed them.   When we used
the afternoons to wander about with our host, becoming
learned in this or that farming operation, and seeing with
his eyes deep down into Nature's very heart.   It all seemed
so safe, so lasting; it was so certainly a place where change
never came, never could come, that we were not heartbroken
when, the harvest supper over, in the great hot barn, lighted
by a yellow moon that rose suddenly over the top of the

fir clump in Lowood, we realised that our stay at the North Farm was over, and that we must go. We had obtained all we came for—health and an intimate knowledge of country life—and we were young and eager to begin life once more for ourselves. Besides, we could return at almost any time : and so good-bye. Ah me ! it was a long good-bye, and more than fifteen years had passed before we came again, and entered those once all-familiar, all-hospitable portals.

It was an eerie sensation, and one experienced always, we take it, by those who come back on a very familiar occasion to a very familiar spot, and one that makes us perceive no one person who is really there, but the forms and faces of those who once were component parts of the place, only appear to come round corners suddenly, and vanish as we come up to them, eager to speak and to be spoken to.

We knew where to find our good kind host. He had not gone away, but lay very still and quiet under the tree in the churchyard, where the snowdrops in spring-time are like an angel's wing covering God's acre in the early sunshine ; and as we stood beside his grave, his widow with her hand in ours, we could not speak because we knew he had gone away from us far too early in the day, and had fallen because the fight was too much for him to wage alone.

But his work should remain, we thought ; and so turned away while the cuckoo mocked us with his monotonous call from the newly-budding sycamore tree, and went on up the lane to visit the shepherd in the cottage we knew so well. But what a change was there ! the cottages were all fallen down, and a little farther on three were standing, windows battered in, roofs in in places, and only one inhabited as it was wont to be, but the denizen thereof remembered us and came out trembling on his sticks, a young man too, as men should go, at fifty-five, yet too infirm to work, and only anxious that this miserable shelter should be his until he follows his dear old master to the churchyard.

We sat down and looked around us—how familiar it all was, yet how ghastly : here, over there, the shepherd lived, and we could just see the traces of the path from his cottage to the lambing-yard, now all broken down and used for hay, a scanty crop of which had been gathered off the arable land and sold to a neighbouring shopkeeper, waiting his convenience there until he chose to fetch it away. Yonder, too, once lived well-known labourers, the little conveniences put up for them by our host falling bit by bit into decay, or taken by passers-by as the spirit moved them, for there were none left to prevent. The tidy garden, too, was going back into a wilderness, and the place where the beehives stood, and where we helped Betsey Smith to tie crape on the hives when her mother died, as a polite intimation to them of the family bereavement, was thick with nettles, and defied our attempts to pass into the field in the old accustomed way.

Indeed, the whole place was full of heart-breaks : the cottages were all like this, all the men had gone "up country," all the girls had gone away to service, and only old Cherritt was left to talk over old times and tell us how the place had fallen into decay. One after the other farmers had tried but failed, owing to wet seasons and the Squire's rent ; and then the Squire had tried farming it himself, but had only cursed the times and the independence of men who would no longer slave themselves to death for him, to have his rent, and to die finally worsted in the struggle, their capital sunk in the land ; and only a pittance left for the wife who had fought the battle side by side with her husband.

And she stood beside us there in the old house porch, and we thought over the past, and even smiled at all the pictures we remembered so well; the gate was gone in truth, but there was the sty left, where old Billy the pig once lived, and ate every chicken that crept into his warm straw bed; and as long as the sty remained we should recollect how he roused himself and tried to get over the gate after some especially fat duckling, and only succeeded in hanging himself on the topmost bar, where he was suspended, squealing, while we all laughed too much to help him either backward or forward.

The long row of sycamore trees was still standing, but no bees came there now, as they used to when the flowers were out below the leaves, and made such a noise the while that the whole place was in a regular "charm," as they say in those parts; and the slope after slope of lovely fields, where once corn waved in the soft wind, and where our host waged perpetual war with the yellow "charlock," have gone back to a rough sort of grass that it will take months to eradicate, and months more before anything can be grown again there.

But the very sight of them reminds us of our host's cheery patience and his many difficulties, and how once, when he had thought he had beaten that yellow fiend, and he had come in rejoicing and rubbing his hands to think of his enemy's defeat, he arose next morning to find a soft rain had fallen which had brought it all up again as thick as ever, and "I do believe," he said, laughing then, even if ruefully, "that if I dug up a spadeful of earth from the bottom of a well and flung it abroad, the stuff would spring even out of that as strong as ever it did."

Every door is off in the stables, the corners of which are as if bitten off, and the house is desolate: it is impossible to believe it the same in which we had so many happy hours; but that it is, is shown by the very hole in the wall, where one night we saw a rat's eyes regarding us while we were playing whist; and by the crooked stairs, where once we found a governess who was a martyr to neuralgia and stupefied herself with laudanum, until she fell about "all over the place" and frightened us dreadfully for fear she was having fits.

Desolate, dreary, and terrible as is the destruction of the farm, we find it too full of remembrances of good times to be really as disappointing as it was at first; there is no life about it, no trim neatness, no hearty hospitality, yet the past has so much power that the present has much ado to keep itself before us.

Yet when we turn away we realise the difference terribly, and know how bad all this is for the village and for the labourers who are fast being exterminated from these parts, and we pause again by old Cherritt, who wants us and is waiting for us at his cottage door to show us how nice the cottages could be made if only the farm were once more let.

We go to him up three stone steps, worn pathetically thin by the feet of many generations of labourers—silent martyrs who have never realised their martyrdom, happily enough, and who only dread two things, change and the workhouse; and we go into the cottages once more, while the old fellow discourses on his rheumatism which is aggravated by heat, and for which he has a humble prescription to give us, consisting of half an egg-cupful of benzoline oil poured slowly, as he expresses it, into his hips, and when we suggest that a cottage where the windows are glazed, and where the water doesn't *climb* up the steps into the floor, would be a better prescription for it after all, he declares the water is beautiful water, and it would kill him to leave the cottage where once he was born, a tiny atom of a baby, for which it would seem the world had small use, and that the world has treated rather hardly from his birth.

The soft spring twilight begins to gather on the downs, and the thrush sings loudly in the tree over the grave, a sad wind moans across the river, and silence glides over the landscape with her hand on her lips. An inexpressibly mournful feeling seizes us ; we realise that the Italian poet was right when he told us that " Spring restored all things—save our dead and our youth," yet we cannot help thinking that we find both, ay, even if only a pale reflex of either, in the desolate, lonely place that is the North Farm now.

# XV

## A LONELY SPOT

A WINDING lane leads very slowly up the hillside, and brings us where we can see the tiny village nestled down in a hollow round the little bay.  As we climb the lane, where the bold forward honeysuckle is already putting out its blue-green leaves, we look down through bare brown undergrowth to the valley, where there is nothing stirring, and where all the waters seem to have met, for the floods are out.  Each atom of a streamlet, scarcely existent in drier weather, has become a river, and the low heath-set pools have spread and spread until in meeting they have transformed the land into a silent silvery lake.  The mild genial weather has already caused catkins to appear; the rooks over the way have long and serious consultations about renovating and rebuilding their nests, and at early morning the sparrows chatter over domestic details, drawing down anathemas from would-be sleepers on their empty little heads; and here in the lane the very air is full of spring-like promises, and comes to us strong with the odour of newly-ploughed fields, and laden with the timorous cry of the early lamb and the deeper response of the newly-made mother, while a blackbird is singing away as if winter had never been, and there was nothing save spring and summer in the whole world.  Full of the sound of life, yet is there nothing human stirring.

Far away stretches the sea, which heaves slowly to and fro, and appears as free from agitation and hopes and fears as the rest of the world around; while farther still pass ever and anon great ships going out into lands, that are not even names to the few folks who live on the shore below. The sound of the sea on the beach is like some tranquil lullaby, while in the bay a tiny stage stretches out aimlessly just at present, but serving to remind the inhabitants that visitors will come again like the swallows, and wander about the cliffs for a space, wondering at the beauty of the place, and how people can be found to live there all the year round. Indeed, it is a marvellous fact that such can be the case, for there seems nothing to live for here in the dead season, which lasts exactly nine months out of the twelve. Yet there is much to interest any one who knows that whenever he likes he can turn his back on the loneliness, and in a few hours find himself in the rush and roar of London; which will soon cause him to forget the calm and quiet place he left only that morning at early dawn. All along the beach the boats are drawn up and covered with tarpaulin, while just one or two curtsy up and down in the bay, to be ready should a fisherman think it worth while to go out in quest of the fish that at most times of the year abound just outside the bar of rocks that keeps the bay tranquil even in the very worst possible weather.

It is hardly possible to describe to an active mind the curious and monotonous life in our lonely spot. The people seem numb, and only capable of allowing time, like a succession of the waves of their bay, to advance and recede, casting up in its progress very few shells, as it were, bringing few events to their doorsteps; and they never go in search of stirring times, for they are never able to spare the necessary time by reason of their daily routine. So much

work has to be done, week in, week out, in the mere pursuit
of a living that there is no beyond for them, even should
they want it. The men go away, but never far; their fish
live outside, and lobsters and prawns are plentiful in the
bay. Men from the outside world come to them to buy their
goods, and there is never any necessity to leave their mere
monotonous occupations to mix with others, for the sake of
ridding themselves of the fish they spend their lives to catch.
And yet small tragedies are sometimes enacted, atoms of
comedies played, and all the elements of love and death
and jealousy and passion exist here, much as they do in
the larger world. It is sad to watch some of the women's
patient eyes, as they stand leaning against their doorposts
knitting the gloves with which they add a few pence now
and again to their scanty incomes, looking now far away
and now at the small children at their feet, struggling to
climb over the two-feet board in the doorway put to keep
them in for the present; for the women know quite well
that some of the children will escape over the board soon,
very soon, and go away into the outside world, returning
perhaps, but never the same as they were in the days of
childhood. Girls go away to service, boys as sailors; and
many stories could be told of those who went down the
winding lane away to London and never returned, or came
back in poor, thin, faded finery to sleep in the churchyard:
forgiven, maybe, but never forgotten, and serving as a
wholesome warning to others who begin to murmur, and
wonder what the world is like outside the hills that stand all
round the tiny bay.

On the left side a succession of grass-grown rings tells of
the old Roman invasion, and here the older children climb
and play, imitating their long-dead ancestors, and carrying
on a mimic warfare, strangely mixed up in their minds with

Bonaparte and the "Roosians," both of whom are still held up as bogies, and both of whom are yet expected to land some day about here and harry the country round. Indeed, though the men know better, and some read their papers diligently, the women still hold a lingering belief in the almighty power of Bonaparte, and can hardly credit that he is no more. The grandmothers and mothers of the present elder generation recollect the days when the whole coast was alive with expectation, and when some of the gentry kept the horses harnessed in the stables, and a bag of guineas in the secretaire ready for use, should the French land and it be found necessary to flee for safety to Salisbury Plain, which was for some reason or other selected as the rendezvous of the fugitives; and sometimes when the men are all away fishing, and the night gets oppressive by reason of its silence, the women gather together and talk of those long-gone days, and wish on the whole that the coast of France was just a little farther off, or turned the other way, for as long as they know it is opposite, they are never quite certain that they are safe from invasion. Yet they should have a sort of fellow-feeling for their neighbours, for, for some reason or other, most of the inhabitants are Roman Catholics, and worship Sunday after Sunday in the little chapel inland, where once Charles X worshipped when he fled from France, and the small Protestant church has but a dull time of it in consequence. Yet the strife of creeds does not trouble them, and they remain in the religion they were born to, never troubling their heads on the vexed subject, or indeed on any other subject beyond Bonaparte and the routine of daily life. From just outside the village the mummers start on their rounds at Christmas-time, but they do not visit the bay, keeping in towns where they will be welcome, and where they are every year received warmly, and listened to as respectfully, as if any one could understand their curious jargon; into which, much as Charles's head was introduced in Mr. Dick's memorial, Bonaparte has once more crept; and is represented by a gorgeously-attired individual, who is much mauled and evilly handled in the course of the performance. But the mummers are regarded as frivolous in the bay, or rather as if they tempted Providence by travestying an event which was too near a tragedy, to be quite pleasant hearing to any one forced to live there, even now.

Sometimes the whole bay is fluttered by the arrival of strangers who are anxious to see everything, and who go and wander about the Roman camp, much to the disgust of the children, who resent the intrusion into their playground mightily, and have small information to give any one who is rash enough to go there in late autumn or winter. A stranger in summer is well enough, and expected, and for him are culled the sparsely-growing flowers, which, tied in a tight little bunch, and feeling very warm from the combined effects of the sun, and the small damp paws that gathered them, are thrust into the visitor's hand, and never fail to draw from him the rarely-seen and much-prized reward of a penny. But a stranger in winter must either be mad or one of those extremely ignorant people, who wish to find out the simple secrets of the birds and cliffs, that are known to every small boy and girl in the bay, who can never understand that the sight of the sea-gulls' breeding-place in May is a marvellous and wonderful spectacle, or that the knowledge of the site of the peregrine falcon's nest is a valuable possession. Perhaps it is because for them seasons are more than people, and weather of more consequence than events in history, that they trouble themselves so little about the outside world. Whatever occurs there, May is to them the time when the

I.

eggs can be gathered along the cliffs; or August the season when the mackerel flash their silver skins outside the bay, playing along the tops of the waves, and almost calling the boats to come out and have a game of hide-and-seek. The new year may be saddened by the death of a great states-man. What is that to them? for here the pall of winter seems to lighten a little; the days begin slowly to lengthen, the mornings are a wee bit brighter. Away on the hills the green corn grows lustily. The tarpaulins have been once and again taken up from the boats, and John or James has thought seriously of pitch and tar and beginning to work; and so the dawn of the year is full of all the promise of waking life. As we wander away, looking back now and then at the group of cottages, whence the blue peat smoke curls lazily into as blue an atmosphere, we almost wish that for us life could be only marked by the faithful sunset or sunrise, and the revolving seasons, that doubtless would really bore us to death, but that seem strangely attractive in this very lonely spot.

## LEAFY JUNE

In June the height of the year's pinnacle seems reached. After the death of Midsummer-day it is all down hill; and though the weather is perfect and warm and lovely, it is the beauty of an English matron that charms us then; whereas, in early June, flowers—not fruit—deck the brow of the year, and she has still the fresh young loveliness of a maiden. In the silence of the country everything then is at its best. The trees are still rustling to the songs of the birds, and each hedge has its garlands of wild roses, and its golden honeysuckle crown; while in every ditch, on every hillside, the stately foxglove stands, bending down with its own weight of blossoms, some of which are already gone— stolen, as the children believe, by the foxes themselves, for Sunday wear, and to prevent them from the dear delights of popping them vigorously on their dirty little paws. The barley has come into ear; and the wheat has the fine delicate hairy line down it, that tells us it is out in bloom; while scarlet poppies, faded to a sad pink where the sun has shone unchecked, peep out of the fields and nod to the big white marguerites and yellow corn-marigolds that are everywhere. The birds and creatures seem tame just now. As we lean over a gate and look lazily into a neighbour's field, we watch a great hare canter slowly from the hedge towards the middle of the grass. There he seats himself, his white tail just showing and the light shining through his erect ears, with which he listens for every sound. He sits motionless, although one or two carriages pass near by; but presently a small white dog pats along, and he is off straight for the wheatfield to the left, where we know a partridge has her nest, and has just hatched out eight of the small brown balls. Every village pond has its families of wee yellow ducks, and some are quite big, and adventurously "fend for themselves," standing on their heads in the water and paddling their feet out behind as they grub up the weeds, and endeavour to maintain their balance at the same time; while the air is full of the cluck-cluck-cluck of the matronly hen, as she marshals her troop of chickens to and fro, and casts contemptuous glances at her friends' families. The big cows, sleek and sweet-breathed, stand knee-deep in the pasture, that when the wind blows one way looks like a silver sea, by reason of the many-toned gray and brown grasses; when it blows another, is all gold, by reason of the buttercups; and when it blows not at all, has a pink flush all through, from the crowding ragged-robin that perks up its red head all over the place. In another field the hay lies in long brown swaths ready to carry, with a square of trifolium left uncut, making a wondrous patch of colour; while in a third a stack-making machine seems slowly to climb up an ever-growing haystack, the wonder and admiration of half-a-dozen mares and foals that look on motionless, save when a swarm of flies becomes more than they can bear, when a tail is uselessly swept over the wrong place, or a foot is angrily stamped, or a foal returns for nourishment, which it seems to take savagely, bumping its own head and its mother's side indiscriminately. Later on, when shadows fall on the river, you may hear the swish of a line as a fly is thrown to attract the attention of a lordly salmon, or the more insignificant trout; and then in the dip, where the bracken grows profusely and leads up to the clump of firs, the rabbits come out and have a regular game at hide-and-seek.    There is no more beautiful sight in the world than an expanse of newly-born bracken under the shade of the solemn dark-robed fir-trees.    The lights and shades are unequalled, and the sheen on the tops of the fronds literally glitters as the gentle air moves the ferns, or a rabbit pushes his way eagerly through them; while graceful shadows glide over the polished bronze-coloured. ground, deep with fir needles and cones, made rough and shabby by the squirrel's tiny teeth extracting the seeds therefrom.

Below the pine wood is the rabbit's favourite resort: there you may watch the great heavy mothers sit and gaze at the little ones gambolling, while others venture into the neighbouring field, where they excite the wrath of the keeper by eating out square patches all along the edges, and causing the place to have a most bare and untidy appearance.    But in June the keeper never goes out without his gun, though he spares the hares, who are more decent in their ravages, and making narrow paths for themselves in the growing wheat from the hedge, nibble here and there in the centre; and so, while doing almost as much mischief as bunny, are not so open as the smaller creature is, in their devastations. But the gun is wanted for other purposes too.    No hawk must hover over the high field on the left, where in serried ranks stand dozens of coops full of pheasants that are being reared for the three days' battue-shooting that will end the keeper's year.    On the heath beyond are occasional hawk traps, but should the birds escape these, they fall victims to one or the other of the ten keepers, who, turn and turn about, night or day, never leave the fields until the 4000 pheasants

reared therein, are turned out into the woods, and given over
to the care of a few hens, who chaperone them carefully, and
call them regularly to their numerous meals provided for
them by their keepers. As we were leaning on the gate
watching the little atoms fly, or creep, or run, according to
their ages, towards the keeper, a sudden cry spoke of a
victim caught in a trap. It turned out to have come from a
lurcher, whose too inquiring mind had led him into difficulties, but as he was claimed by a man and woman who
had unfortunately lost their way, and innocently asked for
directions from the keeper, he was let off with a caution,
and limped away too much hurt in mind or body, even to
look at a rabbit as long as he was in sight. But he caused
quite an excitement among the hens, who at the first sound
of danger jumped up and down and fussed about in the
coops, calling anxiously in shrill spasmodic gasps to their
foster children, eager to see them in safety. All round the
coops were great branches of firs to keep off the sun, which
certainly had not been very ardent up to the day or two
before, and to serve as a species of covert from the hawk,
and also from the aggravating jackdaw, who torments the
keeper dreadfully, for although he does not eat the little
creatures, he has an odious habit of twisting off their heads,
and leaving their dead bodies as a little surprise for him
when he comes along. The woods where the pheasants will
ultimately reside until the day of their death are in June at
their very best. The great chestnuts' broad leaves stand out
stiff and straight, and though there is then no great difference
in hue, all being green, and simply shading from dark to
light, the trees have an appearance of plumes of deep shade,
and peace and silence; only broken by the thrush's warble
or the song of the blackbird, or the monotonous call of the
cuckoo; that they have in no other month, for July always

turns the leaves dark altogether, and brings silence to the birds, and sleep and quiet to the whole land. Still, before this time came, we were determined to see for ourselves a little more of the ways and manners of the birds in this particular spot, and one evening found ourselves again near the place.

The air was heavy with the scent of hay. Far across the meadows the whirr of the hay-making machine and the creak of the waggons, and an occasional shout, marked where the greater part of the country population had vanished to ; and there seemed no one at all about. It was almost the first real day of summer : long sprays of wild roses, blushing pink and white, hung droopingly over the hedges, while all along the top climbed the yellow honeysuckle that looked down upon the magenta foxgloves, and spreading bracken, as if it held but a poor opinion of anything that grew in a ditch, quite oblivious of the fact that its own roots were there too. Away to the right stretched a wood, then quite at its best, and to the left was a long wide field, filled with low gray-painted habitations, row upon row, like a collection of extremely miniature tents. There are few things more fascinating than a deliberate lounge over a gate on a summer evening. There is the chance of seeing the *vie intime* of the wily rabbit, and the timorous hare ; or of noting the manner in which mamma wagtail scutters about feeding her tiny off-spring, who are too lazy to feed themselves ; and looking upon the low gray houses before us as possible shelters for large families of chickens, we put our arms warily on the gate and proceeded to watch their manners and customs, secure in seeing something new. But we were not left long in con-templation ; suddenly appeared a tall figure, clad in the orthodox keeper costume of velveteens and gaiters, and having slung across him a linen bag, very full of something

soft.   Far away over the field his double appeared engaged
in scattering the contents of his bag, while on the extreme
left was even another, who at the sight of us made for the
gate, and looked at us with an evil and suspicious eye.
"Do you want anything?" said number one.   "I wanted
to watch your birds," answered we, in meek accents.   "Then
you'd better come along with me," said the keeper; and
opening the gate ushered us into the field.   "Them's the
pheasants and them's the partridges," and so saying he pointed
over his shoulder with his thumb ; "and if you want to watch
them you shall, but there is nothing to see."   We had our
own opinion on this subject and walked forward, while the
keeper stooped to pick up something over which he proceeded to shake his head dolefully.   It was the body of an
unfortunate little pheasant bereft of his head by a marauding
jackdaw, a member of which extremely tiresome family hung
suspended by the neck in the middle of the field as a
warning to others.   "I should not mind so much, really,"
said the keeper, as he conveyed the headless corpse to a heap
of tiny victims, "if they creatures wanted food ; but a jackdaw is nought but mischief; he simply pulls their heads off
and leaves them.   Oh ! they are the knowingest birds ; but I
thought yon had frightened them away.   I have seen them
fly across the field and sheer off when they saw one of their
friends hung up, but I suppose they have got used to the
one over there, and I must try something else ;" and the
keeper meditated profoundly on deeds of darkness.   Close
to the heap of dead birds was another one composed of
numerous rats, with which an unfortunate squirrel was tied
up, he having been shot because he "happened to come
along"; and weasels and stoats and a miserable jay were
nailed to a tree as a wholesome example to their friends.
On the entrance to the field were several coops containing

partridges, of which the keepers most highly disapproved,
holding that these birds do ever so much better when they
are left to their own natural mothers ; as they refuse the food
that suits the pheasants, and require the tiny yellow egg of the
red ant and other natural dainties ; besides being extremely
difficult to rear ; for they are so very tiny that they are often
walked on, and trampled nonchalantly to death by their
foster mothers, the hens ; who, if disturbed, start up heed-
lessly, and tramp heavily over them as if they were so many
flies.   In several cases, too, wild partridges have been
known to come up to the coops and draw off all the tame
ones that, having been artificially reared, are too " nesh "—
*i.e.* tender—to stand what would suit the ordinary wild-
reared bird.   In plumage they are singularly like the baby
pheasant, who, however, stands considerably higher on his
legs from the very first day.   When the partridges are about
a couple of months old, they are turned into the corn-fields,
where they " pack " like grouse into companies of forty or
fifty, and get away first by flying and then running along
the ground quickly, and then with more flying until they
find a congenial spot where they will sometimes lie so close
while the corn is cut that they fall victims in twos and threes
at a time to the reaping-machine.   But if the keeper dis-
approves of the partridges, he has an endless amount of
affection for the pheasants, 2000 of which are in this field,
and 2000 more in a similar one across the river, and raised,
as is the one we inspected, from all fog and damp that
wreathes the little stream.

As we approached, the long grass suddenly became alive.
Through tiny tunnels, worn through the tall herbage by
constant passing to and fro of the little mites, the birds
began to run, or else flew towards us from the more distant
crops like a flock of sparrows, or came rushing from all

parts of the field to greet the familiar figure. But before they reached him the foremost bird paused, and ere we could realise what they were about to do, they have "spied a stranger," and were back, each to their own particular mother, and peeped at us shyly from under the sheltering black feathers of some matronly hen. They were all ages, from the denizens of the lower coops that were six weeks old, and already beginning to assume their second plumage, when a slight redness on the breast denotes the sterner sex; to the wee atom of a day, who resolutely buries himself in the warm under-garments of the biddy who hives him; motionlessly keeping one beady eye on the keeper to remind him that though she will not move, she would still take a little from the bag, containing a delicately - cooked and compounded mixture of egg and meal and other mysterious dainties. Until the pheasants are about ten days old, they will not even enter the tiny boarded and wired-in runs that remain in front of coops; but after that they roam bravely, coming back to the call of the hen, unless it should happen to be a wet morning, when, if the keeper is not extra careful, the heavy moisture contained in the thick grass that surrounds them, clogs their wings, and then, according to his account, the very poor-spirited creatures "jack-up," and lie down and die, not having energy to rise superior to the cold and clinging wet. Until they are about two months old, they are fed five times a day, and all night long two keepers walk round and round the field on the look-out for stray dogs, and men and women, who, if perceived, pretend innocently that they have lost their way, and beg for directions; and if not seen possess themselves of as many of the birds as they can, finding a ready market for them on rival estates, where the keepers gladly take them at from 2s. to 3s. a bird. But the opportunities for poaching are

small, the watch, day and night, being incessant, and as
soon as all the coops are full of birds that have to be reared
in the season, a fine wire will be stretched completely round
the field, and this will be attached to a gun elevated in a
tree, so that if any unwary soul enters, his foot catches in
the wire, the gun is discharged, and the keeper is down
upon him in an instant. Should a dog enter the field at
night and slink up to a coop without the keeper seeing him,
the hen cries at once, and the dog goes off; but enemies
are rife, and the trouble that begins with collecting the eggs
to prevent the hen-pheasant sitting, never ceases until the
day when a great battue disposes at one feel swoop, of
nearly 2000 of these birds that feed out of the keepers' hands
and come to their call the very day that they are ruthlessly
slaughtered. The pheasants are turned into the wood when
they are about two months old, but naturally much depends
on the season : this one, when we were there, being an
exceptionally good one, the mild winter having caused the
birds to lay early and well ; the wild pheasants having in
some cases just hatched out their second supply of eggs,
they being generally allowed to rear their young themselves.

A sitting pheasant is a delightful sight. She often
chooses the centre of a gorse bush, and if you go quietly,
noting the regular little tunnel she has made for herself, and
so avoiding her eye, you can look down on her beautifully-
marked back, and sometimes see her rise and leave her exquisite olive-coloured eggs for you to gaze at uninterruptedly.
Damp, cold springs are enemies to the birds, for, as the
keeper plaintively remarked, there is little they can do
for them : "If the gale that spoiled our trees had been a
month later I don't believe we should have saved a bird :
the wind was bitter—peewits could not face it even, and
just by yon hedge I found quite a heap," said he, "that had

run there into the 'loo,' and they were there dead : poor
things, our birds must have gone had any been hatched out
then." A keeper, to be a real good one, must be born to
it ; he must have had his father's experience, and his bringing up must have been among the birds, for there are
endless details of management that cannot be learned from
a book or from other men, but must be inherited and
imbibed with the air they breathe. A good keeper easily
obtains corresponding wages. Here are ten and a head
keeper, in and around whose houses the birds are hatched,
told off to those two particular fields, and the 4000 birds
provide " His Lordship " with exactly three days' sport—
save the mark !—during the whole year. The keepers
heartily despise the most unsportsman-like battue-shooting
of the present day, and declare it goes to their hearts to see
the creatures they have tended fall in hundreds round them,
to be ultimately sent in hampers to Leadenhall Market ; but
as they justly remark, " It's the gentry will have it like this,
and 'tisn't for us to say what we think." As we looked at
the rows of coops, and watched the keepers tending the
birds while two of the men prepared to begin their watch
for the night, by loading their guns and " seeing to things
generally," we thought sardonically of " agricultural depression," and the miles and miles of habitationless heath,
and the quantities of untenanted tumble-down cottages we
passed by on a not very extensive driving-tour in this same
neighbourhood.

## A QUIET CORNER OF ENGLAND

As we leave the tiny station and begin our winding way up a wide dusty road, we seem to cast from us our last link with the outer world. The train goes puffing slowly away towards the busy north; and as we drive on and on, a strange dreamy feeling begins to possess us, and we appear to ourselves cut off entirely from all our fellow-creatures, for beyond a bent labourer too weary even to step aside as we drive past, or an occasional dog that has not energy either to bark or wag his tail, we see nobody and meet nothing until we arrive at our destination. But before this our driver draws up suddenly, and points with his whip, first to one side and then to the other of the white way. On the right is a marvellous avenue of beeches, untouched as yet by autumn's hand, through which the sunshine is filtered until the leaves look like an emerald-tinted rain, so close are they together, and so gracefully do they hang; but which evidently leads nowhere, and is a purposeless beauty in these days when everything has its use, or must cease to exist at all; for on the left is the Manor-house, with its old, old hedges of yew, and its Charles II gables, as gray and as varied and seemingly as lasting as the distant hills themselves. A house with a story this; a story of murder and great wrong, which even in this prosaic present is about to be righted, and things

are to end happily when the lawyers have tardily done their
work ; and as we look back on the old quiet place we cannot
help feeling that it seems waiting for right to be might, and
that when the king enjoys his own again, the house will know
it and will look less grim, less gaunt, than it does at present.
The whole quiet place is full of this sort of memories and
feelings, and is utterly unlike any place possessed of the
railroad demon. Few people care to drive the long five
miles between the town we are steering for and the
nearest station ; so the place remains much as it was when
Cromwell came down the long hill the inhabitants call the
High Street, and in the dead of night seized the Levellers
in their lair, and put down with an iron hand their attempted
rebellion. Indeed, it requires very little imagination to
fancy that time, otherwhere so full of work and advance-
ment, has here stood still ; and while people have fallen
necessarily by the force of years, houses remain as they
were when Charles I. lost his head, and the Protector was
all-powerful in England. Indeed, the church that crowns
the town and is the pride of the country-side is older much
than these comparatively recent days ; and as we stand in
the great quiet churchyard and note the beautiful Norman
arches and the quaint gargoyles, and the elegant later spire
that can be seen for many a mile, it gives us a curious indescribable feeling of how little time really is, when we remember that the very same bells in the tower may have rung
to commemorate many a victory ; the names of which were
a weariness to us in our early days, by reason of the dates
which accompanied them, and which had all to be remembered. All round the churchyard a quiet little stream runs,
bordered on one side by graceful willows, and on the other
by a double row of limes, odorous and lovely doubtless in
summer, but now yellow and sad, and dropping every now

and then a leaf, that falls with a sigh to the ground as if grieved to its heart that the summer is over.

This still time of the year suits the place better than any other. The gentle gray atmosphere clings lovingly to the grayer houses, and seems to make them more like houses in a dream than ever. The soft swish of the scythe, as the venerable clerk (who has been fifty years in that office and seen eight vicars of the place) mows slowly down the rank grass on the crowded graves; the crack every now and then of a dead twig or leaf falling; the wind that moans softly through the willows; and the occasional sharp ring of a pail on the paved yard, when a gossip pauses a while in fetching water to talk leisurely over passing events,—are all the sounds we hear. No carts or carriages seem ever to pass, and when we ascend the steps in the church tower and look over the aisle, on the roof of which Cromwell drew up the mutineers to see three of their number shot, as an example to the rest, in the churchyard below, we can see nothing save old men leaning, doing nothing, in the arched doorways of 1066, and three or four women standing in a curiously old-world picturesque group looking up the street, as if they were expecting a mediæval procession down the hill, and exactly as must have stood many a one of their lineal forbears, to watch their men come home from the civil wars; or, pleasanter pastime, from hunting in an adjacent forest, once the people's property, but now enclosed, and cut down until there is little save the name of a forest left. But even now one of our gossips tells us that he remembers poaching there well, and he, leaning heavily on two sticks and much bent as he is, lifts his old head, and his eyes twinkle merrily as he recounts, how he raced many a time from the wood to the town, with a deer slung on his shoulders; only reaching sanctuary in time to lift one of the heavy table-lid tombs down there in the church-yard and cast in his burden, and cover it up again, before the keepers were on him to find him peaceably employed in harmless agricultural pursuits.    Then coach after coach passed down the street, and at certain curves of the route mysterious exchanges of deer and game of all sorts were made for money; and with the boot full of contraband goods on went his Majesty's mails, and none save the poachers and the guards were any the wiser.    The prospect from the roof is not very extensive, not as extensive as is to be obtained at the top of the town, so we turn back to investigate the two old, old rooms, with a lock put on by a locksmith of Henry I.'s time, and with curious little personal reminders of the priest who long, long ago lived there, and kept watch and ward through a gap in the walls on the relics of the saints kept in the side-chapel below. We can see exactly where he stood his bed, because he had a tiny shelf for his candlestick; and he must have been a chilly soul, for a rude stick below the heavy beam tells us where he hung up a curtain between his sleeping-place and the small heavily-framed windows, that are the identical ones through which he must have looked on many a dark winter's night, on many a bright summer's morning.    But the whole of the church is full of such little stories.    Here, on the old lead which lines the font is chipped by a dagger's point, " Anthony Sedley, prisoner, 1649 "; giving point to the story of the mutineers shot down in the churchyard from the Silvester aisle; while in the Silvester aisle itself there are tombs after tombs, inscriptions after inscriptions, from the Edmund Silvester who " decessid the xxvii dai of janvari, 1568," to the last of the name, who was only buried some year or two ago, and had so marched with the times that he spelt Silvester with a " y," regardless of the fact that his ancestors stared him in the face and gave him, so to speak, the lie.

Then there is the Bartholomew aisle, where one Richard Bartholomew did, in 1668, erect a monument to his family, and wrote an epitaph thereon that seems almost as fine as Shakespeare. Reading first the names and ages, evidently belonging to his well-loved children and parents, there is surely something infinitely touching in his lines, which are as follow :—

> " Lo ! huddled up together lie
>     Gray age, green youth, white infancy ;
>     If death doth nature's laws dispence,
>     And reconciles all differense,
>     'Tis meet one flesh, one house, should have
>     One tombe, one epitaphe, one grave,
>     And they that liv'd and lovèd eyther
>     Should dye, and lye, and sleep togeyther.
>     Go, reader, whether go or stay,
>     Thou must not hence be long awaye."

He was evidently much addicted to poetising, for on adjacent slabs are two more rhymed epitaphs; but time with a jealous hand has rendered them well-nigh illegible, and we can make nothing satisfactory out of them.

It is sad to think that no member of the family lives in or near its birthplace, but that America has the sole representative thereof—who takes a warm and kindly interest in his native town, however, and has once or twice paid a visit to the bones of his ancestors, among which his own will never rest.

Opposite the Bartholomew aisle is the Tanfield Chapel, where lie low the parents of the wife of the Lord Falkland, who fell in the Civil War.

A stately structure this, and in perfect order too for

the rent of a pretty little house in one of the side streets is
set aside for its maintenance, and it is as fresh and bright as
if erected yesterday.    Here, as well as in the farther aisle,
affection wedded to sorrow has given birth to poesy ; and,
after a long setting-forthment of her husband's virtues, Lady
Tanfield ends her plaintive moanings thus :—

> " Love made me poet,
>   And this I writt
>   My harte did doo itt
>   And not my witt."

A sentiment that carries its own apology with it.

Just outside the Tanfield Chapel is a more modest slab,
on which is written, after the name and date (1677)—

> " Here may I rest under this Tombe,
>   Not to be moved till the day of Doome,
>   Unless my husband, who did me wed,
>   Doth lye with me when he is dead."

But as no name is added beneath his own, it is to be feared
that a second marriage interfered with this idea.

There is colour in this old church that, though doubtless
startling to the ultra-Calvinistic mind, is very beautiful indeed to those who do not see in it the mark of the beast.
A wondrous inner chapel standing in the nave is alone
worth the visit ; and the pulpit, gorgeous in scarlet and blue
and gold, restored, it is true, or rather repainted only, is the
same that saw Cromwell march in at the grand west door ;
yet it lacks just a finishing touch, for it is almost too far
from the beaten track for any one to offer the few necessary
pounds to finish it, and the inhabitants have already done
nobly by their pride and glory, and have given all they can.

Perhaps the most curious indication of how far out of
the beaten track is this quiet corner is offered to us as we

again pause for a moment in the churchyard ere returning to the street; for here is a tiny spot of ground, enclosed by a severe brick wall and planted with a couple of trees, and that marks the end of a neighbours' quarrel, two of whom each claimed this particular corner as their own especial burial-place, tracing their ownership back almost into the Middle Ages; but the vicar came to the rescue, and pointed out that nothing but lawyers' bills was likely to come of the dispute, and recommended that the place should be a debatable land, planted and enclosed, and the property of both, neither of whom should insist on being buried where there was room for one, but certainly not for two.

The street has dozens of houses all more or less beautiful, large ones, speaking loudly of the palmy days when rich merchants made the place their home and held high state therein; some with quaint oriel windows all more or less irregular; and small ones full of quaint folk, almost as old in their ideas and ways as their dwelling-places, and as content to meander on in their still lives as are even the houses to hold them. Back from the street stands the priory, gradually and slowly dropping to pieces. Here once lived Lenthall, Speaker of the Long Parliament, and here a ghastly murder was committed, the murdered man sleeping within the church near by. And here year by year decay goes on unchecked, and makes us long for the hand of the restorer to save what remains of a marvellously beautiful and interesting structure. There seems no link at all with the present here—all is of the past; yet when we stand on the highest point of the street and gaze down it, a face looks wistfully into ours, and a tremulous old voice asks us for news of the war with Egypt, then just over and done with. He cannot read, poor soul, and as we reassure him and tell

him the war is over, and pity him for the anxiety his three
sons must cause him, he draws up his still vigorous frame
and says, "I don't mind; 'tis for Queen and country, and
'tis better any way than starving on the land, that won't
keep none of us much longer."    Another link with the
present is supplied on Sunday, when a quavering chorus of
small boys and angular women try to sing all up the hill in
imitation of the Salvation Army; but find the steep incline
and the clashing bells just too much for them; but on
Monday we are once more in the past, for we awake to
find ourselves in the midst of a fair, collected round the
"Tollsey"—*i.e.* the market-place—where boys with whip-
cord, wee bits of wool, and other emblems in their hats,
and neat servant lasses stand demurely in rows waiting to
be hired; and as we prepare to plunge once more into the
busy world, we look back regretfully, and rather think of
doing as some of the young folks before us will do, viz.
turning up again about the middle of October, when at a
second edition of the fair, called a "runaway mop," they
will have the chance of re-hiring if they have been unlucky
in their choice of a situation.

# XVIII

## BINDON ABBEY

CLOSELY surrounded by a thick belt of trees, Bindon Abbey is invisible save to the traveller who knows of what he is in search. Even in late autumn, when all secrets are disclosed that the trees kept closely during the summer, it is easy to pass close by the abbey and remain ignorant of its existence; for it is so hidden among the undergrowth and so guarded by thick-set hedge or great tree-trunk, that nothing can be seen until the old gateway is pushed open, and we find ourselves in the enclosure that once held one of the oldest of England's monastic establishments. It is a sad and solitary scene in autumn: the square fish-ponds are almost full of scarlet or yellow or brown leaves, forming a dense carpet at the bottom of the clear ponds, from which the fish long since vanished; while on the mossy paths, on which the feet of the unwary are apt to slide, the leaves are thicker than ever; and tiny bits of stick, or pine-cones bitten roughly by the squirrels searching after the hidden seeds, or even great branches that crumble when we touch them—so rotten are they—tell their own story of the wind that rushes down the valley, finding out all the weak places, and scattering in showers all the leaves loosened by the first touch of autumn's finger. It is very silent in Bindon in the late autumn: no birds sing then, save the bold red-

waistcoated little robin, who perches and chirrups where
once was the high altar. Perhaps we hear the sudden cry
of the jay or the harsh impertinent croak of the gray-headed
jackdaw; but otherwise there is nothing here to remind us
of life. All belong to the past; and albeit a flourishing
garden has taken the place of some of the monastic building, it is quite easy to trace the chapel foundations, and even
see how and in what form the whole abbey once existed.
There is, however, very little of it left : sundry round bases
of pillars, deeply embedded in moss and the blue-green
shiny-leafed periwinkle, show where the nave must have
been ; while where the curious white-veined ivy, that puts
out small feet and boldly clings everywhere, creeps over the
walls that the tide of the Reformation laid almost level with
the ground, the main building must have reared its stately
pile. Overlooking the fish-ponds are the quiet walks, where,
when the mists begin to rise at sundown, it requires small
imagination to picture the gray-habited monks walking,
their hands folded piously in their long sleeves. The
fish - ponds are perhaps the most curious feature of
Bindon, and are almost unique. They are a double set,
and are fed by a tiny stream that burrows underground, and
enters the enclosure, close by where was once the principal
entrance : an enclosure which in spring is bordered closely
by such quantities of primroses that it is turned into cloth
of gold. The ponds must have been stocked from the
neighbouring river, where fish abound even now, and where
salmon are caught constantly for the London market; for
the ponds are too narrow and shallow to have been aught
save a species of larder, for the monks to have ready, should
they be unable to go to the stream itself, and there angle
for what they might require. Or it may be that the monks
dreaded even so much contact as that with the outer world,

and had their ponds stocked for them by the villagers near by, who must have found much of their occupation gone when the abbey was handed over to the secular powers, and the monks and the building disappeared almost together. For all round the abbey are famous wild-fowl haunts; and just at twilight, across the last ray of yellow light that haunts the stream, we can see occasionally now the whirring snipe, or the heavier duck, as they come up to rest by the bridge among the close-growing rushes, after feeding on the mud-flats at the mouth of the little river locally called "the harbour."

Almost the prettiest part of Bindon is the space where the dead rested, and where many an empty open stone coffin tells its own tale of scattered dust and utterly vanished life; while one or two tombs, bearing traces of handsome brasses, point out where the abbots themselves were buried. When excavations were made there many years since, bones were exhumed; and on those that were once feet, shoes were found: thus proving that the monks belonged to St. Dunstan's order, for all who did so were buried clothed "in a clean hood, boots, and cowl," and if a priest, in a stole also. There was also discovered the sepulchral statue of a child, being about two feet in length, and habited in the dress and ornaments of an abbot—a presence accounted for, by the county history, by resorting to the ancient custom by which one of the children of the choir, on the festival and during the whole octave of Holy Innocents, was in cathedral churches permitted to wear the insignia of a bishop, and in abbatial churches those of an abbot. Hence, if the juvenile bishop or abbot—as we may suppose was the case at Bindon—happened to die in the course of the festivity, he would be represented in the ornaments he was permitted to use during that period. Probably, however, the antiquarian will say that the figure

is only an ornament from a reredos or from some part of
the decorations of the building. At Bindon the abbot had
a right to all the wrecks and waifs and strays along the
neighbouring rocky coast, from whence the sound of the
ground-sea reaches us when the wind is from the south-
west; and if we please we may imagine how on stormy
nights prayers would rise from the altar for the souls of
those going to their doom in the darkness, their property,
strewn on the beach, being carefully looked after next day.
When Henry VIII pounced on the abbey, he handed it over
to Thomas, first Viscount Bindon, who, undeterred by dread
of the consequences of sacrilege, raised "ane faire house"
from the ruins, which tradition says was burned to the
ground in the time of the Civil War. It is difficult, even
when contemplating the ruins, to realise that this peaceful
spot could ever have been the scene of such cruel destruction. It is easier to raise again the lovely abbey church,
and hear strains of praise pour out from the stained-glass
windows; and easier yet to understand the quiet contem-
plative life that must have had such a charm for studious
souls in times so rude and tumultuous. Yet the fish-ponds
and a green mound in the centre of the enclosure tell their
own story of a due attention to the comforts of life, and
point out that meditation was doubtless assisted by good
wine and a generous diet. Perhaps, if we too wish to medi-
tate therein, Bindon is at its best in autumn. And yet, though
the autumn suits it well, in summer it is very lovely, and
cool and quiet when all outside is garish and hot. In spring
it is well-nigh perfect : everywhere are primroses and violets ;
wan anemones peep out from among the last year's leaves ;
the blue periwinkle dots the walls and looks with great eyes
into the open coffins. Indeed, Bindon has a season for
every mood—a time to suit each one that walks therein.

## A DESERTED GARDEN

At all times of the year the garden is left solitary and alone. It is quite at the end of a long, lovely, country lane that passes it by, leading away to the open heath and the dip in the range of hills that means the sea.

No one could tell that the garden was there, for a long row of silent trees keeps guard over it, and seems as if it formed a thick wall expressly to keep out intruders.

In the lane in spring-time can be seen the most marvellous collection of mosses; and as the tiny brown bubbling stream, that crosses and re-crosses the road, making melody at all times of the year, runs its course, it passes by deep dells carpeted with the fine fern - moss, every tiny frond exactly like a perfect fern, and every morsel of a different shade of green or yellow, until finally it seems to be lost in the garden, which it truly enters, but does not there appear above ground.

But we find it again in the open heath, where it sparkles brightly among its dark surroundings, and goes on its way, doubtless to join the bigger river below the hills.

Just by the garden the brook is obstructed by a moss-grown branch of a tree, so small that any ordinary stronger stream would have brushed it away long ago, but this thread of water is too tiny; and so only becomes for a while a miniature whirlpool of froth, in which go round and round wee acorn-cups, pine-needles, or the shiny stiff beech-leaf that in spring is being reluctantly displaced by the new-comer ; then the stream creeps under the detaining branch, and after a very little way goes into the garden.

There is an old gate, green and decrepit with age, that we come upon in an unexpected corner of the lane ; sometimes tall campions and nettles stand in quite a little hedge along the bottom of the gate like a rank of lank weedy soldiers guarding the entrance ; while here and there a blossom peeps through one of the upright slats of the gate, that is only hanging by one rusty hinge.

True, the other, at the lower part, is there, but it only extends a ragged end that catches the raiment of the un-wary, or grates with a harsh cry against the gate as we open it and, regardless of the agony we cause several spiders, and of the destruction to the flowers, enter the garden.

The latch is gone : a piece of wire twisted together takes its place, and has to be re-twisted round the post before we can go on ; and as we pause, as we always do just there, we note the bright sunshine in the lane, filtering through the crooked oak branches that form a canopy and almost meet ; and then look at the contrast of the dense gloom just behind us, where, even in spring and summer, cool, damp, and dark chilliness replace the warmth and colour we find but just outside.

As we linger, we can see what used to be carefully-kept gravel paths, now closely dressed in a mossy green slippery robe that moves under our tread, while the beds that once were gay with a thousand highly-cultivated blossoms are now deep in weeds, and only to be discerned from the grass itself, by moss-grown stones that had marked the borders, but that now are rapidly disappearing into the ground.

In the winter it is comparatively easy to see exactly how the garden was originally laid out, and almost to discern positively where my lady has walked pensive at evening, watching the rooks fly home across a lovely sunset sky to the trees below the hills; where they have built since time immemorial. We can almost trace her footsteps as she went down past the clipped yews, long since returned to their original shape; yet even now grotesquely displaying an occasional resemblance to the peacocks or strange mysterious creatures they were once supposed to resemble; towards the big gates that are entirely gone, and are only apparent to those who, from a couple of moss-covered square stones, can mentally erect a stately portico, crowned by the crest of the family whose very name now no longer survives.

In winter there is very little undergrowth; the tall bracken below the pine-trees on the mound to the left of the garden has died down into a brown sably carpet; the lank grasses and lush verdure in the garden itself have vanished; the hedges are no longer entwined with bindweed and hops and the fantastical clematis, but are bare and slender, and allow us to see where the kitchen garden once was; and where the square beds before the manor were long ago filled with rare bulbs from Holland, or with lovely homely flowers, whose presence would now be scouted by a head gardener who "respected hisself," and are only to be found in cottage gardens or in those belonging to folks who rise superior to the riband bordering abominations of the present day.

In the spring the first signs of life come on the thin brown willows; here the stir of the sap is first seen; and then they are decked with the soft gray velvet palms, that when partly out and perceived from a distance seem to flush to pink, though there is not a shade of that colour upon them when we are close to the trees on which they are growing. Then they become golden, to tell us they are ready to give place to the leaf, which generally comes far too soon and robs us of the palms before we realised that they existed.

Turning away from this, we see that the kitchen garden is a strange medley. There are tumbled - down portions of the wall still left that evidently formed the stay for stores of plums, and perhaps of peaches ; and in the crevices grow tall wallflowers, a very small yellow or brown blossom on the top of a thin long stalk, while the glossy dark-green foliage of the periwinkle climbs all over, and bestows upon us a very occasional gray-blue blossom, as if to show what it could do if only we would allow it a little more light and air.

Some time later on, the ivy puts out pale - green shoots that in autumn become curious leaves all lined and patterned with red and yellow ; and in one place a white-veined leaf every now and then comes out to show us where to find that curious ivy that seems to have little feet to climb over everything, and so requires no nailing to attach itself to the wall it honours with its presence.

Every crevice of the wall has a moss to fill it up ; and red lichens, and yellow ones too, that in spring suddenly acquire with the rest of creation an indescribable access of colour, do their best to dress the place gaily and make up as far as they can for the loss of all care or all culture that the garden experiences.

Gooseberry and currant bushes still abound ; an unexpected strawberry leaf marks where the strawberries once doubtless existed in profusion ; but though the apple-trees have a very occasional apple still on them, the only fruit besides that we can find is the hard blue sloe, that takes away all taste from the roof of the mouth, or tightens the skin of the lips with its acrid taste; or a red-faced crab, that it is impossible to think of without a shudder.

At the bottom of the garden is a hedge that in spring is covered with the white bloom of the blackthorn; and here a thrush regularly builds her nest, while in the arm of a moss-grown apple-tree overhanging it we find the lovely home of the chaffinch, so like the tree itself that it requires very practised eyes indeed to see it at all.

We doubt much whether we should ever have done so, but the birds in the garden are so tame; they are less cautious than those outside, and allow us to perceive many of their little ways, that a less unsophisticated bird would carefully hide from every human being; and so we watch the chaffinch feed her babies, or see the sparrows talk at each other in the hasty happy manner possessed by all sparrows, or note the distant and haughty manner in which thrushes exchange remarks, until we feel, if only we had a little more time to devote to them, we should begin to understand all they say to each other, for we are quite convinced they talk, and talk intelligently, on all subjects that are found of interest in the bird world.

In all our visits to the garden we have never come upon a single trace of the house, and we can only imagine where it may have stood by the presence of the more elaborately designed arrangement of flower-beds; where sometimes, especially in autumn, we discover a rare blossom that we have seen in no other place, and can find no name for.

We are loth, too, to take other better-instructed folks to our retreat, for fear it may become common, and be no longer the place of refuge from all mankind that it is at present. One of these flowers is a large, pale yellow globe-like creature, transparent and tremulous. It looks like a soap - bubble, so frail and lovely is it; and another is pink, and hangs pensively on a stem that seems too fragile to hold it up properly.

However, they are very seldom seen, for sometimes the plants come up bearing no flower, and sometimes we are afraid they have gone entirely away; but last year they were there safely enough, and it remains for this autumn to show us if they are still extant.

Here also we find in spring great clumps of wallflowers, an occasional meagre single hyacinth, its white or pink spikes looking curious indeed among the maze of bluebells that crowd all over, and make the open part of the garden appear at times as if a blue table-cloth was laid there for some fairy gambols, or as if it were in readiness for an al-fresco party who were about to be entertained thereon; while marvellous tawny polyanthuses and thin red-stained primroses contrast strangely with the pale yellow blossoms of their wilder sisters.

There are one or two alleys between beech hedges, where the brown leaf hangs persistently until the new foliage comes in spring, and here there are ever warm and sheltered walks. They all lead in one direction from different starting points, and through them we reach the brown knoll, sur-rounded by a ditch and a peat wall, where the fir-trees live, and where we can see all over the heath, and follow the course of the little gray river until it widens out beyond the mouth of the harbour to the open sea itself.

Can anxious-eyed maidens or matrons have used this place as a watch-tower, we wonder; long, long before the beech walks were made; from where they could gaze on the wide expanse before them, looking for lover or husband

returning to them from fighting the Danes in yonder marshes;
or from hunting with the king along the hills, parting with
him, maybe, at the gate of the great square castle that still
stands in the gap or "corfe" from which it takes its name?
For from thence they could see the long red road, and
the high causeway between the meadows, or turning once
more inland, could watch the other roads that led from the
county town, or, farther away still, from the capital itself.

Naturally we cannot tell, but the voice that sighs perpetually through the pine-trees seems essentially the voice
of the past, and has a mournful way of interpreting nature,
who seems to confide her secrets to it, secure in her knowledge that few mortals are able to discern the meaning
thereof.    Is she at rest, and revelling in the golden silence
of autumn?    The wind in the pines croons a perfect lullaby.
Does she crave for sympathy in winter when storms rend
her, and the rains come dashing down?    The pines creak
and sway and croon as they lean down towards her, as if
to show they understood and pitied her agony.

In spring the song is one of hope, while in summer the
aromatic shade is made vocal by the music that replaces the
song of birds; for within a pine wood it is rare to hear anything of these small creatures, save the scream of a jay, the
coo of a wild pigeon, or the twitter of a bird, as it pauses
there for a momentary rest, ere pursuing its flight.

To hear the songs of thrushes and blackbirds in per-
fection, you must perforce return to the garden.

There they sing on, undaunted by the gloom and damp
and decay.    Even a nightingale has been known to build
there, and then at late evening the whole lane resounds with
the marvellous willowy music.

But the saddest and most suggestive corner in the whole
garden is a small plot portioned into six square pieces; it is

away from where we suppose the house to have been, and is not too near the kitchen garden. On all sides it is surrounded by a thick hedge, and at one end is a gate that has once had a lock on it, while at the other is a tumbled-down summer-house, in the thatched ragged roof of which numberless sparrows build unchecked ; while under the eaves a house-martin one summer made himself a residence, and successfully reared a large and promising brood.

Can we not see that this was the children's corner ?

Surely this plot, rather larger, and at the head of the rest, belonged to some elder sister, who may have sat here working her sampler, and keeping one eye on her own property, and the other on the conduct of the little ones, who were doubtless toiling away at their gardens, digging up perchance more flowers than weeds.

Absurd as it may seem, and waste of time as it doubtless is,—for very likely the flowers we notice may have been planted by him or her who owns the garden now, and may never have been seen by our hypothetical maiden,—we cannot help thinking as we sit here, in her old place, that she must have been a gentle, patient child, most likely a blue-eyed creature, with soft brown hair, and pensively pleasing expression of countenance ; for we find at different times the bell-like lily of the valley, the homely hen and chicken daisy, clumps of lavender, and many old-fashioned flowers whose very names we have quite forgotten.

Then in one corner is a myrtle that sometimes flowers, for here it is warm and very sheltered, and by the summer-house it gets the sun, and we cannot help believing that she planted it for her bridal wreath, and we wish her happiness —ay, almost while we laugh at our folly.

Next to her we find the Scotch brier rose, with its yellow

buttons, blossoming out freely, or find red and white, strong-scented, prickly creatures, scattering their leaves generously at every breeze that blows; and we think of the owner of this plot as a child of strong character, well able to work her way through the world that existed outside the garden; and so did not trouble about her at all.

Another of the plots had an undecided owner evidently! Here is a big old gooseberry bush gnarled and venerable, and taking up a great deal too much room; while wild parsley smothers the one or two blossoming plants that still come up by fits and starts, and a curious bean-like climber twines all over what was once a handsome standard rose.

And so going on all through the six, we like to fancy all sorts of different children owning the garden, and we must confess to a thrill of rapture, when, in the summer-house, we came upon some roughly-cut initials and six different notches by one of the windows, that at once represented to us the divers heights of those whose kingdom this once was.

Alas! no date was appended, only the mere dents and cuts that made the letters. Still we could not but feel our children a little more real, even while we had to confess they were no more tangible, than they had been before our discovery.

Away from the children's corner there is a deep, silent pool, sometimes covered with duckweed, and then later on fringed with tall grasses and rushes, that lean down and look into it as if they tried in vain to discern its secret. There is never a ripple on its surface, and it always appears to us as if all the long varied history of the garden had been confided to its keeping; and that being so, it would never betray its trust.

Surely many a tempest-tossed soul has gazed into the water, and found help and peace in contemplating the intense quiet and the unruffled face of the pool; or maybe it holds beneath its surface the unburied body of some one who found the burden of life too heavy, life itself too unsatisfactory to last, and who cast himself in, endeavouring to make the calmness of the pond his own.

Can we not picture it all? A hurried look around, the last glance at the sky, a plunge, five moments' struggle, a ripple or two, and then calm peace gathers once more over the pond, that keeps one more secret as faithfully as it has always kept all that it has heard.

Indeed, indeed, the whole garden is a storehouse of fancies and unwritten stories, legible enough to those who know it well and often wander there. It is entirely out of the world, and so peaceful and restful that it is like an unsuspected church in a silent corner in London, into which you may enter from the hot, noisy, summer streets, and at once be in an atmosphere scented, cool, and prayerful, in which you may rest a while, neither praying nor even thinking, yet inexpressibly refreshed by the few moments' retreat out of the noise and glare of the city.

And although the lane that represents the city to us for the moment is neither noisy nor hot, it is yet outside our garden, and open to intruders, who in winter come for the holme or holly from which it takes its name; or in spring and early summer for the golden, sweet-scented cowslips, that spring freely ever in a broad bright field, beyond which lie three or four unnamed tombstones, discovered long ago, when the little church was built that crowns the lane.

Perhaps some of our six children sleep there unmovingly through all the lapse of slowly-flowing years. Perhaps the elder sister, whose bridal wreath may after all have been woven for her marriage with death alone, there found balm for a broken heart.

But all is naught save speculation! Nothing lasts, save the immortal range of hills beyond the garden, that are now as when the garden was in its prime; and as we stand at the gate, and try to avoid the rusted hinge that always stays us, while we retwist the wire fastening and prepare to plunge into the world again, we seem to part with a multitude of ghosts, who doubtless, as evening creeps up, and the moon rises high in the sky, walk hand in hand in the garden, and talk sorrowfully together of the days when they and it were in their prime.

## A HEATH FIRE

JUST a tiny little puff of smoke over in one corner of the heath, and then, before any one could realise that the furze-bush attacked had really caught fire, a suspicious crackling sound could be heard, like the snapping of small dead twigs, a dry acrid taste was given to the air, the smoke extended yet a little farther, and now the whole brown and purple expanse was in a blaze. And yet not quite a perceptible blaze, for great clouds of black smoke, eddying round and round, gathering volumes as the fire spread, quite obscured the glow that usually characterises flames, and it was only as the smoke hurried past that we could really see what had been done by its passage. As it steadily advanced it burned like some hungry monster, devouring and licking up every bush or clump of beautifully blooming heather, leaving desolation where it found a perfect autumnal picture, and turning black and twisting into grotesque forms every furze-clump that it had not time to eliminate altogether from the face of the moor, over which was its triumphal progress. Presently it came to a hedge that surrounded a clump of fir-trees : here clematis was in full bloom ; honeysuckle flowers had given place to the brilliant red clumps of transparent berries of August, brambles were just fruiting, and sundry stunted nut-bushes were embellished with the unripe nuts

that are never permitted to ripen, but are bitten out of their
sharp-tasting green hulls by impatient children long before
they are ready to be eaten; the hedge-bottom was deep in
lush verdure; great seeding thistles were heavy with puffy
white barbed seeds, eager to float gracefully about the
moment a breeze came strongly enough to spread them
apart; tall campions stretched up their heads, and meadow-
sweet and hemlock crowded together and filled up all the
odd corners. But there was now an end to this: the fire
leapt eagerly forward, hurrying towards the pine-trees. In
an instant the hedge was a ruin; and pausing for an instant
as if to gather itself together, the fire, raising its head like a
snake in the act of listening, suddenly climbed the trees,
rushed like an electric current from twig to twig, from
branch to branch; and then, twining for a second in a tall
column of smoke and flame combined, over the head of the
tree, seemed all at once to leap headlong to the ground,
leaving its victim black and bare, and passing to the next,
repeating the process until all the trees were destroyed, each,
as it were, singly and silently as far as concerned themselves,
although the fire itself roared and cracked and bellowed,
like a fiend newly released from Hades. Now, however,
matters threatened to become serious. Once over the next
expanse of heath and the fire would do incalculable damage;
for it would come to a farm where as yet the fields were
uncleared, and haystacks and adjacent buildings and all
would perish, could the enemy receive no check. Presently
a steady stream of men commenced coming out from the
little town, and began to lay plans for action. The fire
seemed still occupied with the trees, but here and there in
the heath sudden jets of smoke and tiny crackles of flame
spoke of what was to come. The men armed themselves
with long fir branches, and commenced beating out one by

one the small fires as they arose. Then, as if the fire suddenly perceived their tactics and was determined to be even
with them, it threw itself from the trees, and began to creep
eagerly over the low-growing French furze, and spreading
bracken, and heather, until all fell back before its heat and
marvellous strength. Presently all sorts of creatures crept
half-scorched out of the cover that was fast failing them ;
clouds of wild pigeons had ere this escaped from their
shelter in the pines, while sundry jays and magpies, disgusted at others' capabilities for mischief, had flown screech-
ing and scolding out of the blinding smoke ; and now rabbits
and hares and even partridges began to run steadily towards
the belt of men, losing dread of their natural enemies in their
fear of the terrible fire. There was a moment's pause, while
the terror stayed for an instant to slake his thirst at a small
heath-set pool, and that very momentary halt gave the men
a little advantage ; some had been turning up great sods of
the heath and saturating them with water to put the fire out
when it came, and others, whenever they could face the
smoke, threw great spadefuls of sand sideways into the blaze,
thus trying to choke what water seemed powerless to stop.

The least pause of the oncoming fire was of incalculable
value in the fight, and now every advance-guard of the
enemy thrown forward, and beginning their ominous crackle
that told of the spreading of the foe, was immediately surrounded and beaten to death by the long branches, the
regular swish-swish of which could be heard even over the
bellowing of the fire, that when baffled momentarily appeared
to increase in rage, if not in force ; yet presently it seemed
to halt, to pause again ; at the turned sods more sand was
thrown over it, and it almost seemed powerless to advance ;
then at every corner some one met it with sand, or water, or
the beating branches. It paused again, finally halted, and

began to go out almost as suddenly as it had begun. By this time the number of men on the heath had visibly increased; every hand on the farm had been employed keeping the buildings and haystacks wet, to be ready to fight the enemy. A band of men stretched right round the cornfields, and by the time the fire was reduced to a smouldering, inoffensive creature, snapping out now and then as an occasional bush gave a hint of blazing up, it had almost reached the first barley-field, where the ripe grain would have fallen an easy victim to its rapidity. It had been found impossible to beat the fire in front, but advancing as it had done, exactly like a belt of skirmishers, it had been gradually hemmed in sideways, and thus was reduced to a point where it was finally beaten to death ignominiously every time it attempted to reassert itself. Gradually night had crept up, and now it was comparatively easy work; each spark that looked like a late glowworm, and that might have passed unnoticed in the sunshine, now attracted immediate attention, and was at once put out, while every smouldering bush or half-charred tree was watched anxiously until the sun rose once more, and looked down on a terrible scene of desolation. The place for miles round smelt like a newly-blackened cork; all the heath was like coal, and the pine-trees, that only yesterday wore the dull blue-green of autumn, with deep red trunks standing knee-deep in fir-needles and cones, while the sun shone on the bracken that had just begun to turn brown and give forth the scent that marks its dying, were like weird, ghostly finger-posts, standing up, lean and twisted and agonised, year-long monuments to the carelessness of him, whose thrown-away cigar-light or newly-emptied pipe was doubtless the cause of a fire that will for months give a desolate, dreadful appearance to the heath, that in general not even the dreariest month of winter can rob of its unchanging beauties.

## IN A VALLEY

THE valley lies low, between two ranges of hills — one guarding it from the great wide sea; the other standing as a shield from the winds that blow freely over the open moor, which in autumn lies like a spreading purple garment for miles and miles inland, and in winter is the haunt of many a bird. The valley is perpetually sad, and is generally filled high with a soft gray mist, that occasionally, before a very hot sun or strong wind, rises and drifts gradually away, only to return at evening, and sink down once more, covering the whole place as with a veil.

Profound quiet and peace brood in the valley, broken only by a harsh cry from a sea-gull, driven inland for a while; or by the chip of the stonemason's hammer, as he works perpetually at the quarries, that yawn like so many graves, on the side of the farther hills, close to the never-ceasing, mournful-sounding sea. On an autumn afternoon it is inexpressibly impressive to wander up the rough clay lanes that creep up the hillside; and, triumphant from the climb, gaze from our vantage-ground into the valley below us, or on the sea on the other side, where, as the mist rises, we can watch the great ships suddenly loom beneath us — homeward or outward bound — and disappear again, cloudless as is all around, into the gray distance; or catch the steady flap-flap of the cormorant's wings, as he flies heavily along towards his resting-place in the rocks yonder.

In the valley the heath has already ceased to glow redly under the sunset, and has become brown and dead; while patches of a yellower hue, and an indescribable faint odour, tell us that the stately bracken has begun to fade, and has been cut in places, for bedding for the cows or rough ponies that stand meditatively dotted about the heath, and that belong to sundry folk, who inhabit cottages that look like big excrescences in the heath, and are only marked to us as habitations, by the thin blue line of smoke that, as the mist clears away to make room for the sunset, rises into the sharp autumnal air.

Over by Holme the trees have begun to alter, the gaunt pine-tree being alone unchanged, while deep scarlet chestnut-leaves and saffron-hued beeches give emphasis to the scene, that would otherwise lack a distinctive colour; for in autumn the valley has only shades of gray or dull purple with which to deck itself for our delight. Just yonder, too, are the oak-trees, generally the last to change their livery; and below these we can watch the stately pheasant stalk, dragging his plumes after him like a lady's train; eager for the acorns that fall ever and anon with a dull thud; while at a little distance the sharp rattle of guns, one after the other, tells us that the pheasants' days are numbered, and their feast will only be a very short one after all.

From the top of the hill we can hear the long surge of the sea as it flows in on the pebbly shore, and then retreats with a prolonged murmur, strangely like the sigh of some unsatisfied soul, and that mingles even more strangely with the never-ceasing harsh cry of the jackdaws, which whirl and manoeuvre round the grim old castle, the beautiful ruins of which stand as if guarding the gap in the hills from which it

takes its name.    It is difficult, when we survey the peaceful
monotony of the valley, to realise that this was once a battle-
ground, and that the delightful quiet was continually broken
by the clash of steel, the whiz of arrows, and, in later days,
by the boom of artillery; and we realise very forcibly how a
place, like a man, has its day but once, and that it must be
satisfied to know that, its time done, it must contentedly
sink into an honoured old age, certain that for it, at least,
there will be no return of ancient glories.

And in our valley they seem quite content.    Here and
there there is an isolated farm-house, standing all alone save
for a handful of labourers' cottages nestling up against the
barns as if for warmth and shelter.    But it is heart-breaking
work to farm there, for the mist is a terrible enemy; and
the great gales, that seem to use the valley as a speaking-
trumpet, arise at most untoward times, and generally spoil
all that the dim fog has left.

Silence and damp ever seem to brood on the doorsteps;
the very fowls are never dry, and have a most draggle-tail
appearance; and the stone walls, that in places give the
valley a look as of a disused churchyard, are gemmed with
yellow and gray lichen, and are generally humid and dark
with exhaled mist.    In the hedges by the roadside everything runs riot in the autumn; great straggling arms of
clematis, called old-man's beard, twine among the hips and
haws, just now superabundant; oak-apples, and the lovely
bedeguars on the wild roses are close together, and hang
round the gateposts that mark the entrance into one of these
lonely farmsteads.

It is curious that any one can be found to farm in the
valley, but no one can dwell there without sharing in some
sort the silent self-contained life of the lotus-eater.    Day
succeeds day, as the waves follow each other on the sea-

shore beyond the sheltering hills, and things always seem as if they must surely be better in time: for occasionally, especially in spring, things appear so cheerful; all the hedgerows are crowded with violets and primroses and newly-uncurling fern fronds, while in low-growing spots the willows are golden with palms, while the peewit flits about with its welcome cry, and everything is so full of promises of better days, that some of them must surely be kept! The stonecutters have work to do; and as the great horses walk backwards and forwards in the fields, followed by birds eager for the worms newly turned up by the plough, the despondent farmer looks forward hopefully, and already sees yellow ripened grain where at the time is only the blue-green of the wheat just peering above the earth. There is not much hope left in autumn. The faint green sky, in which glimmers a bright star that speaks of the frosts to be, is not long in retaining any tints of the sunset; and as we turn regretfully away from our hill-top and wander down the sticky road, we watch one after the other of the windows in the farms faintly light up, as the housewife trims the ungenial paraffin lamp, that always smells, no matter how great her care; and we can well picture to ourselves the sigh with which she turns from the gray gloom outside, to the heap of work that scarcely seems worth doing, for surely it will have to be done all over again in a few days. But such is life—more especially is life like this, in the valley!

## AN AUTUMN FLOOD

OVER the lowering gray sky great masses of darker cloud began to drift. The wind rose suddenly; and, as if the heavens had opened, the rain rushed down in long slanting lines that seemed as if they never would come to an end. Every now and then the wind threw itself against the house, hurling streams of water, as if some one were busy with a bucket. The trees bent hither and thither, and with every motion lost handfuls of the deep-red or yellow or brown leaves that were making the wood beautiful even in the very hour of death. The poor late flowers were soon no more; and a yellow lovely rose clung close to the window until the rain was too much even for it, and it fell, a sodden heap of dank brown petals, and was drowned in an ever-increasing pool in the gravel-walk below.

But if the garden became a scene of desolation after twenty-four hours of such rain as surely never fell before out of the tropics, beyond the garden, which is raised a little above the rest of the world by reason of its being the site of an old castle, the scene was curious indeed. At first the river was only troubled, seeming worried and anxious with its extra work; but presently its ordinary pale-gray countenance began to change into a deep muddy brown colour. Miniature waves, that grew bigger and bigger as

more water came down from the hills, began to quarrel with
the banks, where thin reeds shivered and moaned in the
tempest ; soon the banks gave way by imperceptible degrees,
and then a deep brown sheet of water crept slowly but
steadily over the wide valley between our garden and the
line of hills. It was strange to see how rapidly green
meadows disappeared; how suddenly fences but just now
high and dry, and three quarters of a mile from the banks,
stood miserable and creaking, as the ever-increasing bulk of
water eddied and crept through the flats ; twining strange
water-weeds and broad dead lily-leaves round the posts, that
in an ordinary season stood knee-deep in kingcups or
cuckoo blossoms ; and strange it was to fancy the great
elms gazing meditatively down at their leaves falling, and
circling in the river which had heretofore existed for them
only in the distance. The willows along the little channels
cut through the meadows to drain them were quite in their
element : and as their spare yellow leaves left them—first in
regular showers and then one by one—almost appeared as
if they would like to follow them, and leaned and swayed
backwards and forwards, their long thin arms tossing about
as a banshee's are supposed to do.

But now the river has crossed the road, and leaping
headlong into the farther fields, has set afloat the carefully-
thatched peat-stacks that were to serve as fuel for yonder
cottages all through the coming winter. Now it catches up
and whirls round in its course sundry baskets and hen-coops
left out in the meadows by the village ; and now it swoops
round one of those queer slate-coloured boxes that are
supposed by the ordinary intellect to represent a shepherd's
hut, but that are known to the initiated as constituting a
vote for their possessors in the neighbouring borough-town.
But even the river in flood is powerless to remove one of

these abuses—it is too well rooted for that; and on the
water rushes, leaving the little house standing solitary and
miserable, surrounded by a waste of waters. The rain falls,
and falls, and falls. At the end of the third day the road is
beginning to be washed into holes; and it is no longer safe
to ride out on either side of the town, or to drive either;
while walking is impossible, and has been since the early
part of the second day. Only the willows now mark the
boundaries of the fields, as the fences have gone or are else
completely submerged; and if it were not serious it would
be comic to stand on the bridge—almost as old and as
strong as the hills themselves—and note the divers queer
" fish " that swim gallantly down with the stream, bound for
the sea. But when piggy's body floats by no one can help
remembering that he was to have gone towards making
Christmas merry in some poor home. And when drowned
hens and a cat or two (doubtless hardened poachers, by the
way, and deserving of their fate) drift under and come up
on the other side of the bridge, it is not pleasant to recognise, or fancy we recognise, some well-known friend.

Yet it is even more terrible to watch a mysterious heavy
something coming along, caught every now and then in a
current and hemmed in against some obstruction, only to
come on quicker than ever as the main body of the stream
again takes it; until by the time it is heaved against the
piers of the bridge we are almost afraid to look, for fear that
it is some labourer or child, caught—as they have, alas!
been caught—in well-known lanes now turned into water-
courses. But the something turns out to be nothing save a
huge bundle of reeds, and soon drifts away, looking more
human than ever as it passes over the flooded meadows.

And now boats begin to appear on the scene. Adventurous boys put out to sea on rudely-made rafts, steering

them by the aid of an oar protruding from behind. But this is dangerous work, and soon ended by their elders, who —excusing themselves to themselves by saying it is to take care of the youngsters—get out all the available boats in the place ; and soon the meadows are dotted by red and brown sailed flat-bottomed boats, and by small gray canoes that go cautiously about the fields. It is difficult work, too. Unknown stumps of trees or remnants of fences unseen in the muddy depths are perilous objects to steer against ; but as the rain stayed for a while, and it was necessary to see if help were wanted in any of the cottages dotted about the heath, canoes went forward as pioneers for larger craft ; while between the little villages and the town a regular ferryboat began to ply. It was a wild scene, if a picturesque one, that became miserable when the floods began to subside, and promised to be worse when the water had drained away altogether. But of that there was small chance ; for a lovely day now and then was succeeded by a regular downpour that kept matters *in statu quo*. For example, on Sunday we would have a day when the air seemed like liquid gold, and a deep-blue sky was repeated in the expanse of the flood ; on Monday we would wake again to the wild rush of the rain and the eager war of the wind as it tore down the valley. It had not been so bad for more than thirty years, and it was to be hoped that thirty more years would elapse before we are inundated again ; but they were worse off then, than even we were, if we can credit the oldest inhabitant, for then the greyhounds were drowned in a stable where we find it extremely trying to have a couple of inches of water : and, farther away by the shore, the whole front of a cottage was washed out and an old bedridden woman taken out to sea in her bed and drowned in it. But, recollecting all we imagine we saw and yet fancy we see, especially at twilight, and allowing for the lapse of time and the extraordinary way in which history is enlarged by being talked over, we are inclined to think that our specimen of an autumn flood was as bad as any, either in ancient or modern times.

## A SMUGGLERS' HAUNT

JUMPER'S HOUSE stands quite alone, facing the broad expanse of the wide sea. It has a jaded and worn expression, and appears continually looking over its shoulder, as if expecting to feel the hand of the bailiff thereon, or the strong arm of the law grasping it suddenly when it least expects to be found out. It is a solitary spot; for miles in front of it extends a long reach of shingle, on which it is almost impossible to walk, and where sundry flowers seem to spring out of nothing, and to drag on a stunted existence, appearing year after year in just the same places, and with just the same number of flowers and leaves; much as if the identical plant had hibernated under the stones, perking up again when the mist and fog, which brood perpetually over the shingle in autumn and winter, disappeared for a while before the rousing south-west wind of spring, and allowed the sun to become visible again after its many months of absence. But in the old days Jumper's House, unlike the flowers, blossomed best in the rain and fog that came drifting along the sea and the shingly shore, and hid everything from the eye of the intruder. Then Jumper's woke to life indeed, and the inhabiters thereof gave up all pretence of tending the sheep that gained a frugal sustenance from the scant verdure on

O

the beach and the short dry grass on the hillside, and
turned their minds with great assiduity to cheating his
Majesty's—nay, even her Majesty's—revenue, and became
smugglers of the real old-fashioned kind. Not that in
summer the owners were not open to offers, but in the short
light nights there was not the chance of escape from the
hated "venters," as there was when the sea came booming
in through the lowering fog; or when the frost and cold hung
about and covered the whole place with a damp white rime,
which hung about the men's hair and beards, turning them
"white in a single night," and embellishing them with icicles
that decorated them grandly, and tinkled like bells as they
walked, said our informant, gazing with aged and lack-lustre
eyes at the dull October atmosphere that surrounded us;
and then looking once more at the house, that, with
shattered windows and tumbled-down porch, seemed quite
as melancholy and hopeless as our venerable friend himself,
who had but a poor opinion of the march of ages, and a still
poorer one of the preventive officers, who seemed to him the
embodiment of everything that was wrong and horrible. But
then he and Jumper's had flourished together, and he remembered how this used to be the rendezvous for many a
mile round of all the smugglers in the country-side, and he
could point out with pride how admirably Jumper's was
situated, and what conveniences were there for carrying on
what he honestly regarded as a perfectly correct and laudable
business. For Jumper's House could survey the sea for
miles, and leaning its back comfortably against the hill
behind it, could furtively regard over its shoulder the valley
to the left that led up to the village, where the inhabitants,
"from parson downwards," were one and all interested in
the boats that went out, ostensibly for fishing purposes, but
really in answer to the mysterious call of a sea-bird, heard by

watchers along the shore, that meant that the ship was waiting for them in the offing, and would be ready to discharge its cargo about midnight or a little later, when the boats would drift out silently into the freezing fog, and return full of kegs of brandy and rum, which were carried up towards Jumper's on men's shoulders, their footsteps in the shingle being obliterated by the last man drawing a piece of net over them, as he followed, walking backwards up the steep ascent.

It was curious, standing on the shingle and listening to our old friend, to realise how these things used to be not so very long ago, and to know that in Jumper's itself existed great double cupboards in the chimneys, where tobacco and spirits could be hidden, in less time than it takes to tell of it, and where the great disused barns were once kept sparsely filled with furze, or straw, or anything that could cover the kegs hastily, or conceal the trap-doors that led into caves, grubbed out for temporary hiding-places; but oftener than not the "venters" themselves were "in the swim" too, and when a cargo was run at Jumper's would find it imperatively necessary for their walks to lead them in exactly the opposite direction. To own Jumper's House then was almost as good, in the eyes of the neighbours, as to own a patent of nobility, for it was, as it were, the key to the whole position. In the kitchen, now rapidly falling into decay, all arrangements for the night's work used to be made, and while the so-called farmer retired to rest, to be ready to give an account of himself should unwelcome visitors come along, sons, grandsons, and nephews and friends, all went off to their work, being quite sure that watch and ward was kept at Jumper's, and that Jumper would be ready to lend a hand with the cargo or to give them a signal of danger should it be necessary; thus being to some extent equal to either fortune. "That was good times, that was."

said our old friend, rubbing his knotted old hands, and
leering up at us out of one wicked old eye; "but neither me
nor Jumper's much good now.    I can't work, and nobody 'll
live there; for they du say as it be haunted.    I wish it was
haunted, for there 'd be a real good set of fellers once more
upon hearth, and I often comes and looks in to see if I can
see they ghosteses; but not I, and I'm afeard, even if they
came, they couldn't bring back the sperets too.    They sort
of sperets don't rise much," and he chuckled at his joke
mightily.    It was rather an uncanny feeling with which we
regarded the house now.    In front of us sea and beach
were alike gray; the sea heaving in slowly, and as slowly
receding from the pebbles into the mist again that lay in a
long unbroken line as far as we could see; while inland the
dim fog wreathed itself all along the hills, and filled the
little valley with its clammy folds, and around Jumper's the
fog seemed heavy indeed, and with small imagination we
could trace figures ghostly and weird, that appeared to wait
round the front door, for our old friend to go and let them
in.    They need not have waited: the front door, that yet
bears the marks here and there of the coastguards' cutlass-
handles as they demanded admission in the King's name,
hangs on one rusted hinge; the stairs down which the old
farmer came, rubbing his eyes, and asking the cause of this
intrusion on his slumbers, are not safe for the most careful
foot to climb; and the window where the oft-repeated signal
was made, that told the farmer the kegs were ready to house,
is broken entirely, and allows the hoot of the owls that at
times roost there to be heard by passers-by, and doubtless
gives rise to the idea that Jumper's House is haunted.

It is astonishing how distance from a railway keeps people
from going with the times, and on what curious nooks one
may alight if the beaten track be left, and a desperate plunge

is made into that unknown desert that lies in England five or six miles away from the iron road.  It is only the fact that coastguard stations and men are closer together and less "bribable" than they used to be, that does not make Jumper's House still an eligible residence, for all the spirit of the folks is towards the life of the smuggler, which they regret fiercely, as they long more than ever in these hard days for the good old times.  Yet the old inhabitant dies out, and the young men go away, returning occasionally only at Christmas or Easter, when they are conspicuous among the congregation at church by reason of their raiment, which sits uneasily on the shoulders of those whose fathers still wear gorgeously-embroidered smock-frocks ; and also by reason of the embarrassed air that pervades the parish, until they are off again to their shops and counting-houses ; and in a very few years there will be nothing much left of either Jumper's House or its ancient guardian, who, as he pocketed our shilling with much more gratitude than a more honest, or less unsophisticated individual, would have done half a sovereign, turned back again to contemplate its damp, uncomfortable countenance, where, doubtless, he will remain off and on, until he joins his old companions whose ghosts he so anxiously looks for to revisit their old-time haunts.

## DEADMAN'S BAY

THE winter wind moans fitfully over the heath and comes laden with salt against the window; a driving mist fills up the space between us and the hills, and, penetrating into the house, makes everything we touch feel clammy and damp. Each bare tree, gemmed with rain-drops, asking for more, as the old folks say, groans audibly as it sways now this way and now that. As the mist thickens and drifts by in solid masses it requires small imagination to discern whole sheeted troops of spirits, with veiled bent heads, driven before the wind; while, when it lifts for a moment, we can see great dark lowering clouds, like armed giants, travelling faster and faster before the rapidly-rising tempest. For the wind that began by moaning has passed on through the screaming stage into that mood when nothing seems to stand before it, and is roaring madly. The very house seems to rock, and the trees begin to swing regularly backwards and forwards like so many pendulums, or as if they were vainly trying to keep time with the wild song sung by the mighty whirlwind. Not an inviting day to stir abroad this; but we are impelled to go out and face the storm. We hear the sea grinding on the rocks, and we are possessed with an unconquerable desire to do battle with the wind, and see for ourselves how the great white waves are churned into foam among the breakers, and to feel the wild spray from them in our faces. Besides, we are weary of staying indoors. Yet as we turn into the miry red road we are almost tempted to go back. All across the meadows tiny atoms of dry sticks and morsels of grass are blowing like a storm cloud; the little river throws itself against the old gray bridge, as if impelled by the general disorganisation of nature to rise, and for once to assert itself against a barrier that has ruled it insolently for ages; and as we begin to mount the rising ground and get more in the heart of the storm, we almost fear we must give in and go back; but opposition makes us obstinate, and, breathless and beaten about ruthlessly, we come as near as we dare to the place we set out to reach. Words are almost powerless to describe the intense noise that goes on all around. The sea and the wind yell and scream one against the other; occasionally we hear the dull boom of the ocean among the rocks below as the wind stays for a moment, as if pausing, as a beast does, to spring with a deadlier aim, but then, stronger for the moment's pause, it comes tearing along, until we are forced to lie down prone on the cliff to escape being blown into space by its fury. The cliff here is steep, too, and curves round into a tiny bay. At one end of the bay a range of ebony rocks runs out sheer into the sea; but one can see small evidences of them now. The sea is one mass of leaping, springing, yeasty billows, that recede, showing momentary glimpses of the black boulders, only to throw themselves against the cliff side, as besiegers throw themselves against a redoubt, determined to carry it at all hazards.

We cannot see very far. Occasionally away to the left looms a great black island, standing calm and quiet amidst all the noise and turmoil, and then as the fog lifts a little more we catch sight of a vessel labouring heavily to keep away from the shore, where certain death and destruction await her.

It looks like the veriest cockle-shell as for one moment it rides triumphant, and for the next is lost suddenly to sight beneath an enormous billow, as it seems to us gone for ever; but it emerges, and heads for the open, and we are beginning to thank our stars for its escape, when suddenly the wind swoops down on it; it shivers for a moment, and then, O heavens! resistless, powerless, in the mighty grasp of the storm, it begins to recede, and is blown suddenly, irresistibly, closer and closer inshore. Some one rises and rushes from our side, making for the coastguard station, a couple of miles away; we creep closer and closer to the edge of the cliff, and by the time we are as near as we can get we can see the ship close under us, and note the men rushing about the deck exactly like ants when their nest is overturned. Some are climbing the rigging, in a vain, mad attempt to rise from the jaws that wait to engulf them, but before they have reached any height the ship comes grinding, crashing on to the rocks. A quiver for half a second runs through it, and positively, in less time than it takes to tell it, the whole vessel has entirely disappeared, casting, as it went to pieces, the extreme top of the mast and some cordage not a dozen yards from where we lay regarding one of the most terrible spectacles that surely was ever seen. The hopelessness of the ship, the impossibility of in any measure helping the wretched creatures that disappeared before our eyes, was the worst part of the sight. The wind and sea completely obscured any sounds or cries, and as all disappeared into the boiling vortex, just as if some gigantic animal had swallowed all at one gulp, we saw none of the sufferings or death-struggles of the victims who day after day were found along the shore, stripped to the skin by grinding against those awful hideous rocks. By the time the rocket-apparatus arrived the wind was a little abated, like some passionate creature that wreaks its mood on some inoffensive thing that has not harmed it, and is sobered by the act. The storm began to lull, the mist got a little less dense, and the rain stopped, and when we rose, sodden and grimy, from the ground to examine the sole wreckage that was safe on mother earth, the coastguards announced that the storm was nearly over, and that this was the worst and quickest wreck that had ever been known on all that dreadful line of coast. "Yonder is Deadman's Bay," said the man grimly, "and fearful have been the loss of life and ships there; but I hold this should be called that, before he. Many's the small boat and vessel that has come grinding in here; and we never knowed it until some atom has come in with a name on it perchance, or a body come to shore, and then we hear of a missing boat, and we puts two and two together, and finds out where he comes from. But do 'ee go home, sir, you're wet through, and come along when 'tis calmer, and I'll row you round; for there's no way down the cliff, and there's nothing to be done for they poor chaps." We took his advice and went home, and it was on a very different sort of day when we next visited the bay.

As we rowed round the reach of rocks the sea was one sparkling surface of glittering diamonds. A soft air came from the land full of the promise of very early spring; a "wind-hover" was hanging in mid-air, seeking what it might devour in the way of mice, or even an extraordinarily pre-maturely-hatched small bird; and all the sound we could hear was the gentle lap-lap of the sea on the stones, and, very far away, the cry of the pewit, inland, as it flew about seeking for a spot for its nest. We did not speak, and then,

as the boat went as near the shore as it could, we saw all
that remained of the ill-fated vessel. A great deal of wreckage had been removed. Some had even turned up in the
Isle of Wight. Yet enough remained to speak of the extraordinary manner in which the ship had rushed to her doom ;
the force of its striking the shore being so tremendous that
great boulders had been displaced by its entry among them,
and they now held down by their weight sundry long broad
timbers, that will doubtless remain there for some time yet
to come.

There was nothing save the long line of rocks to speak
of the deadly character of the bay, but that on nearer
inspection proved quite sufficient; for, quiet lovely afternoon as it was, the sea was surging round them and sucking
through little crevices in a manner that was highly and un-
pleasantly suggestive, more especially as long trails of seaweed rose and fell, looking marvellously like strands of
human hair, drawn over and obscuring mercifully a drowned,
dead face ; while the tall white cliffs, ridged and holding
here and there a clump of rough grass, looked down on a
shore where not even one small boat could be safely beached
(unless on very extraordinary occasions of special tides) by
reason of the grim jagged rocks that lie, like adders in the
grass, ready to seize and " do for " any unwary intruder.

" Deadman's Bay " in truth, for the future to us at least,
who had seen so many perish under its now smiling waters ;
and somehow to us the sweet, thin, yellow spring sunshine
was a delusion and a snare, or a mask that hid the face of
a grinning skull. As we turned away the evening mist rose
along the horizon, prophesying east wind for the morrow ;
and as it crept up hand-in-hand with the darkness and
brooded over the bay, it seemed to us as if a band of ship-
wrecked spirits hung above it, seeking restlessly and ever-

lastingly for the bodies that they had lost there, and which are so seldom recovered that the neighbouring churchyard has but few monuments to tell the truth of all the evil that is done every time the great south-west wind rises and works its wicked will in Deadman's Bay.

# WINTER WALKS

THE wind sighed sadly round the house, and every now and then one of the last relics of the summer fluttered slowly down through the chill air, and lay, a darker brown speck on the dark-brown beds already cleared and put tidy for the long winter sleep before them. Except for the wind, that moaned like an unhappy spirit, yet had not strength enough to move the long, thin, naked arms of the trees on the lawn, there seemed no sounds in the whole earth, and a gray mysterious gloom hung over the horizon, clung about the trees, and seemed almost like a pall placed gently by a loving hand over the dead earth. It is well to turn away from the garden on such days as these, and, boldly fronting the chill air and the damp, that cling closely round us, seek in the woods and fields relief from the sense of decay that must oppress us at home. For in the garden we have so much to remind us of past summer glories and autumn wealth that we can see no beauties there. Limp and dismal look the pure white chrysanthemums that were so lately our pride and joy. The ferns are bent and blackened, and lie as if rent and torn out about the borders; and great gaps in the hedges only remind us of the sight they were in May, full of scented blossoms and glittering silver flowers, a temptation to every child who passed, to possess itself of some of the abundance, and so rouse the anger of Joe—the red-eyed spaniel—who appears to consider himself the custodian of the garden, and severely reproaches any who are bold enough to intrude themselves within the sacred gate. But Joe leaves his post for the superior attractions of a ramble outside, and, sagacious creature as he is, walks decorously enough at our heels, until we are far enough from the haunts of men for there to be a chance of encountering a rabbit. Then he is off like a shot, to appear ever and anon at the top of some tall bank, and, casting an eye at us, as he wags his feathered stump of a tail vigorously, seeming to appeal to us to career with him through furze and over dead bracken; and when not even a series of smothered yaps induces us to follow him, he goes off again, rustling wildly through the deep masses of dead leaves, and causing his progress to be marked by the uprising of sundry solitary birds, that were sheltering a little in the undergrowth, before making their way to their rendezvous for the night. A heavy blackbird, or a thrush, or a screaming jay, makes its exit; but we are too near human beings yet for Joe's search for a rabbit to be quite as successful as he would doubtless wish it to be. So on and on we tramp, past a great holly hedge, green and glossy and cruelly closely cut, and ornamented here and there with a turret-shaped excrescence in rings, that is doubtless considered in the light of a crown by the owner thereof; and at last we reach a turnstile, over which we may lean for a few moments and feast our eyes on the scene before us, which is singularly lovely even in winter. Even in winter, say we? Nay, rather should we say because of winter; for when else could we note the perfect loveliness and differences of the different trees' structure, or behold the dense purple haze that hangs about the wood? and that is so dark that the very tree branches we should call black at any other time, seem brown against it; while a flock of tame white pigeons from some neighbouring house gleam like suddenly-falling snow, as they appear for an instant against it, on their flight towards their homes for the night.

And though it is as yet full early, the short December day has already begun to wane. The wind rises just a little and begins to sway the branches to and fro. The rabbits are just visible in the distance; and, as we watch, a stately pheasant steps out of the wood and gazes meditatively abroad. We call Joe to heel, and, regardless of his anguished countenance, and small whining appeals for mercy, we walk on to the top of the hill, and look round us for signs of what species of weather we are going to have on the ensuing day. Here, again, surely the hand of winter has lain lightly as yet; the trees in the wood to the right have still dark-brown patches that tell us that the oak is, as usual, almost the last to give back to the earth the raiment lent him only for the summer; while the red-bronze clumps lower down show that the sharply-pointed leaves of the beech are still faithful, and will hang on until literally pushed off by the freshly-springing verdure.

Beyond the wood, field after field turns round its brown shoulder, as if it were protesting strongly against the inclement time of year, while suddenly comes riding across them a lithe young figure, closely clad in gray, and on a big brown horse that goes as if he were keenly enjoying the canter. The one touch of life is enough for us to conjure up therefrom the sound of the horn, the whimper of the hounds, and the flash of scarlet coats; and we almost imagined our thoughts embodied, as from the wood came the whole pack in full cry, followed by a red flash that was the hunt, and that disappeared over the brow of a dim gray hill almost as mysteriously as it had appeared. But nature seemed alarmed at its passing: whole troops and regiments of sparrows rose from among the ricks that stood in serried ranks all along the side of the fields; flurried rabbits, disturbed at their evening meal, which is taken full early in December, ran about distracted, much to Joe's rage and despair; and even the rooks, who never seem anxious about any one's business except their own, flapped heavily along, solemnly protesting against such a disturbing element; while the wild pigeons flew out of the wood and then returned, as if fully convinced that, though the matter did not concern them in the very least, yet something was going on rather out of the common.

Night was now closing in. The gray fog seemed to rise a little and allow the sky to be seen, while the shepherds walked across from one field to the other with great bundles of swedes, extracted doubtless from the long low heaps that looked as if a giant were buried alive below the hedge, with a scant opening here and there ornamented with a straw chimney as if to allow him breathing places. This gave us naturally a poor opinion of the shepherds, who should of course have chopped up those swedes before this to feed the sheep, penned close beside the ricks; and we should doubtless have moralised over the decadence of the agricultural labourer, as is our wont, had not we suddenly become aware of the sunset. The wind had cleared away the haze—for what we call fog would not have been perceptible to the eye of the true Londoner—and the cloud behind it had all at once opened to let out a perfect wealth of wonderful colour. In front was a great lake of scarlet, and the blackness of the cloud was rent here and there, as if some vast sword in the hand of a valorous knight had cut and slashed at the darkness, leaving gaping wounds as each blow struck home. Everything became mysteriously intensified. The long angular arms of the oaks were each one several and distinct; the purple and saffron leaves on the brambles caught our eye; we became conscious of hips and haws and gleaming holly in the distance; and we heard distinctly the curious, comfortable, harsh cry of the pheasant as he rose from the ground, and settled himself in the branches for the night; as much as if he would declare his intentions to the world of not being again disturbed until the morning. Time to return, too; and once more we faced the road, and came back to our stile, with Joe, the faithful, close behind. But ere we reached it a most mysterious sound struck on our ears. It was like nothing we had ever heard before, resembling in a slight degree the sound we should expect from hundreds of hives of overturned bees: it was yet far too powerful for anything like that; it might have been the whirr of thousands of sewing-machines all at once, or it might be the home of the winds, yet was unlike them all. The farther we went the worse it was, until, when we reached our momentary resting-place, the noise was as if all the watchsprings in the world had gone off, and were going round and round and round for evermore.

But soon we perceived the reason thereof. The little wood was the night-haunt of about ten thousand starlings— rather more than less — and as we waited a while we saw flock after flock, each separate and distinct, fly into the shelter, and, after what appeared to be a moment's discussion of their destination with the entire regiment, rise again and make for a certain tree, or clump of undergrowth, where, with much conversation and rustling and shaking of wings, they appeared to settle for the night. The whole undergrowth of hazel and ash, densely purple with the shadows of advancing night, was alive with them, and indeed seemed to be the favourite sleeping-place of all the birds around; for, aiming for the higher trees, flocks of wild pigeons came scudding by us, and every now and then a lonely robin would hop in, tentatively, as if not quite sure whether it would suit him, or whether he should suit the company.

As we turned away the noise followed us; while across the sky, now a pale pink over which great clumps of gray clouds hurried before the risen wind; big companies of rooks flapped heavily, making for the tall elms and beeches, where the ruins of their last spring nests could be plainly seen, looking weird and untidy, as they swayed hither and thither in the strong north-west breeze.

Next day brought about quite a different state of things, and the whole face of nature appeared changed. The fog, just indicated on the previous evening, had become a real thing; and a low-lying mist clung closely round the house, and, as the late sun rose, just stirred a little, leaving the hard brown ground, climbing up the trees, and finally settling itself among the topmost branches, where it appeared to rest like a cloud, that nothing save a rousing north-west wind could clear away. At times it sank down again, and came like a wall before the window. It drifted in at any crevice; and by the time hands and feet were alike chilled, it vanished once more to its resting-place, where, obscuring every ray of sunshine, it remained never rising or falling an inch for hours at a time.

All along the gate long lines of dewdrops began to accumulate; every sparsely-hanging brown leaf had its own necklace; heavy drops fell from the eaves on the shining laurel-leaves with a sound like a blow. The windows were dewed over, and presently had small puddles in the sills. Each blade of grass seemed pressed by its weight of misery into the clayey soil, and unable to raise its head from the mud, that appeared everywhere and rendered the lawn

singularly unlike the pleasant trim green expanse that it
generally was.   All at once there was a subtle change.   The
air grew colder ; there were no dewdrops at all ; the top of
the gate was covered with a fine white powder, and on every
bare brown twig, over each faded leaf, there was a wonderful
beautiful silver line.   The trees and shrubs became gray-
headed ; and in less time than it takes to tell it all, the earth
seemed to be the subject of a transformation scene, in which
the mist and damp have been converted into pearls, that
would sparkle like diamonds were there the smallest gleam
from the sun.   But there was not ; and as we looked away
through the undergrowth before us the usual dark-blue hue
of winter gave place to soft gray fog, which we could almost
see condensing into frost ; and, gradually creeping along ash,
or hazel, or young oak saplings, it left, as it passed, the lovely
decoration that makes even fog bearable.

The ground soon became hard ; each laurel was still in
its ice-armour ; the last chrysanthemum gave up the ghost ;
and the violets had no scent, though they were powdered
over and looked as if they were preserved, like their foreign
sisters, in sugar and all ready to be eaten : while every now
and then a disconsolate rook flapped heavily by ; and the
pert jackdaws that usually infest the field opposite, only now
and then gave a strangled croak, as if they had caught cold
in the night.

All the birds were profoundly wretched.   Even the
sparrows, who are always apparently jolly, and equal to any
amount of fighting, love - making, or quarrelling, seemed
subdued, and hopped about miserably ; trying here a clod
of earth and there a tuft of grass, regarding both mournfully
and with head on one side as they found not a worm or an
insect on which they could feed.   The bigger birds loomed
through the freezing mist double their usual size, and, as

they hustled through the wintry wood, brushed off showers of hoar-frost; while the robin himself had nothing to say, and sat disconsolate, puffed out in his feathers, until he looked like a badly-drawn copy of himself on a cheap Christmas-card. As the day grew older the fog and the cold increased. The silence seemed almost appalling; for none stirred out of doors that had shelter, and there was not a breath of air to move the mist, or the trees, which remained perfectly quiet in the keen atmosphere. The gloom in the undergrowth increased; and, as we boldly ventured out for just a moment before the curtains must be drawn, we reached the wood at the top of the hill, and looked forward into a gray curtain that hid closely and jealously the view that was ours only the night before.

The effect was weird and ghastly, the silence quite intense, and we almost imagined ourselves in the land of the dead, so impalpable yet so emphatic was the barrier between us and any outside world that might possibly exist beyond it.

It was almost maddening to contemplate the dull gray, that not even the presence of a sunset somewhere in the world could break: we thought of the shivering sheep folded in the empty gray fields cleared for their winter sleep: we passed a couple of enormous giants, who were really two rather small shepherds; and, as we neared home, disgusted with things in general and the weather in particular, we saw the pool under the thorn-trees had begun to crinkle up in little wavy lines in the middle, and had quite thick ice round the edges; and almost before we realised it was freezing, we had entered our own door, closely followed by the fog, and discovered that hair, eyebrows, and beard were all pure white, and that our garments were covered by the same soft mist, made palpable by the frost that generally in the country accompanies a December fog.

## XXVI

## THE FIRST SNOW

COME when it may, the first snow brings with it a certain delightful sense of exhilaration and surprise : it generally follows days full of gloom and depression—days when all is dim and silent, and when nature appears as if awaiting some dreadful blow or sudden catastrophe. All this is changed the moment the first atom of whiteness falls from the dark-brown expanse above. It flutters slowly and with hesitation through the air, and long before we realise that a change has begun, it is followed by a tribe of relations who have no part or parcel in the first-comer's shyness, and rollick madly along, now this way, now that, just as their fickle fancy persuades them for the moment. The first flakes are generally minute, and indeed, if the snow is really an assured fact, the whole downfall is small too as to the size of the different atoms ; but, ever and anon a great white blossom comes down, and, resting on a leaf or on the ground, seems to make certain that the children's anxiety is over, and that there is now no doubt that the snow will lie. Presently the gravel is covered by a delicate silver powder ; the top of the gate has its burden ; one side of our neighbour's chimneys is quite white. The broad laurel-leaves are straight and stiff and full of snow ; each twig is ornamented, and every joint of the trees from whence the branches spring has a heap of its own, and contains almost enough for a respectable snowball. The curious contrast between the blackness of the stripped branches and the extreme whiteness of the snow is well worth observing; and as we gaze across the little park the whole world appears wrapping itself up in ermine; while a faint blue tinge, and a scarcely perceptible, but still quite distinct, movement among the lower brushwood and dark twigs of the hedges tells us that the fall is continuous, and that we have indeed reached the very heart of winter's kingdom.

There is not a breath of wind, and, though the air is so keen that it is really painful to breathe, not a twig stirs, and the few late leaves still clinging to the oak fall ever and anon to the ground, the "last straw" being the snow that encumbers them heavily, while the only tree that appears to enjoy the weather is the sturdy holly, that stands upright and manful, looking like a sentinel on duty through it all. The firs and pines are resigned, but droop their foliage disconsolately, and allow the snow to slide off at the points of their branches, reminding us, we cannot tell why, of people whose idea of shaking one's hand is to hold it for half a half-second and then drop it limply; while late geraniums, left out because of a plethora of these useful plants, and with a hope that the winter may be mild and allow them to struggle on, as they have done often before, to a joyful resurrection in the spring, go suddenly black in the face and die immediately, seeing doubtless that it is quite useless to fight against fate any more.

On and on goes the silent downfall, and very soon the ruts in the carriage-drive begin to be imperceptible. We had not observed any birds about, but somehow or other there are tiny claw-marks on the path before us. Belinda, the white terrier, a model of cleanliness and beauty, goes by on her way to the kitchen fire, and looks curiously dirty and disreputable, and the few late white chrysanthemums on the table turn grimy, and have to be moved where they can no longer contrast with the pure paleness of the earth outside. By the time the gravel walks have become level with the grass borders we discover that we do not like the existing state of affairs at all. The sky has changed, and has a tinge of yellow in it; the ordinary blue, that is winter's colour (just as brown is the spring's, green the summer's, and purple the autumn's), has entirely disappeared. And, creeping steadily down, ceaselessly falls the snow, as if it never could and never would stop.

It resembles a quiet self-willed creàture with whom it is no use to argue, and it goes on and on, filling here a foot-mark, burying there a fern or a newly-opened premature primrose, until we have serious fears of a repetition of the famous, or infamous, storm of 1880, and begin to remember the miseries we endured at that never-to-be-forgotten period.

But when we have cast an anxious eye over our store of literature and counted our papers, and learned for certain that we have coal and food enough for the present, we see that the flakes are quite big and bloated; they get slower and slower; there is a faint line of light over the stables; the snow stops altogether, and the sun comes out valiantly, and shines down, as if it were his time to get up, and the snow were just a small *lever de rideau*—a little something to pass the time before he found it necessary to put in an appearance. At first he looks down on a level carpet, only broken here and there by a footstep, or Belinda's paw-marks; but these imperceptibly become bigger and bigger, until they resemble nothing so much as the traces of some mammoth beast; brown patches appear in the flower-beds; the pine-trees perk up, and, dropping their snow-garb altogether, seem immensely relieved, and look as if nothing at all had happened. We forget our fears of a blockade, and are almost sorry to see all the pretty white stuff disappear, and give place to a slush that is almost unspeakable.

We talk of the first snow with regret. It disappeared, we say, because the earth was too warm to receive it. We feel almost inclined to blame the earth for that extremely agreeable fault, and we talk of seasonable weather and snowy Christmas with gusto, listening patiently and with attention to our dear friend, the "oldest inhabitant," who always waxes more than ordinarily garrulous when Nature does anything out of the usual routine, and invariably has a store of anecdotes that lie asleep until awakened by a rap from Nature's wand, that arouses them and makes us profoundly thankful that we have nothing to do with the good old times of which she is part and on which she loves to dwell. And we are very angry when reminded of our fears, until there came another storm.

There was a little wind on that occasion that slunk in at the keyholes and moaned reproachfully round the corners of the house, while it blew the snow in at crevices, the existence of which we were profoundly ignorant of before.

The moment a footprint was made it was filled up : there was no chance of the sun coming out : the birds knew all about that, for the sparrows got up in dozens under the hanging eaves and chattered deliriously as if they were holding an indignation meeting ; while robins first of all sought shelter among the tree-tops, and finally perched lower and lower in search of a haven from the storm, until they found one in the underwood, where they remained wedged tightly into the bushes as long as the snow fell.

The few bigger birds that remained went about like

sturdy beggars, almost losing their dread of human beings in their intense craving after light and warmth and food.

It was impossible to go out, for soon the snow became level with the threshold. The horses kicked impatiently and ceaselessly against their stalls, and the extreme quiet, marred only by the melancholy soughing of the wind, seemed quite unbearable.

Still the snow fell, and fell, and fell, and we came at once to the conclusion that if snow is anxious in the least to keep up its character for delightfulness and beauty, the first snow—delicate, lovely, and full of surprises—should also be the last snow ; for if it comes often, or indeed more than once, it earns nothing save our undying hatred, and a resolve on our part to flee to other shores where snow exists only as a lovely legend scarcely believed in.

Yet snow is, after all, like many another thing, for surely a repetition of most events is generally a gigantic mistake !

# XXVII

## DOWN TO SEA

THAT there is something good in even the greatest evil is a truism beneath contempt, as far as repetition is concerned; and the good concealed beneath the snowy aspect described in the last article, is the fact that at no other time of year is it so desirable to visit that obscure locality " down to sea."

There is something delightfully vague in the description of the spot, where vanish at a certain epoch of frost and snow all the able-bodied men and boys about a little town that we wot of; the loungers at the Cross, who represent charity, inasmuch as their presence at that fascinating spot is never lacking, are conspicuous by their absence; and if we drop in by accident at a friend's house and demand luncheon, we are met by a scared look, and a muttered apology for the bareness of the board; giving as a reason that all the food in the place has gone with the eldest son and heir " down to sea "—a reason that at once suffices for the utter absence of butter or eggs or meat, that is apparent to the meanest intellect.

Perhaps one of the worst points about living in the country is this utter inability to rise superior to any extra strain upon our food resources. Long custom has enabled our butchers and bakers to know exactly how much we

ought to consume in a certain space of time; and should any
untoward event render an extra amount of nutriment necessary, we can only obtain the same by humbling ourselves to the
lordly creatures, who are supposed to exist for our pleasure,
but who are really our masters on this point at all events,
and who, if properly cajoled and flattered, will either take
from some one else, or will produce, next week's provisions,
secure in being able to get more by the time we require it
from the county town.

It were well to pause here and remember with a sigh
and a smile our own especial butcher, who has long since
departed into a land where lamb and mint-sauce are not
presumably a part of one's religious observances, as they
were with him in this sublunary sphere ; for he never allowed
us any before Easter Sunday, and insisted on his best
families having a quarter then, whether they liked it or not,
treating our remonstrance as utterly irreligious and great
nonsense : although we declared that our family was too
large to indulge in such luxuries : and remarking that we
might just as well try to do without beef at Christmas as
lamb at Easter, and he should not allow either as long as
he was our butcher.  He had queer touchy ways, too, that had
to be respected ; and though we were lucky enough to have
secured his warm friendship and thoroughly liked him, and
though he once gave us a saddle of mutton for an emer-
gency dinner-party, that had actually been chosen and
duly labelled by one of the County, we have known him
positively refuse to serve a customer again who had once
bought of the opposition butcher, and to inform the mother
of a large family of hungry sons, who had sufficient temerity
to send for a third leg of mutton in one week, "that though
sheep had four legs, mutton had only two, and she must
either have a shoulder or a loin, or nothing at all."

No persuasion would induce him to send us in a bill except at Christmas; and it really seemed quite immaterial to him whether he had his long blue scrawl paid or not; for the longest delay never caused him even to hint at payment from those he honoured with his friendship. Perhaps one of our happiest recollections of the town is his jolly face and his jollier laugh at any of the numerous entertainments we used to organise; and we really were honestly grieved when the poor old fellow died suddenly, very soon after we had given the last private theatricals to the townsfolk that we were ever fated to take part in.

Although our affection was great for him, it yet was undeniably uncomfortable to be in his power when going "down to sea" was the fashion of the day; for part of the performance consisted in taking about five times the amount of food that would have been consumed in double the time at home; and we have known things swept off at early dawn, before the female portion of the household had arisen, which they had comfortably contemplated the night before, secure in the knowledge that the men were safely away, fully provisioned for so long as the frost was supposed to last. We must own ourselves to being too old—or something—to care about this sort of entertainment ourselves; but sometimes when the frost has been especially bitter and long, and the days and evenings are dull, as only country days and evenings can be in the winter, we make up our minds to have a regular good long walk, and set off down the lane for the happy hunting-grounds in the mouth of the harbour.

The lane itself is a most delightful place at all times of the year, and though empty enough on this bitterly cold, gray afternoon, has memories that charm us almost into forgetting all the present and make us young again. It is well to pause for an instant and look at the dear old house

down the avenue, at the very top of the lane, ere plunging
into the mass of white snow that lies before us.  It is a
mournful sight; the keen breeze moans through the
stripped branches of the creepers, and howls along the
verandah; the nursery window hangs upon one broken
hinge; the yard is deep with weeds, and crowded by the
debris that tells of the sale and removal of a family; and
as we turn away we recollect with a curious rush, as if
memory's gates had suddenly opened wide, the thousand and
one days of happiness we had spent in those rooms and
among the gardens, now given over to the bailiff, who once
lived in a tiny cottage close to the sea.  Little boys, prim
in Scotch kilts, come prancing along to tell us it is church-
time: the bells are ringing sharply; it is very hot and
drowsy; one by one the boys fall asleep, the youngest on
his mother's lap, the eldest leaning warm and heavily
against our shoulder.  Then it is after the early dinner: we
wander out into the garden; the air is heavy with the smell
of fruit; bees hum lazily; geraniums glow in every corner.
Then the picture fades: the boys are all grown up and
gone away; every one has gone away; and we wake from
our dream, feeling as if we were very old, and life has little
left to give us ere we go away too.

It is a bitter cold afternoon—the coldest of a cold season
that began with a bitter enough frost, it is true, but with
clear, blue, windless skies that made the "seasonable
weather" almost bearable; then came the snow; and then
pitiless winds swept over the hills, and twisted and tore the
limbs of the leafless trees, while over all lay the silent covering.  Fortunately for us, though the snow lay long, the wind
blew it away from the roads, and heaped it under hedges
and ditches, leaving sufficient dry road visible, or we should
never have been able to set off on our walk down to sea.

The real sea lies just five miles away from us, straight
over the range of hills that looked like a large collection of
twelfth-cakes; but the harbour is easily reached, being only
about two miles down our lane, past the river that had
frozen hard enough to bear the one or two adventurous
skaters that were going solemnly up and down the small
space that was safe, undaunted by the fact that the tide was
plainly perceptible through the clear ice, and gave rise
to unpleasant suggestions in the timorous or imaginative
minds, as small atoms of rushes or green grass were carried
along under their feet, and seemed to insinuate that thus
would be carried away any one who fell in, and could not
be rescued very speedily indeed.

Turning away from the noise of the skates and the
shouts of the boys just let out of school, we realise that it
is very quiet in the lane this afternoon : the only sounds
are the bleating of the tiny lambs as they creep up to their
mother's sides, and the deeper notes of the ewes as they
welcome their children. The white snow glitters in the
turnip fields and rests upon the gate-tops; and here and
there a disconsolate red-winged thrush, with all his feathers
puffed out, hops weakly in the dark-brown furrows of a
ploughed field, striving to find something eatable.

Little flocks of fieldfares flit to and fro on the same
errand, but these are very few and far between, for the
cruel, keen weather has slain them by thousands, and the
poor little creatures crept into rabbit holes and ditches for
shelter, only to die there, starved by cold and hunger.

An occasional robin, very stout, very bright about the
eye, and looking more like a diminutive and rather tipsy
beadle in his scarlet coat than a respectable bird, starts a
weak little song every now and then ; but the gray cold is
too much for him, and appears to depress even his cheery

little soul; for by the time we reach the end of the lane and come out on the open heath that lies between us and the harbour, there really is not a sound of any living creature to be heard. Even Joe, the red-eyed spaniel, seems suppressed, and keeps close to heel, pricking up his long handsome ears every now and then, as he catches the regular puff, puff, puff of the little steam-tug as it strives to keep open the channel in the lower part of the river, or when the ice suddenly gives a loud crack like a pistol-shot; but this is not often, for Nature seems completely paralysed for the nonce, and lies still and quiet, with her gray face looking strangely like the face of a dead creature turned up to the grayer, more silent, sky.

Yet by the side of our path through the heath there still runs a little stream of water, a warm spring that has never been known to freeze; and here is seen the haunt of the snipe, and the occasional home of the woodcock. As Joe, suddenly warmed to life by the sight of this happy hunting-ground, rushes at the water, one rises and departs like a heavy flash of lightning; and then, a little farther on, up gets a snipe, with its rapid whirr of wing and curious call, only to dash head first into the nearest spring for shelter, as if he were quite aware that we had no guns with us, and that walking-sticks have nothing but their appearance against them.

The walking becomes very heavy now, and even Joe's spirits seem abashed; he does not as usual rush and jump and bark madly at any small bird that comes in his way. When he is out simply for a walk and not on business, then he is discreetness itself and a pattern dog indeed; and he even allows to pass by him, unchallenged, a yellow-billed blackbird, that suddenly darts out of the sparse shelter afforded him by a stunted hedge on the right, with a snail in his beak, the shell of which he proceeds to crack artistically and neatly on a stone before he demolishes his prey, a feat we both stop to watch ere coming right out on the open heath, with the " sea " just in front of us.

It is really a marvellous sight, and one well worth the long, cold, lonely walk.

A little—a very little—imagination, a few bears and rein-deer scattered about, and fancy would suggest that we are at the North Pole. As far as the eye can see there is nothing save a white expanse of snow ; the gentle sloping lines that suggest small hills, lying in the shelter of the taller, lovelier ones behind them, are covered with it, and there is nothing between us and that farther shore, save a wide unbroken expanse of deep green ice, white and flaky close beside the bank on which we stand, where the rushes are ringed at equal distances with ice-circles, that tell of the rising and falling of the uneasy tide.

It looked like an unbroken surface of ice ; and somewhat appalled by the silence, and wondering still at the absence of our friends, we were turning away, when even as we were doing so, we saw that a tiny thread of water glittered a long way off, suggesting the channel that was still open ; and as we began to realise this, we saw gliding down it, like the very ghost of a boat, a small gray canoe, silent as the dead, propelled by a gray-clad form, that passes away into the distance towards a dark heap on the waste of ice, that would have been unnoticed by us, had not even the passing of such a quiet boat as this caused the wild-fowl of which it was composed to rise suddenly and fly hurriedly away towards the shore.

Every now and then we heard the deep boom of the large punt-guns at the mouth of the harbour ; and presently wedge-shaped collections of wild-fowl fly hurriedly away from what we know must be the scene of slaughter; still it is very quiet here yet. By the side of the bank the eel-peckers, their occupation gone, have tied up their boats, and only the tiny decked canoes of the wild-fowlers glide up and down the narrow channel that leads out to the sea.

Depressed by the silence, and chilled almost to the marrow, and entertaining but a poor opinion of our friends who had so long been missing from among us in this weary place, we were turning away, when suddenly one of the inhabiters of the canoes turns his skiff suddenly, and comes up to the side of the ice, on which he steps, and then drags his boat after him towards the shore. He has recognised us, even though we have not a notion who he is; and with the evident freedom of an old acquaintance demands to know what we are doing there. It is only when he speaks that we recognise a friend, otherwise we should never have known who he was, for his attire would have effectually disguised him from his nearest and dearest: he was almost unrecognisable in an old gray smock-frock that just reached below his knees, while on his head was a remarkable cap, with a point back and front, of this same cheerful shade, that came down well over his ears.

We replied as well as we could that we had been anxious to see how the harbour looked just then, and that having satisfied our curiosity, and having also most probably caught a violent cold, we were about to return, when our friend smiled sardonically at our weakness and suggested that we could not do better than stay another half-hour, for "flight" would be beginning, and then we should be able to understand the fascinations of going down to sea; always supposing, he added, "you can keep that confounded dog well to heel."

Joe, the priceless paragon and pet of our kennel, is not

accustomed to such language, and felt deeply the further in-
dignity of being muzzled in handkerchiefs and tied to a
stake at the far back of a curious erection that we proceeded to build hurriedly, after our friend's directions, out of
some great bundles of furze that were lying handy, in a
manner suggestive of the "Swiss Family Robinson," at the
bottom of a ditch, where we were instructed to "lay low,"
having first of all buttoned coats tightly and turned up cuffs,
until any vestige of white that had once decorated our
persons had vanished entirely.

By this time the faint yellow gleam that formed the
apology for a sunset began to creep over the gray mass of
cloud, that seemed to lie upon the hills, so heavy and dense
was it, and to be reflected in the expanse around us; deep
silence, deeper than ever, reigned everywhere; here and
there the ice groaned and slipped away from the bank as
the falling tide deprived it of all support, and the rushes
rustled sharply and sadly in the little breeze that began to
moan among them.  An indescribable feeling of melancholy
seized us, and we were beginning to wish we were at home,
when presently something dashed madly by our hiding-
place; our friend fired, and a small dark thing fell close by
the bank, while the echo of the gun rushed round the hills,
as if the shot were answered by concealed sportsmen among
the hollows.

"That was a snipe," muttered our friend fiercely between
his teeth; "so look out, keep still, flight is beginning."

Gradually the pale yellow light increased; it flooded the
gray, and was reflected for miles round on the icy surface;
and as it broadened and glowed, the wild-fowl, with queer
ghostly cries, rose from their haunts in the harbour, and
floated away towards their feeding places.

Every now and then a shot sprang from our hiding-place,

out boomed the big guns in the harbour itself, and then as the sunset faded quicker than it had come, and all became gray once more, the sounds were answered by small guns from different spots on the river bank towards the town, where all those worthies who were not "down to sea," were lying in wait for the birds as they came past them, hurriedly flying up towards their feeding places, hoping to reach them safely before night fell.

In less time than it takes to tell it flight was over, and as we moved stiffly and uneasily from our heath shelter, and loosened Joe, who looked reproachfully at us and trotted away resolutely towards home, our friend informed us he was disgusted to find he had had no luck, for but one red-head, two widgeon, and the snipe could be found, and that he hoped next time we came down we would try and bring our guns and be of some use ; and then he announced he would walk home with us, as he wanted more food, as he and his men had not a morsel left.

We felt so guilty—having been made the confidant of his mother in the morning, who had plaintively shown us her empty larder, and had added, " He doesn't even bring us home any wild-fowl to compensate for this,"—that we could not enter into this question at all, and simply asked him where he was staying.

" In yonder cottage," he replied, pointing across the harbour to what appeared to be a small chimney in the heath on the other side, to which also belonged a tiny square patch of light that indicated a fire or lamp was somewhere about, and that looked singularly inadequate accommodation for any one reared as our friend had been ; and we were astounded to discover he found the locality and spot so pleasing, that he had no intention of returning to the haunts of civilisation, except to obtain food, as long as the weather, which he described as "glorious," remained as it was then, as there was simply no end to the sport to be obtained.

As he talked we had left the bank and come almost back to the lane by the open spring; Joe, who had waited for us about ten yards from the place of his degradation, as if to show us that the spot, not our company, was hateful to him, made a sudden dash forward, and presently in an adjacent ditch we heard a rustle, then a yap from Joe, and a sort of despairing and strangled quack.

"Ah!" ejaculated our friend, "there's a cripple," and off he went after Joe, returning shortly with another victim to add to his store, followed by the spaniel, looking years younger, and with an absurdly self-satisfied expression on his countenance while he amicably wagged his stumpy tail.

"It was a duck," said our friend. "If we had time I daresay we should find one or two more about; those birds that are wounded at sea generally creep up into these fresh-water ditches and lie there a while—the salt water makes their wounds smart, you know. After all," he added brusquely, "that dog of yours is not such a fool as he looks, he found that bird quite cleverly. You had better come back, both of you, and spend the night at the cottage; I'll show you some fine sport just before daybreak."

However, the offer did not tempt either Joe or myself: still our friend waxed so enthusiastic that we were almost sorry when we parted at the Cross that we had not promised to try for ourselves the fascination of a night in the harbour.

But when we were snugly ensconced by the fire, Joe hunting in his sleep that unfortunate cripple in the ditch; and we heard the bitter north-east wind rise, howling through the house, and were informed by the gardener that the snow had drifted into the greenhouse a foot high, and had seen for ourselves a gentle snowstorm career about the passages, notwithstanding that we had stuffed sacks under every door and possible window, we came to the conclusion that we were infinitely better in the apology for a shelter a country house is in any stress of weather, than even sharing in that blissful sport that is only to be found " down to sea."

## BACK FROM THE ROAD

It is only just back from the road, that, ankle-deep in mud in winter, and in dust in summer, creeps down a hill away to a little town, crowned by an old, old church, and washed by the broad blue sea.

But it might be miles from anywhere, so dense is the gloom, so great is the quiet that surrounds the place, and that appears like an intangible wall keeping off all evil intruders.

Another wall exists, crowned in summer by many coloured snapdragons, that grow all along the top, and with every niche full of moss, and here and there a hart's-tongue fern, or the tiny spleenwort. And when we push open the faded green door and come out into the square before the house, we are insensibly reminded of sixty years ago, and tread softly, lest we should arouse sleepers, and awake them rudely to the fact that time has gone on although they have remained stationary.

The place is beautifully kept; there is not a weed on the gravel path or in the flower-beds, quaintly bordered as they are by a notched bone-edging, made from the bones of cows' ankle-joints, in a way that is never seen now; and where columbines and Canterbury bells are nodding to each other in the soft wind; while beyond the deep green lawn a tiny fountain rises and falls monotonously and musically, under the shadow of a dark, broad-branched cypress, that is as the very embodiment of resignation and prayer, and seems as the guardian-spirit of the place.

The lawn slopes quite down to the river, which appears to run slower here, before dashing over the weir away out to the sea, beyond the sand-banks that glitter and gleam like silver in the bright sunshine ; and on one side of the lawn is a paddock, separated from the garden by a wire fence, on which an old pony rests his head and watches us, sure that we shall remember him, and rub his ears in the way he particularly affects, and that reminds him of early days, and the dear young master he loved ; but he too has learned to wait, and only turns his eyes as we walk up and down, and evinces no impatience, sure that what to-day lacks will be supplied by to-morrow, and if not then, at latest the day after.

Indeed the whole place suggests waiting, as if life existent here in bee, or bird, or flower, paused for a while, expectant that some day or other a ripple of laughter or chime of voices would ring out, and fill the silence with human life again.

There is no hint or touch of death ; even in autumn, when the road outside is strewn with dead leaves, and twigs, and beech-mast, inside the wall are no signs of coming winter, for the shrubs are evergreen, and the cypress and ilexes change their raiment unnoticed, save by the gardener, who might be a brownie, so unperceived is he, and so fond of working at early dawn, when the windows of the house have their blinds drawn, and no one can look at him as he sweeps, and weeds, and brushes.

The house itself is square and commonplace, with thin white pillars supporting a somewhat crooked porch, at which a stranger perchance might even smile, but to us who know all the secrets, it represents the united efforts of the young

pair who designed it and saw it carried out proudly beneath
their own eyes, as a shelter below which they could sit hand
in hand and watch the baby-boy play and laugh on the lawn
underneath their seat, secure that in so watching him he
would not stray down to the river, or wander away to stroke
his pony in the paddock.

Inside the porch is a silent, wide, dark hall, cool in
summer by reason of its marble pavement and shaded open
windows, and hung on each side with soft-toned copies of
well-known Italian pictures, done years ago by the bride and
bridegroom on their lengthened honeymoon, and brought
home with infinite peril—so she says, smiling even now—
across land and sea to deck their home, now building for
them in this quiet beautiful corner of England. It is
curious to note how insensibly but surely houses become
exactly like their owners; naturally the mere furnishing of
them gives them a stamp of individuality; but time does
more than this, for as months and years go by, the walls seem
to inhale some of the vitality of their inhabiters, and become warmed and almost living as the same people, year
after year, pass their days and nights between them.

Or else how account for the blank expressionless look of
an ordinary hotel, passed through continuously by different
folks, not dwelt in or cared for, but simply used as a shelter?
or for the warm, "crowsy," genial face of another one, lived
in by generations of the same family, and each corner of
which has its own story and its own associations? or yet
again for the aspect of this same house should it change
hands, ay, even keeping the same furniture? for then does
it not seem cold and resentful as it puts on a very different
aspect to greet those to whom 'tis only a house, and not as it
was erstwhile, a store-place of memories, nay, even a temple
sacred to the holiest of holies, a happy honoured home!

Dreaming here on the threshold of the one place we would bring before you, there is no limit to this fancy, for the house, built as it was in love and smiles, and consecrated by loss and sorrow in the lapse of years, bears out entirely our theory.

Not even the veriest iconoclast of these days of ours could help realising it, and pausing bare-headed on the doorstep ere rushing in to see if he could secure something "high art" or "Queen Anne" with which to mock at —though he knows it not—his own well-loved shams and Tottenham Court Road emulations, that yet lead his soul from entire revelment in crude blues and reds to better, because quieter, things.

For not even he could help feeling the repose and resignation that could ever be found here; and although he may turn away disgusted when he sees the faded, gaudy Brussels carpets of sixty years ago, and feel conscious that there is nothing here that will harmonise with his surroundings, he will allow there is something felt but not expressible, that causes him not to sneer at the poor, ugly old things; and that, somewhat curiously, makes him think of his mother and the days when money did not represent the be-all and end-all of life; and when hurry, that kill-joy of the present, was not for him, and he had leisure to enjoy the sense of life, and the thousand and one scents that make up one's very early recollections.

But although we may enter the house and reverently converse with the past among its shadows, strangers may not come in yet, for only yesterday did the mistress leave her quiet well-loved house for a quieter and better-affectioned one in the beautiful little churchyard, round which the river runs, appearing to keep away all noise from the silent spot; and so her presence still seems to linger here.

Yet when to-morrow comes all the world will rush, not realising that the auctioneer's Lot 1 and Lot 2, that mean to them but a sordid bargain, represent the different notes in her song of life as surely as the dots and lines on a sheet of music paper can mean an epithalamium, or a funeral march, or even a march to victory! For she was fifteen years old when the battle of Waterloo was fought, and remembered hearing the news the very day she began a wondrous work of art, that is now framed and hanging over the low bookshelves in the drawing-room as an evidence of what she did before she took to painting in the delicate subdued style that characterised her later days.

It is indeed a curious device, and, on a black cloth ground, represents a cornucopia full of flowers, all manufactured from small atoms, and in successive layers or petals of cloth, in some cases true to nature, while in others truth is sacrificed to sentiment ; for a blue passion-flower is made from tiny morsels of a fine pale material, of which the gown was composed which she wore the first time she met her future husband ; and the white silk honeysuckle, perfect in form if not in hue, is made from the soft shawl that enfolded her one baby, the day he opened his calm gray eyes on this quiet corner of a noisy world.

It took her years to complete, for many events passed by and she forgot from time to time her handiwork ; but as life gradually schooled the somewhat impulsive maiden, forming her into the calm matron, well-balanced in mind and manner, she deemed it wrong to have aught incomplete that she had once commenced, and so finished it and hung it up above the bookcase, proud, though she confessed it not, that she, who was thought unfeminine because she could do most things best as companion to the man she loved, had thus vindicated her character, and had given proof that she could do frivolous and womanly sewing, should it be necessary for her so to do, as well as, if not better than, the most blushing, retiring wife or maiden in her neighbourhood.

The screen in front of the just-extinguished fire has no such happy memories as these ; for it was begun and ended in feverish anxiety to find in constant employment, that had no dual associations about it, some other object for contemplation than the dead faces of the husband and child who perished together in the river below the garden, and who were brought home and laid in the chamber above this one, just five-and-fifty long weary years ago ; for how could she paint when beside her easel stood his ; or ride, when his horse was neighing impatiently for him in the stable ; or think of reading the book where his paper-knife was still where he had placed it, and from whence it was never removed for many years, and then only by accident, of which she seemed to take no notice, though we who loved her knew well what the heedless action of a young child had done ?

Nay, rather, she seemed to take to the child, and after time went by, and she had been thirty years a widow, he used to be here always as a grown man of five-and-thirty, and his boy rode the old pony who to-morrow will be shot kindly, for there is none to love and tend him now his last friend is dead.

But the screen represented to her a passage from passionate despair to calm hope and prayerful waiting, and to her every stitch represented its own place in the progress ; here false stitches displayed backsliding, eyes inflamed with tears, hands tremulous from nights of weeping ; and there a well-formed, fully-shaded rosebud spoke hopefully of religion conquering natural agony, and hope shining where human eyes saw nothing save blackness and despair.

To-morrow the screen will doubtless be sold as rubbish,

and may be bought for the glass and frame, to hold some
fancy work of to-day, wrought by machinery, or in hurried
single stitch, without scarce a thought, and to last for a
short space : and the work she did may be burned as useless.     What wonder that we cannot help wondering if,
when we despise old handiworks and do away with them,
we unwittingly pain some tender spirit who may yet linger
a while or at times amongst us, and almost believe that
we do, so tender do we feel towards all the things she has
made !

We experience a veritable pang as we gaze around us,
and know that now all will be dismantled and despised.
None of the furniture is old enough to be in the fashion,
while all is too venerable to be so useful that it must be
kept.     In the folds of the long chintz curtains in the
drawing-room her child may have played hide-and-seek ;
his little face, that, painted by Leslie, hangs yet over his
mother's chair, and that can never cease to be the face of a
child, may have peeped out roguishly from the faded
lilies of the valley, among their pale green leaves, and
smiled to her, even while she chid him laughing, for she
must have cared for them, as she always placed the folds
herself, and saw that they were carefully sent to be
" calendered " every successive spring.

The lilies are repeated on the carpet, twining in among
the scarlet and blue and yellow roses, whose crude unæsthetic
hues are toned with time ; for the sixty years have done
nought to it save what is kindly, and, while never wearing
the texture, have only softened down its asperities in a way
time alone has, and that he often employs beneficially to us
too impatient, too irritable mortals.

The furniture is solid and heavy, from the great
mahogany sideboard with the cellaret beneath, so like a

tomb that we distinctly remember feeling ourselves impelled to bury the ghosts therein, to the vast rosewood four-post bedstead, with heavy red moreen hangings, in which she slept, night after night, all her long quiet lifetime, and we cannot bear to think of the lodging-house parlours and chambers in which it must end its days.

But although we cannot save it all, some one, we know, will buy the contents of that tiny inner room, that always seemed the heart of the house—broken, maybe, yet still beating—where she always said her many prayers, and where her son slept and played, those five short years of his innocent life.

Here is his rosewood crib, with fluted pillars, loose in places and easily turned in their sockets, that tell their own tale of his restless little fingers, with one side that lets down with a sound that had its own meaning to her ears, and that, caused once by a new housemaid who knew no traditions, brought to her eyes torrents of tears, although forty years had gone by since the child died ; and here in a shelf over the fireplace is a row of small worn books, that, bought for him, have been read by all the child visitors she so loved, and who ever seemed to her to represent her own boy.

Any child, now happy in the thousand and one lovely and artistic picture-books which crowd our nurseries, would disdainfully turn away from these poor, faded little volumes ; their " Beauty and the Beast " has pages a foot wide, covered by designs we long to see reproduced in our dress and houses ; while this one has thin brownish paper, and rough woodcuts, representing Beauty in the dress of the Empire, with a long scarf round her shoulders, and gloves ample in length for a modern beauty's requirements, while the Beast is like nothing so much as a great Newfoundland dog !

This stands by the little collection of anecdotes of Miss Lydia Levity, which was published in 1802 by Darton, Harvey, and Darton, and bears on its pages evidences of profound study, inasmuch as little pencil x's show exactly how much of these anecdotal pages constituted a lesson; and bleared round patches on the thin paper disclose further that the readings were not always without tears; while rhymes for the nursery, an epitome of Scripture history, the Stranger's Offering, and the Parents' and Teachers' Catechism, of dates ranging from 1802 to about 1810, tell that they belonged to her own childhood, and so keep their associations somewhat distinct from those that render sacred the universal "Primer and Original Poems," the date of which is 1824.

Another little volume, bound in rough red linen cloth, with a wavy line across it, has lost its title-page, but is inscribed in her tremulous, fine, Italian hand, "The Child's Book," and contains poems and pictures, of the simplest and crudest, if the most moral designs. Possibly we may save the contents of this little room from the auctioneer's hammer; but as we look round we wonder, when we are gone too, and our belongings in their turn are scattered, if there will be any of the aroma of the past left among them.

This whole place appears to us full of the most delicate fragrance, redolent of hope or love, or pain or fear, and is like some rare perfume, enclosed safely in a crystal flask, that must be shattered to-morrow when the world comes in to buy and sell.

We may catch, as it were, a few drops as the bottle breaks, but the scent cannot last, and once it is dispelled all must vanish like a dream, or like the life that once was lived in all its various phases within these walls.

From this, how easily we come to wonder why we should ever be vexed, or worn, or suffer, when, after all, 'tis all for such a little space, and when life will insist on being allowed to run its own course, however much we try to stem the stream, and call out against the inevitable. The river runs, and happiest are surely those who go on their way with it quietly; not rushing, neither expecting too much, but rather resting, as doth a caged bird—once the first vain struggles are over,—quiet, yet watchful ever for escape, which oft comes not until death opens our prison door.

Thinking like this, we cannot envy the dwellers in great cities, who dare not stay a while and rest without fearing to be forgotten; thinking, wrongfully enough, that were they to do so they would throw out of gear all that complex machinery they call society, yet that looses them down the stream silently enough, should they for any cause cease to be prominent among them. Yet we regret while we think of them, even more sadly than ever, all we shall lose, now we can no longer find a resting-place in our well-known corner back from the road.

# XXIX

## A FUTURE HARVEST

WHAT we have to describe is only a modest beginning, only a small wooden shed and two or three ponds, that express nothing to the uninitiated, but to the votary of pisciculture are full of interest and possibilities of what may be done hereafter. It is in the very centre of the fish country. Past the garden flows one of the world-famed English salmon rivers away to the sea, out beyond the sandy entrance to Christchurch harbour; while in every stream that feeds the greater river the skilled and patient angler may obtain trout or grayling enough to constitute an excellent day's sport. But this is not all the pioneers of this new departure wish or intend shall be in the future. Sport is all very well in its way, and is thoroughly appreciated by our host *pro tem.*, but he has other larger views than these, and intends to help forward with all his power a system that shall result in stocking all our numerous rivers adequately, and bringing fish, as an article of food, from the eminence of luxury, which it occupies at present, within the reach of the poorest in the land. It is a fascinating operation: not so much just at present, when there is no hatching actually in progress, and when all the tiny fish are disporting themselves in the ponds; but in January and February, when the ova are carefully laid down on the glass grills in the hatching-house, where they require most careful watching, the interest can never for one moment flag. The ova themselves are usually spawned artificially, and sent down by enthusiastic friends to be hatched; for the enemies which are perpetually watching to devour the spawn, in nature, cannot always be circumvented, and while the loss there is 99 per cent, there is very little indeed where art steps in to protect the spawn. In nature everything seems to combine with the fishmongers to keep down the supply of fish, and keep up the prices: big, coarse fish wait behind the spawning beds, ready to devour all they can, while all wild-fowl join in the raid, and swans especially do their best to exterminate the unborn fish, as they can, if undisturbed, gobble up a pint of spawn comfortably in twenty minutes. Great care seems all that is required to inaugurate a very different state of things, and the expenses of a fish-hatching establishment can be met comfortably by the profits, leaving a small margin for contingencies; and, of course, the larger the scale of the establishment the more fish could be hatched and disposed of, and the profits would be comparatively greater.

The hatching-house is a rough shed, with a series of grills arranged in long narrow boxes. Here the ova are laid, with a never-ceasing flow of filtered water passing slowly over them. The moment an egg appears to be dead: and to the initiated it is very easy to distinguish between the dead and living by reason of the dead egg being opaque and white, while the living one is described by an enthusiast as having a " delicate bloom on it like that on a ripe Muscat grape": it must be removed, or it will inevitably develop a fungoid growth, that will spread death and destruction among the other eggs, which must be guarded carefully from any deposit, for the smallest grain of sand, of gravel, or of anything in fact, prevents the hatching thereof, and hence the reason of the filtration of the water before it flows over the grills.

But at present the extremely juvenile stages of the fish are only represented by sundry mysterious little bottles ranged in a row on the desk, and which contain deformities that have been from time to time taken out of the newly-hatched spawn, and preserved as examples of the erratic freaks Nature is sometimes capable of. Here are atoms joined together like the Two-headed Nightingale; here an object which has two distinct tails; and in fact there seems no travesty or curious formation that is not occasionally found among the tiny fish. For six or eight weeks after hatching they do not require to be fed, as they are provided with a yolk-sac that nourishes them nicely. Yet still they require constant attention, as they have a disagreeable habit of crowding up tightly into a corner; and occasionally they have been washed overboard *en masse;* and our friend was once met by the pleasing intelligence that his water-cress bed was full of "rummy-looking" minnows, which turned out to be a pet family of trout, all of which fell victims to their premature rush into the outside world. When they have finished their "sacs," they have to begin to be fed in a larger tank, carefully shaded by blue paper shades, which throw quite an æsthetic tint on the water, from much sunshine; and here they receive, six times a day, minute atoms of boiled liver, cut up artistically in a revolving American machine, and rubbed through a very fine sieve. This continues for about six weeks more, and then, when they are between three and four months old, they are turned out into the ponds, where they remain until they are old enough to be sent into little rivers and streams to look after themselves. The ponds are square and concreted, covered at the bottom with gravel, which is carefully raked three times a week, and through which water is constantly flowing, raised by an ingenious wheel from the swift little weir to the level of the house;

R

and with water-weeds in pots standing about in them ; and at first it is very difficult to see the fish, or realise that they are there in anything like the numbers we are told of. They are precisely the colour of the ground itself, but presently we can see the tiny mites, and note with amusement how even in these atoms exists the germ of the habits and manners that distinguish their parents. The little salmon leap, and climb, and have such astonishing strength that they often go "up stream" into the pipes that supply the ponds ; reappearing in a little cup-like place at the head of the ponds, from which they are ignominiously returned, to remain until they are old enough to begin their travels in earnest ; while the trout stem themselves against the stream in the orthodox manner, and scuttle away and lie close immediately the shadow of a person—doubtless suggestive to their inherited instinct, of a fishing-rod—throws itself across the pond. And yet they are tame too, coming to be fed regularly, and when the man, taking a long-handled butterfly net, sweeps down handfuls of gnats on the surface of the water, they begin to rise after them, one following the other, until the pond seems suddenly to become alive with dimples, or as if a smart shower of rain had begun to fall.

In this stage the young fish only require feeding three times a day. Yet even here they have enemies, cats being famous fishermen ; and even an occasional kingfisher has been known to dart down and devour a few dozen, before any one could rush to the rescue. The fish are almost all of a size by reason of the small ones being bullied and illtreated by their larger brethren ; and we noticed one atom with a curious growth over his eye, "caused by his running up against the rake," we were told, whose existence, no doubt, terminated very shortly after we saw him ; otherwise all we saw were fine healthy creatures, very agile, and all with the distinctive marks of salmon or trout visible on their quivering thin brown forms beneath the water. The one great thing that they require is fresh or living water. Stagnant water kills them almost immediately, and when they are sent away by train, the water is kept supplied with oxygen by a pair of bellows, that constantly pumps air into the tin cans they inhabit *pro tem.* In the neighbouring harbour, a little farther inland, tons and tons of gray mullet are destroyed yearly. Oysters have been exterminated, and even eels are becoming scarce owing to the greed and incapacity of the fishermen who exist there — catching and shooting anything, no matter what, that either swims or flies ; and it is refreshing in these days to come across any one whose one end and aim in life is to replenish instead of emptying ; and who, though only an amateur, yet is one of the very few who are ahead of the present moment, and is himself anxious to bring about a better state of things than exists at present in most of our rivers and streams, all of which seem crying out to be inhabited ; and who looks forward hopefully to the time when his and his friend's exertions shall be crowned with the success they merit, and fish shall take its proper place as one of the cheapest and best articles of food that rich or poor can place upon their tables.

## IN THE CHASE

THE Chase is a long thin strip of wooded land that extends for miles and miles through the most unfrequented part of two distant English counties. It has evidently been at one time a dense forest with deep glades, and thick with undergrowth; but it has changed with the times; and indeed it is so dotted about, so closely covered in some parts with graceful thin nut-bushes and saplings, and so naked and barren of aught save furze-bushes in others, that it is only by such names as "Ash oaks," and sundry similar cognomens, that we are able to trace it as we drive along.

We pause for a while on the down, and look around us. There is a perfect chorus of bird notes, blackbirds and thrushes chanting mightily, while a lark is outsinging them all, and almost drowning the notes of the cuckoo, who is holding forth breathlessly and monotonously, much like a Cheap Jack or a member of the Salvation Army, secure of attention if only for the sake of the noise he manages to make, and vying with the corncrake, who is creaking away, and sounding very similar to the squeak of a gate that requires oiling.

The furzy common seems to extend for miles; here and there are thorn-trees just bursting into blossom, with spare trunks and limbs covered with soft gray moss; while just before us rise two solitary lodges, empty, and looking as if they had seen better days, and appearing as if they stood as sentinels to guard a big house, long since fallen down, and disappeared, in the remarkable manner in which old houses and old families do disappear entirely from the face of the earth, in corners of England remote from the metropolis, or distant from a railway line.

It is extraordinary how far we can see, how far we may travel here, and not catch a glimpse of a human being. The small gray thatched cottages leaning up against a church, and with an imposing much-out-of-place-looking house that is the vicarage, which forms a village, are few and far between; and as we enter the Chase and drive between nut-bushes, growing tall and lanky in a manner that would send a Kentish nut-grower out of his mind, we begin to think we are in the Middle Ages, for all the sounds or evidences of life we hear or see.

Indeed, as we pause once more, enraptured at the sight of the millions of wild flowers that would make the fortune of a Covent Garden market florist, we see evident traces of much earlier days than these; for, concealed in the low-growing brushwood, and grown over by bushes of all sorts and sizes, we discover rings of earth exactly like the Ambresbury Banks in Epping Forest; supposed once to have encircled the abodes of the ancient Britons, or to have formed ramparts to the ingenious dwellings of those mysterious and little-known creatures, the earthmen.

Yet surely now we hear voices, and almost afraid that we must have aroused the spirits of the departed, we venture a little farther, and discover that we have stumbled at last on some other humans beside ourselves.

How picturesque is their occupation too! And as we note the agile manner in which the lissom hazel wands are twisted into hurdles, or neatly stacked for firewood among the thousands of blossoms, and listen to the sound of the songs of birds, we are almost inclined to say, "This will we do ourselves," and decline to return ever again to the haunts of men.

Their peaceful surroundings appear to make these denizens of the Chase very silent; anyhow, they hardly ever seem to address each other.  One cuts the hazel into the required lengths, while another, possessing a horse-shoe piece of wood with holes in it, proceeds to knock the stronger hazel branches into these holes, then taking lengths of the younger wood, he twists them round and round the poles until the hurdle is completed, when he knocks the finished work away from the horse-shoe, and it springs into-shape in one moment, and is then put on a pile to await the carter, and another is swiftly commenced.

Although it certainly does away with the seclusion, a newly-cleared copse is a fine and picturesque sight; the trees that are left seem thankful for the fresh air and sun, and the white stumps of the bushes appear to gleam among the flowers; while somehow or other the men engaged in woodcraft appear always ready to step straight into a picture.

After all, too, they are doing no harm, for these hazels are twenty years old and so unfit for fruit, the gathering of which brings in quite a nice lot of money to the women and children, who come miles and miles from the villages round in early and later autumn: first to possess themselves of the young nuts, which are sent up wholesale to town for dyeing purposes, and afterwards for the ripened fruit, which is sold to the one man in the respective villages who is sufficiently advanced to have dealings with London, and who pays them according to the season's prices, which range from 4s. 6d. to 4d. a peck according as the supply is great or small.  Then the copses are alive with people to whom permission is given by the lords of the divers manors in which the Chase is situate, and is received gratefully by those who are unaware or oblivious of the fact that long ages ago these copses were free and open, and were actually all stolen from the public in those bygone years when folks were not so conversant with their rights as they are nowadays. Perhaps it is as well that these woods are enclosed and kept sacred; for otherwise they would hardly be as beautiful as they are in late spring, when the fine small leaf of the hazel has put out its pale green flag, and when the wan anemone, tall scented bluebell, crouching yellow primrose, and dog-violet make a carpet all too dainty for human feet to tread; and we drive on rejoicing somewhat at the wire fence that keeps out intruders, yet allows all these beauties to be visible to us as we pass.

The Chase goes this way and that, first on the left hand, then on the right, and then for a while disappears altogether, and we are many feet above the level of the sea, as it seems to us, and away on an open down.

And what a marvellous view is before us—one worth travelling miles upon miles alone to see!

Away to the left a drifting spring storm obscures our view, or the Isle of Wight should be visible from this spot, lying like a sleeping beauty enveloped in a veil of mist on the far horizon. It is curious to watch the storm travelling quickly, and even reaching to the far-off distant Purbeck hills; whence it hurries along towards that dim mysterious spot known as "the vale," where disappear, so it seems to us, all sorts and conditions of men and women, who, inquired for by us after an absence, have left their erstwhile habitations, and are now to be heard of as "up country" or "in the vale." And the vale from here seems indeed a desirable location: field after field of rich pasture land, bathed in that peculiar local tint of densest blue that seems to brood over fat grazing land, stretches away; here and there a stately church indicates the presence of a village, that is so hidden by luxuriant many-tinted tree-growths, that, were it not for the faint purple smoke climbing up towards the dappled sky, we should doubt its existence; while an occasional great house speaks of the landowner, who obtains, even in these hard times, £4 an acre easily, while the downlands and rougher fields above the vale scarcely realise for their possessor a scanty pound. In many cases, too, the fields are covered by couch-grass, and fast returning to the down by which they are surrounded, and of which they were part before they were broken up, by costly processes, in the flourishing time of farmers : and this tells its own tale of diminished rents, and even, in places, of entire lack of any tenants for the land at all.

It would be easy to wait here for hours, noting the great hills standing out into the vast expanse of land below our vantage ground, and that look as if the vale had once been the mouth of some mighty river, which had washed out these vast cliffs, that look singularly out of place so far inland, and that in more than one case form the sides of a quaint green table-land that resembles a harbour, where stand the fold and the small movable shepherd's house that speak of a not far distant flock.

Presently we glance up and perceive the sheep and lambs on the incline, above the harbour, hanging on, as it seems to us, by their eyelids, just over a precipice that makes us giddy to look at; and we are involuntarily shrinking back at their perilous situation, when suddenly a tall figure appears against the sky-line; he holds out his arm, a sheep-dog darts out from his side round the outside animal, and in less time than it takes to tell it, the flock is to-

gether in safety, on what appears to be the edge of a
razor, but that is really a broad expanse of hill, covered
with the short, sweet, delicious grass that is their delight.

Every nook and corner of the vale seems to have some
wonderful hunting legend connected with it; with the name
of each hill or well-known trysting-place is coupled the
story of some wonderful run: from the story of the fox
which started from one spot, went right down the vale, and
returned safe at night to the place from whence he had
departed in the morning, to the pathetic anecdote of the
tired beast, who lay down under the pony-carriage of a lady
who was resting in a lane, while her children gathered wild-
flowers, and who boldly answered "No" when asked by a
stray huntsman if she had seen the fox; a lie for which she
believes to this day the fox was properly grateful; for she
saw it in his eye when he slunk away into the underwood,
when the hunt had gone quite in another direction to the
one in which he was going.

But just after waiting one moment to look at the little
town of Shaftesbury, perched picturesquely on a hill-top
beyond the down, we turn away from the vale, and its
thousand and one interests, to inspect just one other corner
of the Chase. It is delightful to drive straight away on
these strange roads into the heart of an unknown country,
coming every now and then on a white finger-post, inscribed
with all sorts of names, that have been only to us as marks on
the map and nothing more, and that even sometimes men-
tion places of which we have never heard, but that are
most suggestive by reason of their quaint names; and we
are almost sorry when we reach our last resting-place, and
descend to examine the "Alarm-oak," which is one of the
sights of the Chase.

Full of interest indeed is this quaint little corner.

Not so very long ago it was a sandpit, deep with hanging thorn-bushes and furze, but now cleared and tidy. It
makes a charming change from the wild uncultured land by
which it is surrounded, and through which we have been
driving. Still, if art has succeeded nature, she has not
ousted the traditions that hang about the place, but has
discovered much that might otherwise have never been
disinterred from the dust of ages; for flint implements
were turned up by the spade, and objects that pointed out
the presence of long-dead Romans, the site of whose workshop this was supposed to have been, and many other
things were discovered, that make tangible links between
us and those bygone times. Indeed, the alarm-oak is in
itself a wonderful thing to contemplate, though there is
nothing save a tiny shell of a tree left, in which is planted
a strong young sapling that shall live on, keeping the
oak's memory green, long after the parent is mingled with
the dust.

For here it is said the ancient Britons used to meet,
ere chasing the deer and hunting the fox in the woods
around; called to the rendezvous by the sounding of a horn,
that thus gave the alarm or notice that the huntsmen were
ready: to commemorate which fact, a fine bronze statue has
been erected here from a model of Boehm's, which represents an ancient British huntsman gazing out into the distance, as if on the look-out for the antlers of a stately deer
coming through the forest beyond the oak. Then here in
later days came King John from his neighbouring royal
residence at Toller Royal, where nothing regal remains
save the name, and a legend that the king still haunts the
site of his palace, hoping to discover a treasure which he
was supposed to have hidden there: why no one seems
exactly to be able to state. And in quite recent times the

alarm-oak has been used as a rendezvous by the game-keepers, when they have suspected the presence of poachers, whose guns have been heard in the preserves, shooting maybe at the imitation pheasants that serve to decoy an unwary poacher into firing, to show his where-abouts, yet shall ensure his doing no harm besides. The birds are still of profound interest in this tiny corner of the Chase, and are rapidly making themselves at home in this quiet cultivated place. Down there on the vase that stands by the little bubbling pool a water-wagtail, called there a "sally-wash-dish," had her nest. She had comfortably hatched out her family, and was absent on a foraging expedi-tion, when a cuckoo came along, and doubtless considered her nest a nice place in which to deposit her egg, for when the "wash-dish" returned she discovered this hard and unwieldy addition to her family. However, she rose to the occasion, turned her own children out into the cold world, as expressed by the edge of the vase, and set to work to hatch the cuckoo's egg, regardless of the fact that her infants died of the neglect, and were taken away in the morning by the custodian of the place, while she sat un-moved and watched them thrown away.

She successfully brought out and brought up the young cuckoo, whose wings were in due time cut, while he was set to earn an honest living by destroying the white slugs on the lawn, which is an occupation dear to the heart of one of these birds; but retribution for his parent's crime over-took him in due course, and he fell a victim to a weasel, who fetched him out of the box where he spent his nights, and made an end of him very quickly.

The stately peacock, with his two plain but dutiful and loving wives, is also an object of the greatest interest, for he will allow no one between the wind and his nobility. The retired soldier, who mounts guard over this particular corner of the Chase, is full of what he calls "antedotes" about them, and relates with pride how it is impossible for him to keep a duck or a chicken near the place where they are, because they all fall on them immediately, and exterminate them, much as some noblemen exterminate all the poor folks and their cottages, when they require more ground for their preserves.

"They're royal birds," he said admiringly, "and they knows it too : bless you ! I daren't keep 'em waiting a single moment after their time for feeding, for if I do they ups and sulks and off they goes to the next keeper ; and I have to sort of apologise to they, before they'll come home. It's my belief there isn't a thing they don't know better than I do, and the airs they give theirselves is tremenjous," and putting great emphasis on this word, he looked first at the birds and then at us to see if we were duly impressed by this introduction.

It is pleasant to turn from this overpowering grandeur to contemplate the little birds, who are gradually returning to the Chase, now that robbing their nests, or persecuting them, is severely punished by the owner. Even the rare and delightful goldfinch has been seen again this year, although he has nearly been exterminated in many parts of England, not escaping the wiles of the snarer even in this remote place ; for the bird-catchers actually travel all the way down from London, carrying their long arrangement of nets and sail-cloth and sticks on their backs, through interstices in which we can see the eyes of the poor little "toll-bird," who appears to look beseechingly out at the world, as if he knew the unworthy work he was obliged to do, and begged somebody to release him, or enable him to earn his living in some less dishonourable manner ; but the moment the cage is put down in the open, and he sees the blue sky and the lovely surroundings that were once home, and that are so unlike Seven Dials, he can but sing and attract his free relations and acquaintances into the net spread all round him : though all the time he is singing he seems to know and feel the harm he is about to do.

The bird-catcher haunts a sheltered spot on the downs, or, better still, the borders of any tiny stream that babbles through the close undergrowth of a copse ; for here the birds come to drink, and are easily taken by bird-lime, if there is not room to lay out the net and place the cages in order ; and to these men is due the disappearance of many of the small birds, who, being good singers in captivity, and not being of the restless agonised nature of a lark, can be easily tamed and made companionable in a comparatively short space of time.

Larks, fortunately for them, are so utterly untamable after they once reach maturity, that they hardly pay to snare ; for although very large prices are obtained for a really good singer, they have to be taken so young, and fed so carefully and continually, and so often turn out to be voiceless females, after all the labour expended on them, that no amount of money repays the bird-catcher for all his care and anxiety. Here we must protest warmly, too, against the wretched cruelty of those who snare or buy these poor little creatures. It is useless to expostulate with Bill Sykes, who sees in them nothing save so many pence and a jolly expedition into the country, where doubtless he may get much mental and bodily welfare ; but we do protest against those who buy any British bird, and beg them to calmly study the question before condemning the open-air denizens to a confined lodging in a draughty, hot, and miserable posi-tion, where too often he languishes neglected and unfed, and with putrid water, just to gratify occasionally their love of hearing a bird's song. If they would only know a bird's heart, watch his beautiful pathetic eye, and note his delight in the spring and summer, and his intense gratitude for any food he receives in winter, we are sure that the bird-catcher's trade would receive a blow it would never recover; for no one who knows what birds really are, could make them suffer as they do in a caged existence. If any should doubt this, let them go themselves to the Chase, where birds are welcome and precious residents: they may see rare specimens that are scarcely known by sight to many of us; they may catch the blue glint of the wing of the jay as he darts about—intent on sucking birds' eggs, say the keepers, which we ourselves do not believe he does; they may come across the deliciously-constructed nest of the golden-crested wren; and they may make the acquaintance of small birds innumerable, who have all as distinct ways and manners as have any colony of human beings.

Rare insects and flowers, too, are found in the Chase; and, above all, there is there a sense of calm communion with a lovely side of nature at home, that is discovered in few other spots, and if summer and early spring are selected for the visit, no one could go away disappointed. In winter it must be lonely indeed; and the drive over the open downs, on what can only be called a road by courtesy, that was so delightful and invigorating when we were there last, is turned then into a penance, of which our charioteer speaks with mingled awe and dread; for many a time has he come across the downs in weather when he has not been able to see his horse, and has had to trust entirely to him to take him home safely; and when driving mist or pouring rain or blinding snow has made the journey not only a disagreeable one, but one of the extremest danger.

Indeed, when we heard of how in the great snow-storm of 1881-82 a man was buried here with his horse and cart, and only found again after many days, and how two little girls going to school were also lost on the dreary wilds, we began to look upon the downs in a different light; and though we saw a stone-curlew, and were almost tempted to search for the nest that we knew must be about, we thought it best to press onward to our temporary resting-place in a typical Dorset village, glad to leave the downs, although it was over them that we had to drive to make the delightful acquaintance of the wide and wonderful Chase.

## LIFE IN A VILLAGE

ALL about the country where lies the Chase are dotted tiny villages, all exactly alike, all more or less beautiful.

There is in one place a complete string of them, somewhat resembling solitary gray beads held together by a green slight cord, and that have a family likeness, heightened by the fact that each name has the same prefix, that it would not do to further particularise than by saying that it conveys to the understanding ear the sound of many waters. It is delightful to wander up the steep incline that leads to the first of these villages, and pausing for a moment or two look at the extensive and marvellous view before us : there, nestling down by the banks of the river, is the big market town, whither journey on Saturdays and Wednesdays the farmers, intent on their one piece of dissipation that shall last them until the next week comes round; and nothing better illustrates the usual farmer's intellect, than the fact that the market has been entirely spoiled owing to a division of opinion as to the respective advantages of Wednesday and Saturday for the market—a division resulting in bitter feuds between those who so differed, each of whom still adhere to their own opinion, and so spoil what was once almost the largest market in this part of the country. Looking away from the town, we can see nearly to Salisbury Plain, and then going farther on, between rows of wonderful trees, and past running streams, gurgling over the roads, and never troubling in the least to keep between proper bounds, we reach the first of our villages.

There is not a soul to be seen : all the children are in school, all the wives cooking the dinners, all the husbands in the fields housing the hay that is making the air heavy with its scent ; and we might have stumbled on the city of the dead for all the evidences of human life there are to be seen. Even the animals are drowsy at noontide : the cats lie asleep under the gooseberry bushes, and the dogs snore audibly, stretched out at full length on the stones ; all except the foxhound puppy sent to the farmer to educate, as is the custom in those parts ; nothing daunts him, and he gambols about, seriously annoying the older animals, who are very patient at first, but wax wroth when they discover no mild remonstrance on their part will cause the small nuisance to leave them alone.

Every one is very busy for the hay harvest is at risk ; and though fine enough at the moment, the weather is " casulty," as they say in those parts, meaning doubtless casualty, or not to be depended on. Yesterday, for example, it was easy enough to watch the gathering of a great storm that did vast damage only twenty miles away, but that left our village almost untouched ; for, as generally happened, the hills drew away the clouds that travelled round them, leaving the plains with nothing worse than just a scud of the rain we could see pouring down, as it seemed, in the next parish. The gathering of a storm is a wonderful sight, and one well worth noting: perhaps overnight we may have noticed a faint cloud on the horizon, or one or two fleecy white messengers may have crept over the tops of the hills, reminding us that fine weather is but a transitory possession after all ; still we arise to a beautiful morning and forget our warning until about twelve o'clock.

Then the poplars at the bottom of the field, by the brook, have had an ominous shiver in them, the aspens have resolutely turned their backs on us and shown us their white sides; the animals have one and all been uneasy, and the birds have kept up such a chatter and appeared so anxious to find shelter somewhere, that we know quite well something out of the common must be going to happen.

Presently immense clumps of white clouds with puffy cotton-wool-like tops begin to appear suddenly in the sky; bigger clouds creep over them; it becomes very hot, then very cold, then hot again; a brown sort of hue seems to fall on the landscape; the horses and cows become still more uneasy. We go out into the verandah and look about us: on the flagged walk great round splotches of water, the size of a half-crown, and with rayed edges that tell us of the weight with which they fell, appear all at once here and there; the blue lupins bow to the foxgloves as the drops fall one by one on their tall lanky heads; then the trees all begin to rustle together, the birds fly about screaming, much as a silly woman would do were she in fear of an accident, and unable to do anything sensible; and presently very, very far away we hear a low continuous rumble, like heavy waggons coming home at night when all is still and we can hear them a long way off, and that tells us that the storm has, as usual, broken with all its fury on the unfortunate folks who farm unwisely and not too well in the valley among the hills.

Although the storm itself does not affect the village, as far as it is concerned, these violent convulsions of nature are almost sure to break up any spell of warmth and lovely sunshine in which we have been basking. English weather

very much resembles the English people: once get it firmly
fixed in a groove, and it is almost impossible to alter it; but
once set it roving, and no one can say when we shall have
two days alike once more. We recollect summers in our
village when rain was almost, if not quite, unknown; when
great and unexpected chasms gaped in the gardens; when
the roses, if they bloomed at all, opened all at once and
dropped their leaves before the evening; when geraniums
and calceolarias literally glowed in the sunshine and grew
before our eyes into big shrubs; when the bedrooms were
like a vapour-bath, and the great white moon at night really
seemed to have as much power as the sun had by day; when
the village pond dried up incontinently, and disposed of, with
one blow, dozens of legends respecting its vast depth, its lack
of bottom, and its many corpses whose dead hands were
supposed to stretch out at night, and wave lights to entrap
unwary travellers to join them in their moist retreat; when
sunstrokes were not unheard-of occurrences, and when as
day after day rose as hot, as brilliant, and as lovely as its
predecessor, we began to understand the feelings of the
Israelites when they endured those seven years of rainless
arid heat in the days of old. That year we had a perfect
swarm of humming-bird moths in the garden flitting hither
and thither, and looking strangely tropical and out of place
among our banksia roses and lemon plants and jasmines;
and never was there such a corn harvest before or since; yet,
as we watched the flagging of the old folks and the little
children, we could not help being glad when the weather
broke up, and has remained more or less broken ever since.

But we shall never forget the joy of the first rain, nor the
sound of it, as it fell on the parched leaves of the trees, and
the scent of the earth as it seemed gratefully to open its
baked, cracked lips, and drink in of the abundance. Still,

how it did rain, to be sure ! Presently little rivers rose in the garden and careered wildly down the paths, the house walls became moist and damp, and we soon wished for the fine lovely weather back again.

September had come, and it was of course useless to wish. The flowers were all washed into the earth, the second bloom of the roses was done for ; and by the time it had finished raining October was in, and the first frost cleared the place, and decently buried the summer in less time than it takes to tell it.

Life in a village depends so much on the weather that that is the first thing we remember in connection with it. Unlike entirely life in a country town, it depends essentially on the resources within yourself, if you are able to endure it in the least ; and naturally a great deal depends, as it does everywhere else, on the position in life in which you happen to be placed.

In a country town, life is impossible for any one who has been accustomed to the free and unfettered existence of London, where it rests entirely with yourself and your acquirements, mental and otherwise, to determine who and what shall be your friends ; in a country town in England this is determined for you by your occupation, and also by whether you are or are not a regular attendant at the parish church. And should you live in this latter half of the nineteenth century, be troubled with conscientious scruples and object to the mild ignorant sermons that are generally provided for the ordinary country congregation, and have connections with any sort of trade, you find yourself received into society—save the mark !—on a footing that speedily results in your being entirely forced to exist without friends worthy the name.

But in a country village there are interests enough if you

will but seek them; and if you are lucky enough to care about fishing and shooting, to say nothing of hunting, your life may be a remarkably pleasant one. And that is the secret of the desire of so many young men, country born and bred, to be farmers; horses are a *sine quâ non;* they rub shoulders with those mysterious beings, the members of the county, chuckling to themselves at the stories they know about these individuals, who look upon themselves as locked, beautifully-polished, and much-admired caskets, the interior arrangement of which has never been seen by their tenant-farmers; and they have a free open life, full of ups and downs, and have no desk-work or head-work to addle their brains. Naturally there are as many different types of farmers as there are of any other class of human beings, but they are all unanimous in one thing: in a perfect dread lest they should be eliminated, as the yeoman farmer has been, almost to a man.

They appear to have the same sort of fear of losing their landlord, as a child has who has been taught to walk in a go-cart, and sees with dread that the time has come when they must walk alone. They are perfectly agreed about the heavy over-rent, about the disgraceful inequalities between landlord and tenant; yet are they quite powerless to alter the existing state of affairs, and stand aghast, while a long series of bad seasons and American competition does for them what a bold stroke on their own parts would have done for themselves long ago.

The most disagreeable specimen of the class is the long-sighted toady and sycophant we once met, some twenty odd miles from our village. With small desires and an only child, and a thorough knowledge of stock, he found it easy work to keep his head well above water; his best shooting was reserved for his landlord, for whom he worked at election times, and indeed at all times of the year, with a servility that made our blood boil to see; and his constant attendance at church and Sunday-school, joined to a mean overreaching of others and hard driving of bargains, gave an insight into his character that was truly appalling to contemplate, and that ended, as such an one always must end, in losing the confidence of all both high and low.

Then there was the true old farmer type, pleasant indeed to look upon, pleasanter still to visit, if love of the country were joined to love of early rising : in winter the prayer bell rang at seven and in summer at six, and woe indeed to the unhappy soul who came in late or not at all, giving as an excuse that they had overslept themselves !

Even as we write, the whole scene rises before us ; we never were unlucky enough to have to stay there, objecting, as we do, very strongly to breakfast anywhere before or after half-past eight ; but many a September day have we spent there among the turnips, returning to a gorgeous dinner, before our long drive home again in the dark. The house was once the old manor-house, and still retains unharmed by time all the characteristics of a fine old mansion. The front is gabled, a crest is over the door, and the small-paned windows look out upon a garden that would delight the soul of any one who loved flowers; then one of the ubiquitous streams glides past the lawn, and then come the meadows, rich with grass, and leading to the fields where presently we shall be striding along after partridges. The inherited awe of centuries is in the farmer's voice as he talks of his landlord, and the pheasants that are to be his spoil when October comes in ; but there is nothing unpleasant about it, and he tells us of his own prosperity and his love of the land, much as if bad times were unheard of in that particular place.

Aided in every way by his excellent wife, our old friend,

rents notwithstanding, had made quite a good thing of his life; but this class is almost as extinct as the yeoman, and has given place to a race, uneasy, anxious for more money and more enjoyment, and a distinct dislike to the hard-working lives lived by their fathers before them.

Perhaps the most entertaining part of the day was the dinner to which we returned at six after the sport was over; when the farmer put himself painfully into queer swallow-tails made when he was married, and worn only on occasions like the present; and when his wife, warm from superintending the last touches to the feast, appeared in a rich black silk that creaked and rustled horribly, and crowned by an elaborate cap, the wide strings of which, composed of broad ribbon edged and embellished with blonde, were gracefully reposed on her ample chest until the moment came for action, when they were put behind her by her maid and replaced by her when dessert arrived on the table.

On these grand dinner-party evenings, a waiter was hired to assist the little maid, from the neighbouring county town. It was always the same one; and therefore he took possession in a fatherly manner of the whole establishment, who, mistress and maid alike, followed him humbly, taking his instructions, and watching him as he arranged the flowers and the table in a masterly way, laying up · stores of knowledge to be used in a sort of second-hand manner at smaller entertainments given during the winter to neighbouring farmers.

What wonder that a species of uneasy awe was thrown over a banquet where the waiter was addressed as Mr. Elder, and asked in trembling accents if he had "steeled the knives"—an inquiry he only answered by a superior smile; and not even the alarmed manner in which Kitty was asked what had become of the "monge" when the blanc-mange did not appear at the proper moment, or the way in

which punch jelly was pressed upon us, enabled us to feel
at our ease, or recover from an insane attempt to giggle, that
seized us the first time we dined there in our youth, when
we discovered the fish and soup on the table at once : the
fish neatly tucked up in a fine white napkin to keep it warm,
while we were consuming the most excellent soup that
began the almost endless feast.

Then we had to listen to the name and history of each
fruit on the table; to take part in an animated discussion,
finally determined by a reference to a small book neatly
kept by our hostess, as to whether the pears were this or
that sort, and how old the tree was, or how young, that produced them; while incautious admiration on our part of a
hideous compound called black-currant gin, of which we
cannot even now think without a shudder, resulted in a
long procession of bottles of home-made wines, each more
truly appalling than the other.

However, out of these we obtained a capital account of
the manor ghost, in whose authentic existence we were all
requested to believe, even though the story told us would
seem to do away with him altogether; and as we sat round
the table, covered with a red cloth, as a contrast to the
green dishes, and lighted with wax-candles, in old-fashioned
brass candlesticks, our hostess told us how once the house
was overfull on the occasion of a wedding, and how she
had had to put a couple of girls in the ghost-room, thinking
there would at all events be safety in numbers, and one
would protect the other during the short hours of the
August night.

"I shall never forget the girls when they came into our
room," said she, laughing, "for they tore in in the middle of
the night and told us they had heard a succession of shots
in the next room, followed by the falling of heavy drops of

blood on the floor. I must say I felt a trifle squeamish myself, but Tom got up, and he and I went in, and sure enough we heard the blood dropping too. It was a very still night, with the harvest moon just over the house yonder, and it shone in, so we didn't want any candles; and as we stood there listening it had rather a gruesome sound, but all at once Tom said, 'There's naught but your jam-closet there, missus; there's no room for either pistols or blood,' and in a moment I knew what it was. I'd been bottling gooseberries some weeks ago, and put 'em in there out of the way, and the horrid things had fermented, or something, and gone on working, until they had popped out the corks, and the blood was my nice ripe red gooseberry juice falling down on the shelves, and creeping out underneath; for there! I'd forgotten the best part of the story, which was that the girls wouldn't call us until they saw the blood actually coming into the room—a sight they showed us naturally enough when we came in with 'em. I can tell you they were laughed at, and they don't like being offered ripe gooseberry tart even now! If you'll come with me I can show you exactly where the ghost was."

Ah! we may smile as we walk behind our hostess as she discourses eagerly over her pickles and preserves, and we scent the queer lavender "cupboardy" smell that hangs about the upstairs rooms, each bed appropriately attired in a ghost-like dust-sheet; yet a softer mood seizes us as we realise there is another side to the picture from which sentiment of the finest kind is not lacking.

For few and far between now are such simple pious households as the one at the manor-house, and though the life may not be intellectual or refined, it yet resembles one of those beautiful old-fashioned flowers that have no mark of education or high culture about them, but that yet are so delightful to us, that the mere name conjures up remembrances that no gorgeous attractive greenhouse plant, valuable from its novelty, has power to do; and that has a special scent belonging to it, that lingers lovingly about the drawer where it may have been placed, charming us we know not why.

We can argue away every atom of the *raison d'être* of such a calm eventless life, full of petty cares and exploded beliefs; but we cannot account for the restful delicious feeling that always came over us at the manor, and that comes over us with a strange sentiment bordering on home-sickness, when we lay down our pen for a moment, and see as in a picture the whole scene once more. In our village, life is rather more unsatisfactory at present, for discontent like leaven in dough is beginning to work there, and renders life uneasy and unsettled.

It were well to paint the picture as it is without note or comment, leaving politicians to draw their own conclusions therefrom.

Here, then, is the village; a great avenue of elm-trees whispers and beckons to the stranger; and the village pond on one side adds just a touch of life to the scene, for here the ducks enjoy themselves mightily, and the pigs ront round the edges, wallowing in the mud trodden down by the horses and cows, and rendered by them a regular trap for the unwary. On a little farther are some rows of tumble-down cottages. Will you enter one, and simply look at them ? You will then, we take it, agree that the horses in the squire's stable are better housed than the labourers on his land.

This is April 1883, almost the present day, yet there are small if any evidences of civilisation here : the flagged floor is worn into pathetic holes by the feet of generations;

here is a small-paned window, mended in more than one place by a paper patch ; exactly opposite the window is a door out into the back-yard, and a great wide grate admits as much rain and wind, as it sends warmth out into the room. The grate burns turf and emits a pleasant odour, resulting in a blue smoke that is essentially picturesque as seen among the trees above and around the cottages, but that has small, if any, really warming qualities in the little draughty place ; still, by the aid of sundry curtains and pieces of list, a little heat can be obtained, and it is up the steep wooden steps that we reach the real evil of the place. The bedroom accommodation consists of one room, and a wide landing open to the stairs—no more, no less.

These cottages close together have each their tale of woe. Each of the daughters "went wrong," as the saying is, and one of them has disappeared entirely from our ken ; the others have married, and are now living in much the same sort of abodes themselves as did their fathers before them, bringing up their daughters, who, doubtless educated a little better than their mothers, may insist on a better state of things before they set out to face the world.

People can talk of the ingratitude of the poor ; they who do so do not know the poor. They require so little to be happy; the flowers in their windows and gardens are sufficient proof that they hanker after beauty ; and they are far more pleased with an intelligent appreciation of their difficulties, and five minutes' conversation with any who can take them from their own standpoint, than for all the soup and blankets from the big house, that after all only pauperise the inferior ones, and cause the better sort to regard their vile hovels sardonically, and then look at the big house, where the tradespeople have to wait for their money, not daring to trouble the squire, and take their revenge by pressing the small folk, who would willingly pay if they could.

Then the pig goes to the one shop in the village, and they have to buy back their bacon, mortgaging to do so the minute grunter in the sty, who is to be bacon next year; and though the squire may owe (as in one case we know a squire did owe) over £100 there, for trifles constantly required at the house, that it was not worth while to send in to the town for, he is not troubled of course, and the meat at the big house is as much as ever, notwithstanding his debts. We are very far from advocating any socialistic doctrine, we are simply stating a case; still we would consider labourers, farmers, and squires in the light of one big family, placing the labourers in the light of the younger children, the farmers as the elder sons, and the squire as the father of the lot. What would the younger children of a household say if they saw their father living in careless luxury and they were starving? they do not wish to usurp his place or push him from his throne; they only require consideration and to be allowed to live: the farmer should act as medium to bring the two together, while the squire should act as father, and so let all feel they have an equal right to exist.

Here we have another type of farmer: a present-day man, whose hands are tied by his landlord at the moment, but who does all he can for his people, has a cheery word for all; and all know if wages are slack or houses small that it is because it can't be helped; and they bear it cheerfully, because they know that the farmer suffers too, and does not live in luxury although he has to reduce their pay.

It is very good to wander about the village with his pretty, simply-dressed wife, who does all the teaching and dressing of her children herself; and, year in year out, remains at home, never hankering after change, and simply doing her duty; it is not a pleasant or a cheerful life, but she has an equal mind, and believes in doing the duty that is next.

Her own house is small and comfortless, and in winter the springs break and meander into her drawing-room, and she does wax a little warm over this, contrasting it with the wonderful dog-kennels the landlord has just built, although he has no money to spend on his farm-houses; still she considers her duty to the labourers exists, and has to be done, whether or no the landlord does his to the farmer.

It were well to turn away from this side of the picture to the other that amply represents the life of the village. First, naturally, comes the parson, a man full of vague ideas for the regeneration of his flock, that alternately get him into disgrace with the squire and with his parishioners; he has, curiously enough, the courage of his convictions, and would as soon tell the squire his mind as the youngest boy on his glebe farm.  He has not a pleasant time of it, but he loves his work, and having always some project on hand, has never the time to be miserable or unhappy.  To him comes every mother who wishes to get her daughter a place, or her son a lift up from the agricultural slough in which he was born; every man who has a fancy for bees or flowers finds a ready listener in the parson, and indeed everybody who has something to say finds an ever-open ear at the vicarage.

To see him really at his best we should try and be present at any church occasion, such as the dedication festival on the opening of a new organ; then, indeed, we should be amused.  If the bishop is present, he yet is master in his own church, and treats him much as a captain should treat a figure-head on his ship, as a hall-mark, or necessary embellishment; not to be lightly esteemed or scoffed at, but no more really necessary to the steering, or proper management, than the least conspicuous part of the vessel would be. His wife is used to him, but still is rather nervous lest he should offend some of the proper, somewhat starched, parsons' wives around, who come in their best raiment, much creased, and rather redolent of the damp vicarage drawers, in which they have kept it since the last somewhat similar occasion on which it appeared. Yet our parson knows and respects their small peculiarities, recognising that all, he himself included, have corners round which it is well to steer cautiously, and though all agree in calling him queer and quixotical, there is only about one man in the neighbourhood who would rejoice at his going, and with him we have nothing to do.

Small joys serve as well as large ones to our village friends. A flower-show is the source of much anticipation and preparation; a school feast a somewhat delirious joy; a kindly interest in one's neighbour's business more than necessary, else how should we know when our help is needed? and our sorrows are lightened by the knowledge that profound interest is taken in us, and that we have sympathy freely offered us, and in the consciousness brought home to us, alas! often enough, that suffering is the lot of all of us in time. There is no sadder sight in the world than the display of tan or straw laid down in a London street; it argues that the place is so large there is no one to stay the vehicles or cause them to go by another route. Does illness come to our houses, there is not a child who does not forget to whoop when he comes out of school; not a "trap" whose owner would not drive miles round sooner than break in upon the invalid's chance of slumber!

We never see that straw laid down in London without longing to call and find out all about the illness, simply because we love sympathy so much ourselves that we long to give it to others : only the dread of the footman's astonishment has often kept our hands from the bell, though very likely he was raised in the country himself and knows all about it.

We see gradually the old village life disappearing and nothing seems to be given in its place, yet in our village things go on in the old strain, and we hope they may do so for many years to come. Our farmer looks at his fields, at the unlet farms around him, at his meagre house, his rather strained relations with his landlord, who talks of restoring a second old house on his property because the one in which he lives does not quite suit him, and who yet has no money to spend on his farms, and sometimes speaks of moving away ; but he has sunk so much in his land it is difficult to move, and so we look forward some day to pay him another visit.

Here at the top of the lane is the house the landlord thinks of rebuilding, and before we turn away from our village it were well to pause there a while. Here, too, we get a curious insight into the erratic disposition of the village king, and the whole spot forms an interesting study of character. Here are acres of apple-trees planted all in a minute, irrespective of the time of year, or the soil, or the thousand and one necessary items requisite to secure a proper crop : all bought at great cost, and all utterly useless. There three-quarters of a mile of road, useless and grass-grown, suddenly commenced in an excess of affection for a neighbour's company, to be reached earlier by this route than by the ordinary turnpike road, and as suddenly ended when a difference of opinion as to the pedigree of a dog turned the once dear friends into bitter enemies ; and there again acre after acre of gooseberry bushes, in imitation of Kentish farming ; not considering that what paid excellently well on a line within a few miles of town, could hardly be expected to answer eight miles from a station, and so far from a town, that they would be utterly spoiled before they reached the hands of a purchaser.

But the house itself is full of interest and has doubtless a score of stories attached to it.   In this part of the world, too distant, before the days of railways, for the small or big squires to have much to say to London, there were at one time many manor-houses, each with its family content to abide in the place where it was born; gradually Time's fingers opened the enchanted door that stood between real country and the town, and the whole face of England, the whole aspect of English country life, began to change—doubtless much for the benefit of all.   Yet any one possessed of sentiment can but grieve over these poor old places, some of which have vanished, some turned into barns, some into smaller houses, three being made of the one; and some, like the house in our village, allowed to stand solitary and alone, for none can be found to dwell therein.

It could never possibly be made comfortably habitable either; the passages and staircases are all stone, very narrow, very high, with water dropping on the unwary visitor's head should he not go there in the very height of summer; with great high rooms, hideously out of proportion and paved with stone; and with bedrooms which have rheumatism and ghostly fears rampant therein.

Still, it was once a stately pleasant house enough, extending in great wings on each side of the portion that is left; with fine cellars, yet extant, quite 300 yards from the front door; and with wide beautiful gardens, wonderful with trees and producing strange unknown flowers at odd moments even now.   It is well to stand here for a moment and regretfully take our last view of the village.   We can hear the squire's children calling to each other on the lawn, the cows come treading heavily down the soft lane, with the weary-footed herd-boy behind them, slashing every now and then with his whip at the newly-springing hedges, and whistling dully some Moody and Sankey hymn; a reminiscence of the mission that came to convert us, and that made a hideous noise, going away at last, leaving much evil and little good behind it. The rooks are steadily flying home, a cuckoo wakes up and begins to shout enthusiastically in the elms, the lambs call to their mothers, the sun sets, and a great calm comes over the land.

Far away over the downs we see a horseman galloping home; we take our friend's hand in ours for a moment, and then turn away, watching him with jealous eyes as he saunters home with the step of one to whom hurry is unknown, and certainty of welcome there perfect; and we almost long to stay with him always, learning more daily of the life in our small distant village.

T

## FROM A GARRET

AT first sight the garret might not seem an attractive spot to a stranger: it is dark and low and quiet, with sundry corners from which darkness is never absent, and where at twilight strange forms appear to loiter, as if ghosts were emerging slowly and reluctantly from the bosom of the past.

It requires, too, an adventurous soul to climb the worn steps that lead from the nursery floor, and a wary eye, else surely will your head come sharply against the rafters that are close above; and the stoutest heart quails a little, as the owner leaves the light and noise and merriment of the household, and wanders up the staircase, into what is essentially a museum of long-forgotten curiosities, a storehouse of long-dead days. But once overcome these difficulties, and to any one imbued with sentiment the charms of the garret are indeed apparent enough.

More especially if the first visit should be paid just before the setting of the sun on some fair evening in late summer; then, shutting the door as closely as the loosely-falling latch will allow, the chair, the old elbow-chair that we love, should be drawn up to the window, and opening the stiff casement warily, lest we should shake out the diamond panes of glass, and leaning out just a little, a look should be taken silently at the scene.

There is nothing like it to us in all the world beside. Calmness and peace walk therein hand in hand; reflection and sweet sadness are to be found in the close-growing shrubbery, the home of many of our beloved birds; the garden is old and perchance commonplace, but the flowers are ever fragrant and linger lovingly in our memory now we see them no more; the great white magnolia opens her cup and pours out her scented wealth of beauty into the still atmosphere, like rich wine falling from a silver flagon.; and far away are the hills, for ever new, for ever old, for ever yielding help and counsel to those who can read their lovely lines aright.

All round the garret window climbs the red virginian creeper, brought hither from the wife's old home, and tended with much care until it could fend for itself; and then it became a vast creeper, in less time than it took the eldest child to grow from long frocks into short ones, and then into long ones again; embellishing all the gable-end of the house; and peeping thus into our highest window, became one of the associations with the past with which the garret is crowded.

Indeed, were it now left to its own devices it would form a complete veil over our own window, which is often enough tapped at emphatically by its long tendrils, as if they wanted to shelter from the world outside, and many times have we snapped them off unconsciously, not seeing they had put their feelers in at the hinges.

But we will not lose our sunset view, even to keep out the present day of hurry and rush, and so, like most other things, the creeper has to remain duly within bounds, at all events as long as we have the management of it.

Inasmuch as it always seemed the first hint of autumn and death, as the shortening days decked its long tendrils with glowing scarlet, and faded yellow, and brown leaves; so it, itself, was destined to give us our first hint of our own shortening time; for pointing to it as an example of quick luxuriant growth in a very little space, we were only recalled to the real length thereof, by a small voice that said: " It has been planted twenty years, father; no wonder it is as big and tall as it is, after all that length of time."

And yet it always in autumn makes us instinctively look towards the hills beyond the meadows, where in autumn the heather looks like a pink veil thrown over the purple gloom, that broods for ever in the dips and hollows on the hillsides, and where even winter seems but as a sleeping beauty, wrapped in gauzy mist, and waiting for that fairy prince the spring, to step forth and give his magic kiss; so waking the earth forthwith, and clothing it all swiftly with its flower-embroidered, wondrous bridal robe.

As we gaze at the sunset, now fantastically clothing the quiet pale gray stream in a saffron garment, now dressing the fleecy clouds in all the divers hues it borrows from the rainbow, an ineffable sensation of peace folds us gently in its arms; and we cease to feel conscious of the present, for we seem far away from all its carking care; for an hour at least life can run alone without us, and we are suspended motionless, while all else goes on beside us, leaving us entirely on one side. It is in times like these that we seem to have again communion with those who are no more with us. It is almost possible to feel that, brooding over the past, those inhabiters thereof, who have departed and belong no more to the things of this life, can intangibly be again close beside us, and longing, as they must ever do, to communicate their experience and their thoughts to us, who yet have mouths wherewith to repeat our words, come nearer and nearer in their anguish, to have communion with us, and touch us with hands that only exist in their own fancy, for they have long since fallen to dust and become things that are not.

Sitting here alone in the twilight we cannot but believe we are surrounded by a whole company of voiceless spirits. Fine delicate fancies creep, we know not from whence, into our minds. We have at these moments a certain assurance, so it seems to us, of that future life that is so vague, so impossible, among the rough evident life-struggles that await us downstairs; and we are no longer doubtful, that once free from our detaining, hindering body, we shall be free indeed, as is a bird, once the cage door is open, and he rises joyful to claim the inheritance—the open air into which he was born.

It is not, therefore, on the living that we ponder in our garret, but on the dead.

Dead hours of happiness, dead ere we knew how sweet and dear they were, are ours once more. Dead friends stand beside us, and point out to us how we are able to climb from their graves to higher things, far better than from our own dead selves, whose various forms grow and alter, it seems to us, far more from others' examples or others' experience than our own. And love comes back to us, not grave and wrinkled and strong as he is now, but young and lissom, charming and wayward, as he used to be in the time of roses, so many, many years ago.

Ah! how pitiful it is to us who are older, to stand aside and watch the everlasting, ever-living passion and pain and enjoyment and raptures of young lovers; it hurts us even now to hear their pretty songs, all about love and kisses; for do we not know how the poetry will melt and turn into prose, how the romance will fade before the bread-and-butter side of existence, and become very true, very useful, very lovely at the best; but be no more the sweet laughing cherub he was, than yonder bowl of fragrant pot-pourri is like the rose-bed from which we culled it only a couple of months ago.

It must go, alas! alas! and wise are those who are able to know they have had their day, and gather up their rose-leaves to keep them in a delicate china bowl, content with the undeniable fragrance thereof; and, wilfully oblivious of the fact that death is in the bowl, see nothing there, but the reflex of days that once were theirs.

Ah! is there not in our garret, safely locked away, a collection of letters that we have never yet had courage to look at, since the day we nailed them down, laughing between ourselves at the number, and promising to read them together, when old age sat between us at the fireside, holding one of each of our hands, and making a bond that nothing save death himself should sunder, and then only for a little time?

But were we to open the box, what would not troop out? dead youth, laughter and song, aspirations never fulfilled, hopes disappointed, prophecies of happiness, hideous now with the mockery of their unfulfilment: for old age never came to her and she died; yet still we cannot help thinking that from our errors and mistakes then did we, who are here now, learn much that renders life better and worthier, if not half so sweet; because it is full of purposeful work, which it was not in those early days of dalliance in the rose-bound paths of love.

We have never read over the letters—we never shall—but we know each one well; and 'tis difficult to realise that we, who are more profoundly interested in the good wife's housekeeping efforts downstairs, and in Jim's success at the examinations, than in aught beside, can have been the identical creature, who was once the unassured lover of the wife who lies under her low cross, clasping our baby close to her dear childish breast.

Sometimes we cannot think that this was so. We ponder on ourselves there, until we fancy we are some one we have read of, and have once felt very, very sorry for: we, stout, middle-aged, and very happy with our surroundings, could never have been that lonely miserable mortal, who came back broken-hearted, leaving all he loved in life in the dear little churchyard, nestled down among the hills we loved, thinking that "we" were no more, and only a desolate "I" was existent to represent the household that was to have grown so rapidly, and become full and vocal as a nest is that is filled with birds. And sometimes when we wake at night with a shiver, dreaming that those dreadful days of darkness have come again, yet knowing that they never can, we almost believe that the difference in the identity is such that a separate resurrection will be needed; and that we shall discover that the boy of then, and the commonplace husband of the present, were and are two entirely different folks. Yet then we feel whimsically jealous of the boy, and dare pursue that train of thought no farther, for we cannot tell where it may lead.

But if those early days of love for Mara served as stepping-stones, how much more did the friendship formed in our later years lead us on!

She, too, rests below the hills, whereon how often have we not gazed as we vainly talked about the great mystery that far too early was solved by her whom we so loved! It is impossible, sitting here with the gradual gloom closing round us in the silence of our garret, to believe she lies out there in the darkness — she who was the only other who ever climbed to the garret, and needed no words ere entering straight, unerringly, even sympathisingly, into the mood in which for the moment she would find us.

Far easier than that is to put her chair in the old place, and from the shadows form once more the keen glance, the sharply-defined, clear-cut features, and hear through the soft sighing of the wind, her voice talking over and over again those well-worn subjects of death and the life beyond the grave.

A restless and unsatisfied soul too, clear and ardent, but a Pegasus chained to a domestic car amply laden by her loved ones, and sufficiently so, to keep her in the ruts that jarred her intensely ; for she longed more than she ever said to be given voice to, and wings that she might soar beyond the mere under-air of earth.

Fine, impetuous, impulsive, angry with each sham and pretence of life, unable to stay quiet, ever beating against bars that she never ceased to contemplate, how was it possible that she could pass through life without errors ?—never of heart or brain, simply of judgment, yet errors all the same. Yet from her mistakes have we not learned to avoid similar pitfalls, and from her unselfish courage have we not better learned to appreciate the tender trust of womankind ? She who was always speaking of the mysteries of death has solved them, yet still is very, very silent.

So we are almost sure that she does come to us in our retirement, and is fain to tell us all she knows. As we think of her we almost feel a hand on our shoulder, a touch yet not a touch ; and we know that had she mortal lips, had she taken into the spirit land those we kissed so sadly in her coffin, she would e'en tell us aloud what she whispers silently to our brain, that somewhere or other we shall, must, meet again. And so our garret is indeed a sacred shrine to hold her memory, and it is there we ever think of her; and her presence among us seems always like some faint delicate perfume in old relics from a flower whose name even is forgotten, and whose form is vanished, but yet is so sweet and so subtle that it remains, and makes whoever turns over the drawer about which the scent hangs, think insensibly of purity and loveliness, and late wanderings in an August garden of long ago.

The worst of growing older is that the miles along the road are marked only by tombstones; and, falling out of the ranks one by one, those who started with us in early morning are not there to loiter with us in those pleasant paths where work well done is over, and we have earned the right to rest. There may be new friendships formed, new acquaintances made; but these cannot compare to those who remember us young, and speak of us to the wonderment of the youngsters, who only realise us as wayworn and weary, as having been once as undisciplined, as hopeful, as reckless as themselves.

Yet though people die, things remain — ay, the things we have made ourselves will stay, ironically looking down on their creators lying dead and dumb below them.

Death would not be half so dreadful were it not so defenceless; did all the earthly surroundings vanish what time the poor possessor, once holding so much, now clasping nothing in his nerveless hands, was taken away in his coffin.

But it may not be; and 'tis then our garret comes more than ever into use, for in our anguish we hurry the things so fearfully like to the possessor, who can possess no more, up here, to be looked over and apportioned when time shall give us strength to overlook them again.

What wonder that the time comes never, when we recollect that yonder modest trunk labelled with evidences of the honeymoon tour contains a soft white garment that was once a wedding-dress : ah ! there is no length of life yet given to man that can dull the memories that lie sleeping in its folds.

What number of days can obscure the remembrance of the talks about its purchase, the pros and cons of satin or muslin or silk talked of tremulously, while her head was on my shoulder, and her hands, holding mine, turned and twisted my solitary ring as she coyly spoke of the day, and asked me seriously in which texture she should be clad, and which would please me best ?

Nay, were it shaken out, or used by others, or destroyed even, it would seem like desecrating her grave ; and so we leave the box unopened, and wonder when we are gone what will become of the dainty thing.

Perhaps it may remain here for years, much as the old spinning-wheel yonder has done : in its day it hummed busily enough, and turned out yards of wondrous fine linen, in which members of our house are yet born, and sleep, and are laid out in death ; yet when our youngest, bitten with the prevailing fever of the day, begged to have the poor thing polished and restored to the light of day, to stand in its old accustomed place and do no work, we would not have it so, feeling that, could it but speak, it would surely protest at being dragged from its seclusion and forced to stand, an idle mockery, where it had once been a useful and honoured member of the household.

Yet the "youngest" is the only one of the children who ever ventures near our garret, and who feels there somewhat of what we feel ; and when she speaks not, and nestles there beside our chair, an indescribable something draws away our thoughts to that other youngest child; and we almost believe the little life that was never lived by it, was given to the daughter whose brown eyes and serious expression are not ours, but singularly like those other eyes that scarcely opened on the world they only came into, to withdraw the mother from.

It is singular for us to sit here in the sunset, and to know how divers are our thoughts. The garret is the past, a holy present unto us. To us the sunset represents the bringer-on of night, full of rest and possibilities of slumber; while to her it is a place of the dead, and the sunset is a wondrous foretaste of the dawning of another day, in which, as we gaze over the long red road over which so many of our dearest have been taken to the little lovely resting-place beyond the hills, and where we can see only long funeral trains, and only hear the sad boom of the bell in the square gray tower beyond the river, she smiles to herself as she sees in fancy her fairy prince come riding from the gaunt ruined castle among the hills, eager to claim the bride who gazes at him from the garret window. Her presence, intent as she is on a future, has not much in common with the dark rest and peace that are for ever brooding o'er the garret; and as with a smile she kisses and lightly leaves us, her footsteps growing lighter as she emerges from the gloom, it is easy to believe that the dwellers in the garret are relieved by her absence, and that they come nearer as night draws nigh, secure in their knowledge of a sympathetic presence being alone among them.

And indeed it is well to have such a garret, for around its walls hang undisturbed, pictures seen only by the possessor of them, and that if we had no garret in which to contemplate them, would surely fade altogether beneath the garish light of day.

For certain it were not good to forget the precious jewelled days of youth and early middle life; and it is best sometimes to recollect the time when the very air seemed intoxicating and a summer's morning of beauty was as a gift direct from God.    And so on the west wall of the garret hangs a picture of a summer morning on the river, and gazing thereon, at once come back in an instant the scent of the distant hay, the regular swish of the scythe, and the curious soft grating feel of our boat, as with one vigorous stroke of the sculls we brought her in to the bank, and in the deep shade, cast by meadow-sweet and willow-herb, and over that by a great elm, rest from our pleasant toil, and learn by the help of summer, mysteries just faintly indicated by our favourite poets, whose secrets were no longer secrets when pored over and discussed upon the river's placid breast.

It is good to remember it all: to recollect the swift pass-ing of the brilliant kingfisher, held by us then as the emblem of good luck; or to remember the wondrous hues of the dragonfly as he sometimes pitched on the reeds or flowers above us, and balanced himself just a moment there ere darting away again on another flight; or even again to think over the scented silence of the summer night, when the nightingales were almost silent, yet sang once and again, when least expected, small snatches of their eternal melody; when the nightjar creaked out his monotonous note ; when the dew lay heavy on the path, and the flowers as we brushed by them almost drenched us with their cups over-full and flowing with moisture.

But what did that matter! our fortunes were to be determined that night, and as we set our eggshells, lighted inside by miniature candles, floating down the tiny stream, that farther on flowed into the broader river, we took small heed of all our surroundings in the anxiety of seeing how we should progress in our tiny voyage; wondering if we should float successfully onward, or else sink ignominiously into chaos, represented by the forget-me-nots and flowering rushes growing thickly in the streamlet.

Yet when we look at our picture on our garret wall, all comes back to us: the bark of a dog across the meadows, the grate of the heavy market-carts, groaning as they slowly rumbled up to town, the never-ceasing sighing of the ash trees in the copse, and farther away yet, the song that one of our sisters sang as she tried to. amuse the father, saying with a smile that she need not try her fortune, for that was already settled.

Then the scent of lemon-verbena greets us, a white rose scatters her petals at our feet, and the picture fades silently away. It were easy now to see another picture, one of disappointment and despair; but surely 'tis best to contemplate yet another, when we were older truly, but only just beginning to really live, and this has its own accompaniment of sounds of martial music, and we recollect the band playing in the valley while we climbed the hill, and looked down on the great camp fire, where the flames rushed and sprang from the darkness, straight up into the clear autumnal sky; scattering in their passage through the air wee atoms of burning furze, that as they fell looked like wandering stars, or strange bright insects perishing in the flames below them.

Then the music stopped; we heard the vast sea moaning on the shore below our feet, and looking seaward we saw come suddenly into the moonlight a great ship, outward bound, that passed away almost as suddenly into the shadows on the other side, causing us to think simultaneously of the shortness of this life of ours, and how we emerge but for a moment out of the gloom into the broad light of life, and then disappear into outer darkness almost before our presence on the scene is recognised.

Perchance this cognisance of the shortness of life made us ponder also on how to dispose best of the time we had : I know not, yet somehow the beacon-hill became a sacred spot to us, and life, after that one evening, was never quite the same thing to either of us again.

Slowly, slowly, darkness falls around outside our garret. Yet it does not matter, for darkness and silence suit this resting-place best, and when we contemplate our pictures, aided thereby by the presence of the relics of the past, we cannot help feeling that with the outside world of human folk we have very little indeed to do.   Folks may sneer at us or talk of our little failings and peculiarities, and trouble may come, friends may leave us, and nearer and dearer ties may— nay, must—snap with the hand of time ; yet it seems to us that fates may do their worst, if we are left our resting-place ; and with faith and hope and memory to serve as hand-maidens, contemplate our pictures that only grow the brighter for the darkness and silence outside.

And so as we lay down our pen, and know that we shall wander no more among the hills and dales of Dorset, nor by the bright blue seas we love ; we yet would feel we had done something to hang upon other walls a series of pictures that may in some measure decorate them, or cause food for reflection : secure in knowing that if this do not occur, it is not because folks have no garret, nor eyes to see the simple loveliness, the romantic old-world beauties of this piece of our native land, but because our love has outrun our strength, and our words are not enough to bring the scenes before you, as they rise one by one before our eyes that will never look upon them any more.

If this be so, well, so it must be ; yet we have and retain our pictures, that herewith we show to you, trusting you may care to decorate your walls, as we have decorated those that are never pictureless to us, even if they be only those of a garret.

THE END

*Printed by* R. & R CLARK, *Edinburgh*

www.ingramcontent.com/pod-product-compliance
Lightning Source LLC
Chambersburg PA
CBHW020505270326
41926CB00008B/745

* 9 7 8 3 7 4 4 6 7 9 3 3 6 *